EXPLOITING THE SEA

EXETER MARITIME STUDIES

General Editors: Michael Duffy and David J. Starkey

British Privateering Enterprise in the Eighteenth Century
by David J. Starkey (1990)

Parameters of British Naval Power 1650–1850
edited by Michael Duffy (1992)

The Rise of the Devon Seaside Resorts, 1750–1900
by John Travis (1993)

Man and the Maritime Environment
edited by Stephen Fisher (1994)

Manila Ransomed: The British Assault on Manila in the Seven Years War
by Nicholas Tracy (1995)

Trawling: The Rise and Fall of the British Trawl Fishery
by Robb Robinson (1996)

Pirates and Privateers: New Perspectives on the War on Trade in the Eighteenth and Nineteenth Centuries
edited by David J. Starkey, E.S. van Eyck van Heslinga
and J.A. de Moor (1997)

Cockburn and the British Navy in Transition: Admiral Sir George Cockburn, 1772–1853
by Roger Morriss (1997)

Recreation and the Sea
edited by Stephen Fisher (1997)

EXPLOITING THE SEA

Aspects of Britain's Maritime Economy
since 1870

edited by

DAVID J. STARKEY

and

ALAN G. JAMIESON

UNIVERSITY
of
EXETER
PRESS

First published in 1998 by
University of Exeter Press
Reed Hall
Streatham Drive
Exeter EX4 4QR
UK

British Library Cataloguing in Publication Data

A catalogue record of this book is available from the British Library

ISBN 0 85989 533 5

Typeset in Palatino by Sue Milward

Printed in Great Britain by Short Run Press Ltd, Exeter

The cover illustration is of the Elginshire, ship no. 167, Wallsend
Swan (1891), and is reproduced by permission of the Chief
Archivist, Tyne and Wear Archive Service.

FOR STEPHEN FISHER

Convenor, Contributor, Cajoler

Exeter Maritime History Conferences,

1967–

Contents

Tables, Figures and Maps

Tables

Figures

Maps

NOTES ON CONTRIBUTORS

JOHN ARMSTRONG is Professor of Business History at Thames Valley University, London. He is interested in all aspects of transport history and especially the British coastal trade. He edits *The Journal of Transport History* and is series editor of "Studies in Transport History" published by Ashgate Press. His most recent book was *Coastal and Short Sea Shipping* (1996).

JANET CUSACK is former Senior Lecturer in Physics at La Sainte Union College of Higher Education, Southampton. Early retirement was followed by a switch to History and a PhD awarded in 1996 by the University of Exeter for a thesis on the history of yachting in South Devon, 1640–1914. Her current research interest is eighteenth-century English yachting.

BRIAN DYSON has been Hull University Archivist since 1987. His duties there are wide ranging and include the custodianship of the Ellerman's Wilson Line shipping archive. He edits the journal *Paragon Review* and his recent publications include contributions to *Business Archives*, 'Northern Riches' (with Helen Roberts) in *Archives* (1997) and *Liberty in Britain, 1934–1994* (1994).

ANDREW GORDON is Senior Lecturer at the Joint Services Command and Staff College at Bracknell. He is author of *British Sea Power and Procurement Between the Wars* (1988) and *The Rules of the Game: Jutland and the British Naval Command* (1996). He is an Honorary Research Fellow of the Exeter Centre for Maritime Historical Studies.

ANTHONY GORST is Senior Lecturer in History at the University of Westminster and researches and writes on the history of British defence policy since the Second World War.

ALAN G. JAMIESON was formerly Leverhulme Research Fellow in British Maritime History in the Centre for Maritime Historical Studies, University of Exeter. Currently an Honorary Research Fellow in the Centre, he was editor and principal author of *A People of the Sea: The Maritime History of the Channel Islands*, and has had numerous articles on maritime history published in British, American, Canadian and Australian journals.

LEWIS JOHNMAN is the Quintin Hogg Research Fellow in History at the University of Westminster and is currently working on various aspects of British shipbuilding history since 1945.

NIGEL J. MORGAN is Senior Lecturer in Tourism Marketing at the University of Wales Institute, Cardiff. He has worked in tourism, marketing, public relations and leisure policy in local authorities in South Wales and at the Sports Council for Wales. He has a PhD from Exeter University and has written extensively on tourism and leisure in Wales, seaside resorts, brochures and destination imagery. He is currently co-authoring (with Annette Pritchard) two books on twentieth-century tourism.

SIDNEY POLLARD, now retired, taught Economic History for thirty years at Sheffield and for ten years at Bielefeld, Germany. His latest publication, *Marginal Europe*, deals with the contributions made by marginal regions to European economic development. He is currently working on the history of industrialization and entrepreneurship in Europe.

ROBB ROBINSON is a History tutor and Curriculum and Staff Development Manager at Hull College. He has written widely on fisheries history and is the author of two books on the subject, the latest, *Trawling: The Rise and Fall of the British Trawl Fishery*, being published by University of Exeter Press in 1996.

DAVID J. STARKEY is Wilson Family Lecturer in Maritime History at the University of Hull. He has published widely on British shipping, shipbuilding and privateering in the eighteenth and nineteenth centuries.

PREFACE

In 1992 the Centre for Maritime Historical Studies (CMHS) at the University of Exeter commenced an investigation into 'Change and Adaptation in the Maritime Dimension of the British Economy since 1870'. This research project is concerned with the development of Britain's sea-related interests in the late nineteenth and twentieth centuries. It takes a broad view of the nation's recent maritime past, assessing the contribution that activities such as shipping, shipbuilding, port operation, fishing, maritime defence and coastal leisure have made to the British economy. The fluctuating fortunes of these sea-related activities, their changing significance in an international context, and explanations as to the performance of Britain's maritime industries are further central themes of the work. To further the progress of the project, experts on particular aspects of this broad subject area were invited to deliver papers on their specialist fields to the 1995 meeting of the annual maritime history conference hosted by the CMHS at Crossmead Conference Centre, University of Exeter. The proceedings of this conference constitute the core of the present volume.

The editors of this volume (and research fellows engaged in the project), David J. Starkey and Alan G. Jamieson, would like to acknowledge the support of a number of individuals and institutions in this venture. Underpinning the investigation as a whole lies a generous grant made by the Leverhulme Trust. The authors of the chapters which comprise *Exploiting the Sea*, who all enthusiastically contributed their time and talent to the conference and its proceedings, are warmly thanked. We are also grateful to the following for their considerable efforts: to Simon Baker, Richard Willis, Anna Henderson and their colleagues at the University of

Exeter Press for bringing the volume to fruition; to Sue Milward (University of Exeter) and Richard Gorski (University of Hull) for their word processing and typesetting skills; and to the staff of Crossmead Conference Centre for their splendid hospitality. Out greatest debt of gratitude, however, is owed to the Directors of the CMHS (and directors of the Leverhulme-funded research project), Michael Duffy and Stephen Fisher. Both worked tirelessly to ensure that the conference provided a critical and valuable forum for debating the issues at the heart of the research investigation and thereby fulfilled its objective of invigorating the project as a whole.

This debate took place in the context of a conference that has been an annual feature of the maritime history calendar since 1967. Accordingly, we feel that it is entirely appropriate that this volume should be dedicated to Stephen Fisher, the person who has done more than anyone to maintain the vitality and scholarly rigour of this series of meetings. Though Stephen retired from the academic staff of the University of Exeter shortly before the 1995 conference, his contribution to the study and understanding of matters maritime remains undiminished. Long may this continue!

David J. Starkey

Alan G. Jamieson

January 1998

INTRODUCTION

David J. Starkey

In recent decades, considerable progress has been made in the study of maritime history. This is evident in the improvement in the volume and quality of publications, the establishment of specialist societies and journals, the emergence of a conference circuit, and the introduction of maritime historical studies into university syllabuses. Amidst the burgeoning historiography of this vibrant subject area, there has been a good deal of debate as to the content and parameters of maritime history. Two particularly important points have emerged from this 'collective soul searching and stock taking'.[1] Firstly, the wiser counsels have argued that sea-related activities cannot be understood in any meaningful way if they are treated in isolation from the broader processes of economic, social, political and technological development.[2] In the second place, a broad consensus regarding the topical parameters of maritime history has become evident in recent years. Whereas in the 1970s maritime history tended to be equated with merchant shipping history, now there is general agreement that its bounds extend well beyond ships, shipowners and seafarers to embrace all aspects of man's relationship with the sea, including topics such as resort development, offshore oil operations and port structures and societies.[3]

Taking these two valuable pieces of intellectual cargo on board, this volume examines a broad range of sea-related activities in an economic context: essentially, it is concerned with the development of Britain's 'maritime economy' since 1870. As no such sector exists in the official statistical record, or in conventional divisions of an economy, some consideration of the extent and components of the maritime economy is necessary. Interpreting 'maritime' in its

1

broadest sense, a vast array of sea-related activities hoves into sight. Rendering amenable to analysis a topic which embraces battleship building and Blackpool beaches, bulk cargoes and battered cod, supertankers and sail yachts, requires both definition and prioritisation. As David J. Starkey points out in the first essay of this volume, this is best achieved by adopting Professor Broeze's contention that maritime activities should be classified functionally, that is, according to the ways in which human societies have exploited the sea. In the context of the modern British economy, four functions can be identified: transport, power projection, resources and recreation. In each of these functional categories, there lie a range of sea-related activities, some of which are both more important and more maritime than others. Some distinction should therefore be drawn between 'principal' and 'secondary' maritime activities. Identifying the principal means in which the sea has been utilised entails the establishment and application of two basic criteria. Initially, and quite obviously, a fundamental reliance upon the sea is a prerequisite of a principal maritime industry; counter-factually, if Britain was a land-locked nation then such activity would not take place. The second criterion is a coastal location. Of course, sea-reliant industrial activity, such as the manufacture of marine engines and naval weapons, occurs inland. But it does not contribute directly to the economy of coastal districts, and is not fashioned by the particular physical, cultural and economic influences that the sea imparts upon the land. Accordingly, a coastal site, or operational base, its character dictated by the configuration of the sea–land interface, the culture of its community shaped by the proximity and use of the sea, and its space embodying a factor of production, land, of central importance to economic activity, is an essential ingredient of a principal maritime activity. The industries which meet these criteria are listed according to function in Table 0.1.

Table 0.1: Principal Maritime Industries by Function

Transport	Resources	Power Projection	Recreation
shipping	fishing	maritime defence	coastal leisure
shipbuilding	oil/gas		
port			

This functional division provides a framework for the analysis of Britain's maritime interests. It therefore underpins the discussion of several aspects of the maritime dimension of the British economy in the essays which comprise this volume. Accordingly, four chapters (by John Armstrong, Brian Dyson, Alan G. Jamieson and Sidney Pollard) are largely concerned with sea transport, each providing a different perspective on the factors conditioning the provision of coastal and overseas shipping services; two chapters (by Andrew Gordon, and Anthony Gorst and Lewis Johnman) focus on power projection, more specifically on the impact that naval policy has had upon shipbuilding and the support and supply industries collectively termed the 'maritime defence industry'; the exploitation of living marine resources by the application of steam power in the trawling sector of the British fishing industry is examined in Robb Robinson's chapter; and there are separate treatments of recreational sailing (by Janet Cusack) and seaside resort development (by Nigel Morgan), the two main constituents of the 'coastal leisure industry'.

Several general insights into the development of Britain's maritime interests emerge from these chapters. In the first place, much is revealed about the forces which determine the extent and significance of a nation's exploitation of the sea and its resources. Sidney Pollard cites 'geographical reality' as being a key influence on the vitality or otherwise of Britain's maritime interests. In this sense, as an island state, in a strategically favourable position, with a coastline fortunately configured for port operations, marine recreation and the export of conveniently located endowments of industrial raw materials, Britain was 'lucky' before the First World War. More recently, such erstwhile blessings have turned into handicaps as the foci of sea-borne trade, naval strategy and even coastal leisure have shifted elsewhere. At the same time, of course, human agents have had a considerable influence on the development of the maritime economy. Government policy, whether it has related to naval procurement strategies, railway rate subsidies and excess shipping profits in the First World War, or the imposition of purchase tax in the late 1940s, has had a strong bearing on all maritime activities. Likewise, technological change, notably with regard to vessel size, design and construction, emerges as a causal factor throughout the volume. And that most obvious and controversial of human agents, the entrepreneur, also features regularly, notably in Brian Dyson's discussion of the management of the large-scale family enterprise of the Wilsons of Hull, and, more generally, in Alan G. Jamieson's analysis of the shipping and shipbuilding industries since 1930.

Secondly, there are indications within this volume that close relations existed between the different components of the maritime economy. Some of these linkages were so close and obvious as to be taken for granted. The shipping and shipbuilding industries, for instance, have always been strongly related, not only as producer and customer, but also as investment partners and as servants of that volatile master, world sea-borne trade. Other linkages were less visible. Accordingly, as John Armstrong shows, in late Victorian and Edwardian Britain the coastal trade profited from seasonal surges in recreational business as passengers turned to short sea cruises for bracing air, scenery and an escape from their dreary urban homes. Likewise, recreational sailors, as Janet Cusack points out, have proved to be increasingly important consumers of the products of shipbuilders and the amenities of port operators as the twentieth century has progressed. Elsewhere in the maritime economy, connections between functionally disparate activities can be identified, notably in relations between public policy and private enterprise. For example, as Robb Robinson indicates, fishing vessels and fishermen were recruited in great numbers for military service in the First World War, while Brian Dyson shows that many vessels of the Wilson Line's fleet were hired by the state in the same conflict, and Anthony Gorst and Lewis Johnman, and Andrew Gordon, focus on the state's use of naval orders as a counter-cyclical device to shore up ailing shipbuilding concerns.

This coherence within the maritime economy is reflected in the long-term development of Britain's sea-related interests, a third theme illuminated in this volume. While not all of the nation's sea-related activities have ebbed and flowed in unison, some broad waves in the chronology of expansion and contraction can be discerned. The strongest of these occurred in the 1870–1914 period when nearly every constituent of Britain's maritime economy experienced growth in both absolute and relative terms. This is clear in John Armstrong's discussion of the 'apogee' of the coastal trade, in Robb Robinson's account of the increasing operational range and productivity of British trawlers, and in Janet Cusack's quantification of the development of yachting and cruising in the 25 years before the First World War. As Sidney Pollard emphasises, an 'astonishing' rate of expansion was also evident in the shipping and shipbuilding industries, though according to David J. Starkey the distribution of these burgeoning activities within the UK was extremely uneven, and therefore in the midst of plenty regions such as south-west England largely shed their shipping and shipbuilding interests.

4

INTRODUCTION

If Britain's maritime interests generally blossomed before 1914, the dislocation and contraction ushered in by the First World War were almost as pervasive. In the short term, as the contributions to this volume show, the conflict entailed losses of ships and men to enemy action, the curtailment of fishing operations in the North Sea and beyond, and the prohibition of pleasure sailing in home waters. In the longer run, the Great War proved to be a great turning point in the pattern and vitality of sea-borne trade as 'unfair' competition from the railways severely depressed coastal shipping, while a proliferation of energetic foreign rivals emerged to challenge Britain's sea transport and fishing industries. Though it was not until 1932, as Alan G. Jamieson points out, that the British government fully acknowledged this watershed by bringing to a close the era of free trade, the business environment since 1918 has never been as favourable for Britain's maritime industries as it had been before 1914. As a consequence, these interests have experienced marked fluctuations and periodic crises during the course of the twentieth century. Accordingly, as Alan G. Jamieson suggests, the shipping and shipbuilding industries have passed through four phases of growth and contraction since 1930, while the prosperity of the maritime defence industry has fluctuated in line with the cycle of war/peace/rearmament identified by Andrew Gordon. The underlying trend in each case, however, has been one of relative, then absolute, decline. Only the coastal leisure industry has followed a markedly different developmental pattern, enjoying growth in the interwar years and the 1960s, as Janet Cusack indicates, when other sea-related concerns faltered. Even so, as Nigel Morgan relates, crisis and depression have visited this facet of the maritime economy since 1970.

The final broad insight provided by this volume is perhaps the most important. As Sidney Pollard contends, the economic development of the nation as a whole has largely governed the evolution of Britian's maritime interests. It follows, therefore, that a broad consideration of these sea-related activities provides a good, if unusual, vantage point from which to view the growth of the British economy since 1870. That exploiting the sea has been such a significant facet of recent British economic history renders such a perspective both clear and instructive.

NOTES

1. Frank Broeze, (ed.), *Maritime History at the Crossroads: A Critical Review of Recent Historiography* (St John's, Newfoundland, 1995), ix.
2. See Basil Greenhill, 'Epilogue: *The New Maritime History of Devon* and the Maritime Aspects of History' in M. Duffy *et al.*, (eds), *The New Maritime History of Devon: Volume II, From the Late Eighteenth Century to the Present Day* (London, 1994), 268.
3. See David M. Williams, 'The Progress of Maritime History, 1953–1993', *Journal of Transport History*, 14 (1993), 127–41.

CHAPTER 1

Growth and Transition in Britain's Maritime Economy, 1870–1914: The Case of South-West England

David J. Starkey

As the study and historiography of maritime history have developed in recent years, so the term 'maritime' has taken on a fuller, more literal meaning. Now it is widely accepted that this field of enquiry extends beyond shipping and shipbuilding to include all facets of the utilisation of the sea by human societies. While the exploitation of the sea has assumed many different forms, most guises can be placed into one of four functional categories: that is, the use of the sea as a means of transport, as a source of food and fuel, as a medium for the projection of power, and as a zone for recreation, recuperation and retirement.[1] Of course, an array of sea-related activities might be listed according to these functional divisions. Many of these track back deep into an economy and are located far from the sea; for instance, while the consumption of sea fish and foreign imports, and the production of naval weapons and overseas exports, are, in a sense, sea-related, such activities often take place inland, in communities distant spatially, economically and culturally from the sea. To examine maritime activity in any meaningful way, some form of gradation is therefore desirable, some recognition that certain sea-related concerns are more vital to a nation's economy than others.

In line with this thinking, the present chapter focuses on what might be termed the core of Britain's maritime economy in the 1870–1914 period. While it is acknowledged that a host of sea-related activities of a secondary or auxiliary character had an important bearing on the nation's economy and society, the parameters of this discussion are drawn around six industries that were—and still are—unequivocally sea-reliant, essentially located on the coast, and interrelated in many significant respects. Three of these industries were largely conditioned by the extent, character and direction of sea-borne trade. Collectively dubbed the 'sea transport industries', shipping, shipbuilding and port operation in late Victorian and Edwardian Britain were closely related in that shipowners consumed the products of shipbuilders and used the facilities provided by port owners, while all three utilised, and competed for, waterfront space. The fishing industry, though concerned with exploiting the living resources, rather than the surface, of the sea, had many linkages with the sea transport sector, not least in deploying vessels constructed in British shipyards, utilising port space and competing with shipping for labour and investment funds. The fifth of the principal maritime industries, maritime defence, had similarly strong links with the shipping, shipbuilding and port industries, but was also charged *inter alia* with protecting Britain's sea transport and fishing interests. 'Coastal leisure', the remaining maritime industry, comprised that assortment of recreational activities that together formed the business of the seaside resort. Though functionally and practically very different from the other elements of the maritime economy, the coastal leisure industry nevertheless consumed some of the products of shipbuilders, vied with shipping and fishing interests for access to the waterfront, and flourished in coastal communities which also engaged in other maritime pursuits.

These central components of Britain's maritime economy all expanded in absolute terms during the 1870–1914 period. For instance, as the *Annual Statements of Navigation and Shipping* indicate, most performance indicators in the sea transport industries moved upwards. The capital stock of the shipping industry, as reflected in the merchant tonnage registered, more than doubled, from 5.63million to 11.68million net tons, between 1871 and 1911. At the same time, the output of the port industry, in terms of total shipping movements, increased by 125 per cent, from 117million to 264million tons, while shipbuilding production grew still faster, with 1.1million tons launched in 1911 as against 391,000 tons in 1871. Expansion was likewise evident in the fishing industry, with tonnage registered increasing by 36 per cent, from 252,600 to 344,300 tons between 1871 and 1911. Meanwhile, the maritime defence industry also experienced substantial growth, annual investment rising by over 400 per cent, from £9million to £45.5million over the same 40-year period.

A further performance indicator, employment, can be applied more widely across the maritime dimension of the economy. As

Table 1.1 shows, the occupational breakdown contained in the census suggests that the number of males occupied in fishing, port, shipbuilding and maritime defence activity rose significantly between 1871 and 1911, though a small decline was evident in the shipping industry. In the aggregate, moreover, employment in the maritime industries expanded at a faster rate than the increase in the male population of England, Wales and Scotland, implying that sea-related activity was expanding relative to the economy as a whole. This contention is given added weight by the fact that the coastal leisure industry is omitted from the analysis. Though yet to reach its peak, this recreational business developed steadily in the decades prior to 1914, with seaside tourism notably buoyant. For example, between 1881 and 1911 the aggregate population of English and Welsh seaside resorts increased by over 60 per cent from 995,400 to 1,600,200 inhabitants. Of course, not all of these coastal dwellers worked in resort occupations. But a significant proportion, especially of females, found employment in catering for visitors and holidaymakers, albeit on a casual, seasonal basis.[2]

Table 1.1: Males Engaged in Maritime Occupations in England, Wales and Scotland, 1871–1911 ('000)

	1871	1911	% change
Fishing	47.0	53.2	+13.2
Port	64.5	167.3	+159.2
Shipping	125.7	119.3	-5.1
Shipbuilding	61.8	155.4	+151.5
Maritime Defence	44.1	93.9	+112.9
Total	343.1	589.1	+71.7
Total Male Population	12,660.6	15,969.8	+26.1
% in Maritime Occupations	2.7	3.7	

Source: *Census of the Population*, 1871, 1911.

While such data paint a rosy picture of all-pervasive growth in Britain's maritime economy, this image is not quite so bright in a comparative light. Relative to the economy as a whole, the maritime industries generally performed well. For instance, whereas much of the manufacturing sector was losing ground to foreign competitors, the shipping and shipbuilding industries comfortably maintained

9

their positions as world leaders down to the First World War. Yet caution should be exercised on three fronts. Firstly, according to the 1911 census, there were nearly four times as many men recorded as working 'on the railways' than there were in the shipping industry—397,990 as against 99,199. On the roads, a further 278,423 men worked as 'carmen, carters and waggoners (not farm)', while in the manufacturing sector 104,508 males were engaged in shipbuilding compared to the 480,174 males and 642,041 females employed in textile production. With over one million working below ground in mines and quarries, some 92,171 engaged in agricultural pursuits, and 226,266 male domestic outdoor servants, including 67,228 coachmen and grooms, 118,739 domestic gardeners, 23,151 motor car drivers, and 17,148 gamekeepers, the ascendancy of the land over the sea in employment terms was very clear. Secondly, in an international context, the performance of Britain's maritime industries was impressive in many, but not all, respects. For instance, a range of markers point to the vast extent of Britain's maritime interests. Possessing over 41 per cent of the world's steam shipping stock, launching over 60 per cent of the world's tonnage, carrying 52 per cent of the world's trade,[3] catching more fish than any other nation, deploying the largest naval fleet on the oceans, and relishing the delights of more seaside resorts than any other nation, Britons were pre-eminent in most matters maritime. However, it should be noted that exploiting the sea was considerably more important in relative terms in various other countries. Accordingly, on a tons per capita basis, in 1913 the ownership of merchant shipping was more significant in Norway (1.15 tons per capita) and Denmark (0.34) than in Britain (0.22), while Sweden's fleet was the same size by this relative measure. Likewise, Iceland's fishing industry, though much smaller and less productive than its British counterpart, was proportionately more important to the population; indeed, in the early twentieth century, whereas fishing was a comparatively minor industry in Britain, in Iceland it emerged as the leading sector which to some degree stimulated the 'take off' of the national economy.[4]

A third sense in which Britain's maritime economy was not altogether buoyant lay in the spatial distribution of activity. While the development of Britain's maritime interests entailed the growing concentration of sea-related activities in particular districts and ports, there were other regions which experienced mixed fortunes, pockets of growth emerging as virtually terminal decline afflicted sea-related industries which had been prosecuted on a substantial scale for many centuries. This chapter is concerned with south-west England, a region comprising the counties of Cornwall and Devon, where the pattern of limited growth and marked decline was clearly apparent. Attention is initially focused on the absolute changes that marked the development of the South West's maritime interests. The relative performance of these sea-related interests is then assessed, with the factors conditioning this pattern of transition identified in the final section of the chapter. It is hoped that such a discussion will refine the conventional wisdom which has it that in all respects Britannia truly ruled the waves in the late nineteenth and early twentieth centuries.

Absolute Change in the South West's Maritime Economy, 1870–1914

The maritime interests of south-west England were broad and well established by 1870. With its two long, generously indented coastlines, this peninsular region was favourably endowed for the pursuit of sea related activity. The South West's situation in relation to the Atlantic and southern Europe also proved advantageous, not only from a commercial point of view but also from a strategic perspective. Accordingly, from the 1690s, the region's maritime economy encompassed an important and permanent naval presence, as well as longstanding and strong interests in local and transatlantic fisheries, and in the shipping, port and shipbuilding industries which served the needs of coastal and overseas trade. Moreover, by the mid-nineteenth century, the recreational and health restorative qualities of the region's coasts had long been appreciated, and the foundations of a substantial coastal leisure industry had been laid.[5]

This broadly based relationship with the sea was to change decisively between 1870 and the outbreak of the First World War. During this period, the maritime defence industry and, to a lesser extent, the coastal leisure business emerged as the central facets of the region's maritime economy, while the fishing and sea transport industries experienced varying degrees of relative and absolute decline. These broad shifts can be discerned in the occupational breakdown of the decennial census of the population. At the aggregate level, as Table 1.2 shows, the number of workers employed in the region's principal maritime industries increased from 32,765 to 48,499 between 1871 and 1911, a rise of 48 per cent. Much of this expansion took place in the maritime defence industry. In the 40 years down to 1911, the number of men engaged in navy-related work increased from 10,758 to almost 28,000, an increase of some 159 per cent. During this period, the proportion of the region's

Table 1.2: Employment in the South West's Principal Maritime Industries, 1871–1911

	1871		1911		% change 1871–1911
Maritime Defence (a)	10,758	(0)	27,882	(0)	+159
Coastal Leisure (b)	4,063	(2,465)	6,642	(4,578)	+ 63
Fishing (c)	4,583	(23)	5,218	(2)	+ 14
Port (d)	676	(0)	2,031	(3)	+200
Shipping (e)	9,226	(25)	4,947	(15)	- 46
Shipbuilding (f)	3,459	(0)	1,779	(16)	- 48
Total	32,765	(2,513)	48,499	(4,614)	+ 48

Note: Occupational categories:

a   officers and men of the Navy; Navy half-pay officers; officers and men of the Marines. *1911 figure includes 4,285 shipyard workers resident in Devonport and Plymouth.*

b   innkeepers; lodging-house keepers; coffee-house keepers; inn servants; others—boarding and lodging. *These totals have been halved to take account of employment in inland and 'non-tourist' inns and lodging houses.*

c   fishermen; fisherwomen.

d   1871: dock labourers; wharfingers; navigation service. 1911: dock labourers; harbour officials; navigation service (on shore).

e   1871: shipowners; seamen; stewards, cooks, etc.; pilots. 1911: merchant service - seamen (navigation and engineering departments; cooks, stewards, etc.; pilots)

f   1871: ship, boat, barge builders; shipwrights; mast, yard, oar, blockmakers; shipriggers; sailmakers. 1911: ship-platers, rivetters, painters; shipwrights; shipyard labourers; others engaged in iron or wood ship and boat building. *1911 figure excludes 4,285 shipyard workers resident in Devonport and Plymouth.*

Figures in brackets denote female workers.

Source: *Census of the Population, 1871, 1911.*

maritime workforce deployed in such state-funded activity grew from less than one-third to over 57 per cent. At the same time, employment in the South West's coastal leisure industry increased by some 63 per cent, the preponderance of females in the labour force reflecting the domestic character of much of the work. By 1911, this was the second largest source of jobs in the region's maritime economy, with an estimated 6,642 employees, over 68 per cent of whom were women, engaged in resort occupations. Expansion was also evident in the region's fishing and port industries, though the former increased at a very modest rate, while the latter grew from such a small base that only just over 2,000 men and three women were engaged in port work in 1911. Shipping and shipbuilding evidently fared less well, the number of seafarers and shipyard workers resident in Cornwall and Devon declining appreciably after 1871.

Data relating to the individual maritime industries tend to substantiate and refine this general picture. Growth in the maritime defence industry, for example, is further suggested by the burgeoning volume of capital invested in naval facilities and infrastructure in the South West during the Victorian and Edwardian eras. Such investment tended to occur in spurts. Thus, between 1846 and 1853, as the Admiralty sought to keep abreast of the latest shipbuilding technology, a major engineering works, the Keyham Steam Yard, was built at Devonport Dockyard at a cost of some £1.225million. The construction of barrack accommodation in 1879 and the Royal Naval Engineering College in 1880 added substantially to the Admiralty's interests in Plymouth, though the greatest surge in naval expenditure occurred from the 1890s as the naval arms race intensified. Accordingly, in the decade following the 1896 Naval Works Act over £4million was spent on the construction of a modern shipbuilding and engineering plant, the Keyham Extension, while a further £300,000 was invested in barrack and educational facilities.[6]

The development of the South West's coastal leisure industry is less easy to chart, though there are numerous signs that its two principal components, seaside tourism and recreational sailing, expanded during the 1870–1914 period. With regard to coastal holidaymaking, this is implicit in the population increases which marked towns with identifiable resort functions. Such growth was particularly apparent in South Devon. Torquay's population, for example, expanded from 26,283 in 1871 to 38,771 in 1911, while the same period saw the number of residents in Paignton grow from 3,590 to 11,241, and those in Exmouth from 6,524 to 11,962. Elsewhere in the region, there was an appreciable increase in Ilfracombe's population, from 3,677 in 1851 to 8,935 in 1911, and likewise in the Cornish towns of Penzance, Falmouth and St Ives, which boasted 13,478, 13,132 and 7,170 residents in 1911 respectively, though in each of these cases the population included a substantial non-resort element.[7] There are further indications of resort growth in the numbers of visitors travelling to the Devon coast. In 1913, for instance, the Great Western Railway conveyed a total of 369,145 passengers to Dawlish Warren, Dawlish, Teignmouth, Torquay and Paignton, a rise of 20 per cent on the 1903 figure. Similarly, on the North Devon coast, there was a steady increase in the number of day-trippers transported by steamer from South Wales to Ilfracombe in the pre-1914 era, the availability of alcoholic beverages on the cross-Channel passage proving highly attractive to those facing 'dry' Sundays in Wales.[8]

Recreational sailing—boating, yachting and 'cruising for pleasure'—appears to have developed considerably in the South West during the second half of the nineteenth century. Such activity, which encompassed the aquatic pastimes of coastal communities as well as the conspicuous displays of the gentleman seafarer, had long since been practised in the region's estuaries and inshore waters. But there are clear indications that recreational sailing was not only becoming more widespread, but also increasingly commercialised and institutionalised after 1870. Regattas, for instance, featured ever more prominently in the calendar of attractions at nascent resorts such as Teignmouth, Dartmouth and Salcombe. The number of yacht clubs increased, with the Royal Dart, the Royal Torbay, the Royal Western and the Royal Plymouth Corinthian all established between 1870 and the turn of the century. Thus, whereas in 1852 South Devon's sole yacht club mustered some 85 members, who owned an aggregate of 5,329 tons (Thames measurement [TM]), in 1900 the district boasted six clubs with a combined membership of 282 boatowners and a 'fleet' which totalled 17,572 tons (TM). Sailing clubs also prospered at this time, with no less than 13 founded in South Devon by the turn of the century. Such growth is echoed in the expansion of yacht-building activity. While fewer than 60 yachts were launched in South Devon during the 1875–9 quinquennium, at least 200 of this varied class of vessel were completed in the area between 1895 and 1899. Something of a peak appears to have been reached at this stage, however, for the number of yachts built in South Devon, and the membership lists of local yacht and sailing clubs, tended to subside in the opening decade of the twentieth century.[9]

The South West's fishing industry expanded during the second half of the nineteenth century, though most measures suggest that a decline set in during the 1890s and 1900s. For instance, according to the census returns, employment levels increased from 4,583 to 5,218 between 1871 and 1911, with a peak of 5,760 fishermen reached in

1891. A similar pattern emerges from the figures generated by the statutory registration of fishing vessels. As Table 1.3 shows, the fleet registered in the South West increased from 16,896 to 25,702 tons between 1871 and 1891, before contracting to 21,803 tons in 1911. The quantity of fish landed in the region also fluctuated. Thus, the Sea Fisheries Inspectorate reported that just over 590,000 cwt of fish was landed in Devon and Cornwall in 1886, the figure increasing steadily over the next 20 years to reach a peak of almost 663,000 cwt in 1906. Five years later, however, landings in the region had declined to less than 564,000 cwt and in 1913 stood at just 406,000 cwt.[10]

Table 1.3: The South West's Fishing Fleet, 1871–1911 (net tons; sail and steam; 1st and 2nd class vessels)

	1871	1891	1911
Falmouth	1,113	393	483
Fowey	1,572	2,276	2,417
Hayle	2,235	2,642	-
Padstow	154	156	462
Penzance	732	4,019	4,112
St Ives	-	-	2,525
Scilly	-	13	111
Truro	208	55	154
Cornwall	6,014	9,554	10,264
Barnstaple	189	296	29
Bideford	196	-	98
Brixham	-	-	7,328
Dartmouth	6,236	10,455	182
Exeter	377	371	633
Plymouth	3,326	4,665	2,924
Salcombe	-	-	72
Teignmouth	558	361	273
Devon	10,882	16,148	11,539
South West	16,896	25,702	21,803
England and Wales	12,6917	207,269	190,008
% South West	13.3	12.4	11.5

Source: *Annual Statements of Navigation and Shipping.*

Absolute growth in the South West's port industry was more sustained. In line with the increase in its workforce, the industry's capacity improved in many respects during the late nineteenth century. For instance, in Cornwall, harbour provisions at Par and

Table 1.4: Shipping Movements in the South West's Ports, 1850–1911 ('000 net tons; entrances and clearances; foreign and coastal trade; with cargoes and in ballast)

	1850*	1871*	1891	1911
Falmouth	103.5	146.7	420.5	803.8
Fowey	141.3	142.5	459.4	761.3
Hayle	61.0	167.0	-	-
Padstow	67.2	50.3	68.0	47.6
Penzance	212.7	100.2	460.1	462.2
Scilly	12.2	29.1	27.6	33.8
Truro	119.7	105.1	-	-
Cornwall	717.6	740.9	1,435.6	2,108.7
Barnstaple	65.2	142.2	363.3	396.5
Bideford	46.3	67.0	-	-
Dartmouth	111.3	84.9	252.3	368.5
Exeter	137.5	76.2	145.4	142.5
Plymouth	720.6	888.4	1,502.0	4,915.4
Teignmouth	-	62.7	252.8	244.9
Devon	1,080.9	1,321.4	2,515.8	6,067.8
South West	1,798.5	2,062.3	3,951.4	8,176.5
England and Wales	34,273.1	60,260.2	128,574.0	211,204.9
% South West	5.2	3.4	3.1	3.9

Note: * coastal trade, with cargoes only.
Sources: For 1850, *Accounts and Papers* (BPP, 1851, LII, 213); for 1871–1911
          Annual Statements of Navigation and Shipping.

Newquay were transformed by Joseph Thomas Treffry, while members of the Harvey family invested much capital in the enhancement of Hayle harbour.[11] Devon's port infrastructure also developed during this period, most notably at Plymouth where the construction of Millbay Docks in the 1850s, the steady improvement of Sutton Harbour's facilities from mid-century, and the development of the Cattewater in the 1870s and 1880s added greatly to the port's capacity.[12] There were further signs and causes of the

South West's burgeoning sea-borne traffic in the rail linkages effected between harbours and hinterlands at sites as diverse as Fowey and Fremington, Kingswear and the Cattewater, Millbay and Exmouth. Such physical developments were necessary to

Table 1.5: Shipping Registered in the South West's Ports, 1850–1911 ('000 net tons; sail and steam)

	1850	1871	1891	1911*	
Falmouth	7.3	17.1	18.4	29.1	
Fowey	10.7	15.6	14.4	6.4	
Hayle	-	4.3	-	-	
Padstow	8.2	10.6	8.9	2.9	
Penzance	9.2	8.1	11.2	5.3	
St Ives	10.2	6.4	25.8	67.3	
Scilly	6.8	5.2	0.3	-	
Truro	3.9	4.5	2.4	1.1	
Cornwall	56.3	71.8	81.4	112.1	
Barnstaple	4.9	3.6	2.5	2.0	
Bideford	10.1	10.4	4.1	3.5	
Brixham	-	15.5	13.1	8.0	
Dartmouth	33.7	17.6	2.8	4.0	
Exeter	18.4	12.0	2.4	1.0	
Plymouth	41.8	42.5	35.6	101.8	(10.4)
Salcombe	-	12.2	4.4	1.9	
Teignmouth	-	5.7	2.1	2.2	
Devon	108.9	119.5	67.0	124.4	(33.0)
South West	165.2	191.3	148.4	236.5	(145.1)
England and Wales	2,721.3	4,465.7	6,017.5	8,602.7	
% South West	6.1	4.3	2.5	2.7	(1.7)

Note: * Figures in brackets exclude 91,402 tons owned by the New Zealand Shipping Company.

Sources: For 1850, *Accounts and Papers* (BPP, 1851, LII, 213); for 1871–1911, *Annual Statements of Navigation and Shipping*.

accommodate, and in turn facilitated, the growing volume of traffic entering and clearing the region's ports.[13] Accordingly, as Table 1.4 indicates, total shipping movements handled by the region's Customs Ports increased from under 2million to over 8million tons between 1870 and 1911, the most pronounced increase occurring in the 1890s and the first decade of the twentieth century.

If the volume of shipping activity in the South West tended to grow after 1870, this was not reflected in the development of the region's shipping and shipbuilding industries. In both cases, expansion was evident until the third quarter of the nineteenth century, with marked and rapid contraction taking place thereafter. For instance, as Table 1.5 indicates, the capital stock of the region's shipping industry extended to some 191,300 tons in 1871, the fleet diminishing steadily over the next 20 years so that it totalled just 148,400 tons in 1891. Though the official figures indicate that registrations increased considerably down to 1911, this renewed growth was illusory, for it merely reflected the fact that for technical reasons the New Zealand Shipping Company began to register its large, ocean-going steamers at Plymouth from 1890. If this extra-regional fleet is omitted from Table 1.5, West Country registrations amounted to just 145,100 tons in 1911, a decline of nearly 50,000 tons on the 1871 figure.[14]

Shipbuilding followed a similar path. Steady expansion was evident in the unit size, workforce and output of the region's shipyards during the 1850s and 1860s. However, during the next decade a sharp reversal took place in these trends and the South West's interests in shipbuilding declined precipitously down to the First World War. This is clearly illustrated in the production figures presented in Table 1.6; whereas in 1871 the South West's shipyards produced 7,124 tons of shipping, in 1911 output had shrunk to 997 tons. By this time, moreover, a substantial proportion of the vessels built in the region were intended for recreational use. Indeed, the construction of sailing yachts and steam launches provided a lifeline which enabled the more resilient and adaptable of the South West's shipbuilders to stay in business during the late nineteenth century.[15] This development, together with the fact that a large number of the vessels registered in the region, as well as many of its seafarers, were not actually employed in trading activity, but in recreational sailing, merely serves to emphasise the parallel contractions which afflicted the South West's merchant shipping and shipbuilding industries in the late Victorian and Edwardian period.

The absolute decline of shipping and shipbuilding was the most obvious sign of the changing structure of the region's maritime economy. For centuries, ocean-going and coastal vessels had been built, owned and manned with West Country resources, but from the 1870s this erstwhile significant and widely pervasive activity was to represent a small and diminishing facet of the region's exploitation of the sea. Yet sea-borne trade was still important in the South West as the growing volume of business handled by the

Table 1.6: The South West's Shipbuilding Output, 1871–1911 (net tons; including overseas sales)

	1871	1891	1911
Falmouth	305	222	84
Fowey	219	0	37
Hayle	87	-	-
Padstow	653	0	0
Penzance	493	2,240	105
St Ives	185	0	0
Scilly	0	29	0
Truro	135	24	0
Cornwall	2,077	2,515	226
Barnstaple	624	0	0
Bideford	976	170	91
Brixham	1,083	170	346
Dartmouth	401	457	297
Exeter	50	0	0
Plymouth	1,067	302	1
Salcombe	586	97	36
Teignmouth	260	0	0
Devon	5,047	1,196	771
South West	7,124	3,711	997
England and Wales	237,751	410,885	484,867
% South West	3.0	0.9	0.2

Sources: *Annual Statements of Navigation and Shipping.*

region's port industry attests. Moreover, with absolute growth evident in the maritime defence and coastal leisure industries, and fishing activity of some import, the South West's interests in the sea remained strong. Indeed, in the context of the development of the regional economy, it would appear that sea-related activity, in the aggregate, gained in significance during the 1870–1914 period.

The South West's Maritime Industries in a Regional Setting

The process of industrialisation invariably and inevitably entails contrasting regional experiences.[16] In Britain, the nineteenth century witnessed high rates of growth in manufacturing output, population and consumption in the burgeoning industrial districts located primarily on the coalfields of the North and the Midlands. At the same time, regions beyond the industrial core, including much of southern England, not only evinced relatively sluggish rates of growth but were also characterised by absolute contractions in a range of once significant industries. South-west England typified this latter pattern. Increasingly peripheral to, and dependent upon, 'up country' manufacturing centres, the region experienced a degree of de-industrialisation from the 1790s onwards. This can be perceived in the demise of Devon's extensive woollen textile industry during the first quarter of the nineteenth century, and in the dramatic collapse of Cornwall's metal mining interests in the 1860s and 1870s.[17] With agriculture also entering a prolonged depression as cheap foreign produce penetrated the British market from the 1870s, the economic and social problems posed by the South West's shrinking industrial base were compounded.

Against this background, maritime activity generally assumed a growing prominence in the South West during the 1870–1914 period. This is evident in the growth and distribution of the region's population. Between 1801 and 1901, the number of people resident in Cornwall and Devon rose from 532,000 to 984,000, a much smaller rate of increase than that evident nationally (247 per cent), and one that disguises the absolute contraction which marked Cornwall's demographic experience from 1861.[18] Within the region, however, there were areas which exhibited comparatively high rates of population growth. The most notable of these districts were situated on the coast, their economies reliant to a large degree on sea-related activities. For example, the population of the Plymouth conurbation, a large proportion of which depended on the sea transport, fishing and, most importantly, maritime defence industries, increased from 40,000 to 178,000 between 1801 and 1901, a rate of growth (345 per cent) approaching that evident in the nation's leading industrial towns.[19] Seaside resorts also tended to buck the regional trend; for example, Torquay, Paignton and Exmouth expanded at rates of 462.1 per cent, 235.3 per cent and 104.8 per cent respectively between 1841 and 1901,[20] while rates of 175.9 per cent and 117.6 per cent were exhibited by Newquay and Bude between 1881 and 1911.[21]

Table 1.7: Employment in Agriculture, Mining and Maritime-Related
Activities in the South West, 1871–1911

	1871		1911	
	No.	% of Total Occupied in South West *	No.	% of Total Occupied in South West *
Agriculture	112,928	24.2	75,739	16.8
Mining	33,608	7.2	16,712	3.7
Maritime	32,765	7	48,499	10.8

Note: * The total occupied in the South West in 1871 was 466,828; in 1911
        450,268.
Source: *Census of the Population*, 1871, 1911 (see Table 1.2).

The occupational breakdown of the census further attests to the
growing significance of sea-related employment in the West
Country. Whereas the population of Cornwall and Devon increased
by 6.6 per cent, from 964,500 to 1,028,000, between 1871 and 1911,
the maritime workforce expanded by 48 per cent over the same
period (Table 1.2). Relative to the total occupied in the South West,
as Table 1.7 shows, the growth in maritime-related employment was
still more impressive, for the region's working population decreased
during the 1871–1911 period. Accordingly, as a proportion of the
region's workforce, sea-related employment assumed a growing
significance, increasing from 7 to 10.8 per cent of those occupied
between 1871 and 1911. This growth stands in marked contrast to
the substantial and sustained contraction apparent in agriculture
and mining, two central facets of the South West's mid-nineteenth-
century economy. While employment in maritime activities rose by
nearly 50 per cent during the 1871–1911 period, the numbers
engaged in mining and quarrying almost halved and the agrarian
labour force diminished considerably.

While sea-related employment expanded disproportionately in
the South West between 1870 and 1914, this growth was skewed in
two senses. In the first place, expansion was not evenly spread
across the maritime economy but focused chiefly in navy-related
and coastal leisure occupations. Indeed, the contraction of
employment in shipping, shipbuilding and, from the 1890s, fishing
added a maritime dimension to the process of de-industrialisation
which marked the West Country's nineteenth-century economy.
Secondly, spatial concentration, which entailed a degree of
specialisation, was a marked feature of the region's sea-related

21

industries. Naval expenditure in the South West, for example, was largely channelled into the dockyard-naval base complex at Devonport, though some training and educational facilities were developed elsewhere in the region, most notably the establishment of Britannia Royal Naval College at Dartmouth in 1902–4.[22] Sea-borne trade was handled at a great number of harbours and shipping places along the South West's shores, but Plymouth was clearly and increasingly the region's dominant port, accounting for 43 per cent of its total shipping movements in 1871, a figure that had risen to 60 per cent by 1911 (Table 1.4). Fishing, too, became more narrowly focused in the late nineteenth and early twentieth centuries, with over 65 per cent of the region's fleet being registered in Brixham, Plymouth and Penzance (Newlyn) in 1911 (Table 1.3). Locational changes were likewise apparent in the shipping and shipbuilding industries. A feature of all the South West's ports in the mid-nineteenth century, these activities were waning in importance from the 1870s, a pattern reflected in the concentration of shipowning and shipyards in fewer and fewer localities. By the early twentieth century, the region's shipping interests were largely centred on St Ives, which meant the considerable steamship fleet of Hain & Co.,[23] and Falmouth, the port of registration for the steamers managed by R. B. Chellew of Truro (Table 1.5).[24] Shipbuilding, by this time, was principally undertaken at a handful of yards at Brixham, Bideford, Dartmouth and Penzance (Table 1.6).[25]

Such patterns were not so evident in the coastal leisure industry. A growing number of West Country coastal communities developed resort functions during the 1870–1914 period, many adapting to the decline in their sea transport and fishing interests by turning to seaside tourism and recreational sailing. Into this category belong towns such as Penzance, Falmouth, Dartmouth and Bideford, which not only pursued 'traditional' maritime activities but also accommodated holidaymakers and excursionists.[26] Indeed, in some instances the one begat the other as the instant theatre of the fisherman, the seafarer or the stevedore at work served as something of a tourist attraction. However, even as this recreational business spread along the coasts, some concentration was taking place, for it was the larger, well-established resorts like Torquay, Paignton and Exmouth which experienced the higher rates of business and population growth during the late Victorian and Edwardian eras.

In essence, sea-related activity was becoming more significant in the context of the South West's economy during the 1870–1914 period. But the changing balance of the region's maritime interests meant that this expansionary role was increasingly focused on particular industries and most keenly felt in particular coastal localities. A different light is cast on this pattern of growth and transition if it is viewed from a national perspective.

The South West's Maritime Industries in a National Context

The strength and breadth of Britain's maritime interests in the 1870–1914 period were truly remarkable. Though operating in different markets and according to different influences, each of the nation's principal sea-related industries reached a relative peak at some stage during the late nineteenth and early twentieth centuries. Like the economy as a whole, however, there were major disparities in the regional distribution of these buoyant maritime industries. The South West, while accommodating facets of each of the principal sea-related activities, a distinction shared by few other regions, experienced relative decline in many of its maritime interests. This is again indicated in the census returns. As Table 1.8 shows, the total workforce engaged in the maritime defence, fishing and sea transport industries of England and Wales increased from 238,591 to 443,276 between 1871 and 1911, a faster rate of increase (86 per cent) than that pertaining in Cornwall and Devon (46 per cent). Within this broad picture, a slower than average rate of growth was evident in the South West's fishing workforce, though it still amounted to a fifth of the national total in 1911. Likewise, census analysis suggests that the region's coastal leisure industry, despite its absolute expansion, was growing much more slowly than the business at large, local seaside resorts, for instance, experiencing moderate population increases compared to those exhibited by such booming recreational centres as Blackpool, Brighton, Southend and Margate.[27] While the contraction in the South West's seafaring and shipbuilding labour force was comparatively sharp, there were pockets of relative growth in the region's maritime economy. Quite clearly, as Table 1.8 demonstrates, the increase in employment in the region's maritime defence and port industries compared favourably with the national pattern, the growth in navy-related work being particularly impressive in that roughly one-third of the industry's 85,000-strong labour force was based in the South West in 1871 and 1911.

Analysis of various other sources largely confirms this general developmental pattern. Warshipbuilding and repair work undertaken at Devonport Dockyard, for example, undoubtedly formed a significant part of the output of Britain's maritime defence industry. Moreover, with 17 battleships (including five dreadnoughts), two battlecruisers and 14 cruisers constructed at Devonport between 1883 and 1914—a record rivalled only by Portsmouth—the Dockyard's output was both large in scale and technically sophisticated. Plymouth's significance as a naval base, and the development of training and educational facilities in its vicinity, were further important facets of the region's interest in maritime defence. Indeed, with over 21,000 seamen and marines ashore or in port on census night, in 1911—the great majority in Plymouth—including a sizeable complement of ratings and officers under training at HMS *Cambridge* and Britannia Royal Naval College, South Devon accommodated one of the largest concentrations of naval personnel in Europe on the eve of the First World War.[28]

Table 1.8: Employment in Selected Maritime Industries, England and Wales, 1871–1911*

	Number employed		% change	% change SW	% employed in SW	
	1871	1911	1871–1911	1871–1911	1871	1911
Maritime Defence	31,613	85,206	+169	+159	34.0	32.7
Fishing	21,043	25,239	+ 20	+ 14	21.8	20.7
Port	36,499	128,277	+251	+200	1.9	1.6
Shipping	104,272	99,804	- 4	- 46	8.8	5.0
Shipb'g	45,164	104,750	+132	- 48	7.7	1.7
Total	238,591	443,276	+86	+46		

Note: * The coastal leisure industry is excluded from this table.
Source: *Census of the Population*, 1871, 1911 (see Table 1.2).

The South West's marine recreational industry expanded at a more leisurely pace during the late nineteenth and early twentieth centuries. In fact, it was the genteel, unspoilt character of the region's resorts and coastline which attracted a largely middle-class clientele of holidaymakers, short-stay visitors and recreational sailors to the area. Hence, investment in popular attractions and amenities for a mass market, which proceeded apace in the principal English resorts, and was to transform the coastal communities of Cornwall as well as Devon after 1918, was generally absent and actively discouraged in most of the socially refined watering places of the West Country. Of the south-western resorts, only Ilfracombe, and latterly Paignton, catered for the working-class excursionist and holidaymaker to any great extent, and even here levels of investment in resort facilities and attractions were small-scale and piecemeal.[29]

The relative standing of the West Country's sea transport and fishing industries can be discerned in the *Annual Statements of Navigation and Shipping*. In quantitative terms, these returns generally concur with the employment patterns drawn from the census. Thus, the comparative decline in the South West's shipping stock is once more evident. Whereas the tonnage registered in the South West represented 4.3 per cent of the total for England and Wales in 1871, the equivalent figure for 1911 was 2.7 per cent, and even this exaggerated the South West's real stake in shipping for it included the vessels of the New Zealand Shipping Company. Disregarding such registrations, the region accounted for a mere 1.7 per cent of the English fleet on the eve of the First World War (Table 1.5). The relative contraction of the region's shipbuilding industry was of a similar magnitude. Having launched 3 per cent of the tonnage produced in England and Wales in 1871, south-western shipyards contributed just 0.2 per cent to the total in 1911 (Table 1.6).

With regard to the South West's port and fishing industries, the picture emerging from the *Annual Statements* differs slightly from that gleaned from the census. In the region's port industry, as Table 1.4 shows, entrances and clearances in the coastal and foreign trades increased steadily during the 1870–1911 period, keeping pace with the expansion of the national total so that the South West's share in sea-borne trade remained stable at between 3.4 per cent and 3.9 per cent during the 1871–1911 period. The region's fishing effort likewise assumes a slightly different complexion if its capital stock is examined. Though at least 20 per cent of English and Welsh fishermen hailed from the West Country during the 1870–1914 period, a much smaller, and diminishing, element of the nation's fishing fleet was registered in the region. Accordingly, in 1871, as Table 1.3 shows, just 13.3 per cent of the 1st and 2nd class fishing tonnage registered in England and Wales was owned in the South West, the proportion declining to 11.5 per cent in 1911.

In terms of the quality of the merchant and fishing vessels operated, owned and built in the 1870–1914 period, further discrepancies between regional and national patterns can be detected. As Table 1.9 indicates, West Country vessels tended to be smaller than average, the divergence between local and national means generally widening over time. This was most apparent in the shipbuilding industry, the size of the average vessel launched from south-western shipyards declining from 78.2 to 28.3 tons between 1871 and 1911 as the typical product of the industry at large increased from 323 to 688.7 tons. In contrast, the mean tonnage of vessels registered in Cornwall and Devon more than doubled during this period, though the increase was largely attributable to the 18 steamers (91,402 tons) owned by the New Zealand Shipping Company but registered in Plymouth. Excluding this fleet, the size of the average local vessel had improved to just 130.6 tons by 1911, whereas a mean of 531.3 tons prevailed nationally. Similar trends were evident in the South West's port and fishing industries, with mean vessel size increasing during the 1871–1911 period while lagging well behind the equivalent national figure.

Table 1.9: Average Tonnage of South West Vessels, 1871–1911 (net tons)

| | 1871 | | 1911 | |
	SW	Eng/Wales	SW	Eng/Wales
Port (a)	102.5	180.3	233.3	365.9
Shipping (b)	101.7	221.4	212.9(130.6)	531.3
Shipbuilding (c)	78.2	323.0	28.3	688.7
Fishing (d)	7.3	11.3	13.4	25.5

Notes:
a   Total shipping movements (see Table 1.3). 1911 figure refers to UK total shipping movements.
b   Figure in brackets excludes vessels owned by New Zealand Shipping Company.
c   Figures exclude vessels built for foreigners.
d   1st and 2nd class vessels.
Sources: *Annual Statements of Navigation and Shipping.*

A comparatively large proportion of sailing vessels was a further distinguishing feature of the South West's mercantile and fishing fleets in the late Victorian and Edwardian eras. This is clear in Table 1.10. Steam power was a minor factor in the region's fishing industry, propelling just 6.4 per cent of its 1st and 2nd class craft in 1911, when the national figure exceeded 62 per cent. Shipbuilding was likewise marked by the persistence of sail, steamships representing just a quarter of south-western output in 1911 as against a national figure of 96.2 per cent. In line with the general trend, the region's port traffic and shipping stock were both increasingly dominated by the steamer after 1871. Even so, as late as 1911, sail still accounted for nearly 12 per cent of total shipping movements in Cornwall and Devon, and over a quarter of locally owned merchant vessels, much higher proportions than those current in England and Wales as a whole.

Table 1.10: Percentage of South West Vessels Propelled by Steam, 1871–1911

	1871		1911	
	SW	Eng/Wales	SW	Eng/Wales
Port (a)	33.2	56.8	88.4	95.4
Shipping (b)	1.9	23.2	83.2(72.6)	91.9
Shipbuilding (c)	1.4	82.8	25.9	96.2
Fishing (d)	1.3	46.0	6.4	62.7

Notes:

a   Total shipping movements (see Table 1.3). Figures refer to 1876 rather than 1871. 1911 figure refers to UK total shipping movements.

b   Figure in brackets excludes vessels owned by New Zealand Shipping Company.

c   Figures exclude vessels built for foreigners.

d   1st and 2nd class vessels. Figures refer to 1901 rather than 1871.

Sources: *Annual Statements of Navigation and Shipping.*

Thus, the South West's sea transport and fishing industries displayed an unorthodox commitment to relatively small sailing vessels in the late nineteenth and twentieth centuries. At the same time, these 'traditional' maritime activities were experiencing differing degrees of relative decline. Such broad characteristics were causally connected.

Causalities

The changes which marked the South West's maritime economy during the 1870–1914 period were many, varied and not without apparent contradictions. While the region's aggregate sea-related activity expanded in absolute terms and in relation to the local economy, the pace of growth was generally slower than that pertaining in the maritime sector of England and Wales as a whole. Moreover, this growth was increasingly centred in particular coastal localities, and chiefly evident in the maritime defence industry, which was also characterised by the modernity and technical sophistication of its products, and the coastal leisure industry. The South West's other maritime concerns, in contrast, tended to contract absolutely, as in the case of shipping and shipbuilding, or, like the port and fishing industries, to experience a significant degree of relative decline—weak performances associated with the region's predilection for small sailing vessels.

An array of global, national and local factors interacted to explain this complex pattern. At the macro level, the 1870–1914 period witnessed a marked expansion in the demand for maritime services and goods of all forms. Fostered by the growing intensity and spread of industrialisation within Europe and North America, and the incorporation of primary producing regions in South America, Africa and Australasia into the industrial market, the volume of world trade increased dramatically in the six decades preceding the First World War. This pronounced increase entailed a massive growth in the demand for shipping services, which in turn exerted bullish pressures in the market for new tonnage and cargo- and ship-handling provisions, the business, respectively, of the shipbuilding and port industries. International competition was intrinsic to this sustained commercial growth, and as the industrial powers competed ever more keenly for a greater share in the markets for manufactured goods and raw materials, so political rivalries intensified. Such tensions increased the pressure to expand state military capabilities, a trend amply demonstrated in the acceleration of the naval arms race from the 1880s. At the same time, the social benefits of industrialisation were increasingly evident in the rising real incomes of large sections of the burgeoning populations of the industrial nations. Again, this stimulated demand in the maritime sector. While improving standards of living entailed increased expenditure on food, it also led to the emergence of mass recreational pursuits, general trends which boosted respectively the fishing and coastal leisure industries.

Britain played a prominent role in the expanding maritime markets of the late nineteenth and early twentieth centuries. On the one hand, a significant proportion of the increase in demand for sea-related products emanated from the first industrial nation. A major exporter of manufactures and primary produce, notably coal, and a consumer of vast quantities of food and raw materials produced overseas, the British economy was central to the long-term expansion of international commerce. While this expansive role entailed the exercise of naval power, it also contributed to income growth and the rise in purchasing power which underpinned the development of marine leisure and fishing activity. On the other hand, Britain was particularly well placed to supply the sea-related industries. Of course, a large and expanding domestic market, be it for sea-borne trade, naval vessels or seaside holidays, was an important stimulant in this respect. Just as important, perhaps, was the strength and structure of the nation's industrial base. Possessed of the most productive iron, engineering and coal industries in the world during the mid-nineteenth century, Britain inevitably played host to the many and various technological advances which together transformed the sea-related industries between the 1860s and the mid-1880s. These developments—encapsulated in the steel-hulled vessel propelled by the triple expansion marine engine—not only gave Britain a decisive edge in the sea transport, fishing and maritime defence industries but also facilitated further growth in the level of world trade, thereby intensifying the demand-side pressures in the maritime markets.[30]

This cycle of Anglocentric development impacted strongly on the regional distribution of Britain's maritime industries. As the nineteenth century progressed, major locational shifts and concentrations increasingly marked the nation's sea-related interests, most notably its sea transport and fishing industries. Sea-borne trade, for instance, increasingly focused on the major ports of London, Liverpool, Glasgow and Hull, and on the coal ports of South Wales and north-east England.[31] Likewise, shipping, both in terms of vessel registration and capital concentration, gravitated towards the major ports, while shipbuilding migrated to the Clyde, the North East and other northern districts from the 1860s.[32] Fishing, too, experienced uneven regional development, as the east coast stations of Hull, Grimsby, Yarmouth and Aberdeen emerged as the dominant bases of the industry in the Victorian era.[33] Concurrently, even as demand in the national and global maritime markets was increasing apace, with levels of supply rising in tandem, absolute and relative contractions were evident in the sea transport and fishing interests of other areas, including much of southern England.

That the South West conformed to this latter pattern, yet still became more reliant on the sea in an overall sense, was due largely to the factor endowments of the region in relation to the economic and technological developments of the 1870–1914 period. Some productive factors had little bearing on this transitional process. For instance, there was no discernible deficiency in the extent or quality of the human agents, labour and entrepreneurship, to explain the contraction of the South West's sea transport industries. With agriculture, mining and other industries generally declining in the region from the 1860s, labour was in plentiful supply. It is a moot point as to whether this labour was versed in skills appropriate to, say, the steam shipbuilding industry. But the deployment at Devonport Dockyard of up to 14,000 workers, many engaged as boilermakers, rivetters and other skilled craftsmen, indictates that the South West could provide, or attract, labour of a sufficient calibre to sustain such modern industries.[34] Entrepreneurial ability was also evident in the region's maritime sector. Successful shipping and shipbuilding concerns like those of Hain of St Ives, Harveys of Hayle, Holman & Sons of Topsham and Yeos of Appledore were all established and sustained by archetypal, risk-taking entrepreneurs, while Thomas Gill, founder of Millbay Docks, and Joseph Thomas Treffry of Par, Pentewan and Newquay, performed similar roles in the region's port industry.

At a broader level, there is much evidence of innovation and adaptation in the West Country's maritime interests. The region's shipowners, for instance, having pioneered the use of the schooner rig in the early nineteenth century, turned to the more efficient ketch rig in the 1870s and were therefore still able to make profits from the operation of increasingly obsolescent wooden sailing vessels.[35] Local shipbuilders likewise exploited emerging niches in the market, Philip & Son and Simpson Strickland Ltd of Dartmouth, for instance, shifting from mercantile to recreational craft production in the 1880s and 1890s, while Cox of Penzance and Upham of Brixham cultivated the wooden trawler market well into the twentieth century.[36] There were also effective adaptations to the changing needs of shipping, with extended port facilities, based on rail linkages, established at Exmouth and the Cattewater, Plymouth, and locally significant coal bunkering trades emerging at Dartmouth, Brixham and Penzance from the 1880s.[37] Moreover, there were signs of the ultimate rationality of south-western entrepreneurs, in that many disinvested in shipping, shipbuilding or fishing amidst the regionally-skewed shipping revolution of the late nineteenth century, while others— Holman, Reardon Smith, Anning, T. S. and Marshall Stevens, and countless fishermen—migrated with their businesses to areas of more dynamic growth, generally the major trading ports and the large east coast fishing stations.[38]

While these human factors tended to follow rather than dictate the pattern of change, the physical endowments of the region exerted a strong, if ambivalent, influence on the West Country's sea-related industries. The situation of the south-west peninsula clearly promoted some maritime activity; thus, from a strategic perspective, the proximity of the Western Approaches underpinned Plymouth's expanding naval role, while from a commercial standpoint the distance of the region from the nation's industrial core stimulated sea-borne trade, albeit dominated by an inwards, coastwise flow. The region's coastline, moreover, not only provided the natural beauty, sandy beaches and quaint estuaries sought by the seaside tourist and gentleman seafarer, but also offered a variety of sheltered, deep-water sites eminently suited for port development, naval base construction and shipbuilding production. And in the clay deposits of the Bovey Basin, Lee Moor and the St Austell district, and in the mineral wealth of the Tamar Valley and West Cornwall, the South West was blessed with traces of the high-bulk, low-value cargoes which stimulated so much trade and shipping activity in the industrial era.

The South West's natural endowments also imposed major constraints on its sea-related interests in the changing maritime context of the late nineteenth century. From a locational perspective, distance from the major urban centres, and also from the highly productive fishing grounds of the North Sea, Iceland and beyond, tended to inhibit respectively the development of the region's mass coastal leisure and fishing interests. The configuration of the South West's coastline, for all its scenic bays and estuaries, greatly impaired the traffic of many local ports as vessel size increased inexorably from the 1850s. Even relatively small steamships were unable to negotiate the Exe, the Taw, the Teign and a miscellany of small, but active, trading harbours in Cornwall and Devon.[39] More restrictive still, notwithstanding the local reserves of clay, was the West Country's lack of coal, iron ore and other significant 'industrial' raw materials. While this chiefly accounted for the tardy development of even a small-scale steam shipbuilding industry in the region,[40] it also placed a twin constraint on the sea-borne trade of the South West. At the micro level, the region was unable to fill holds with coal, the single most important sea-borne commodity of the 1870–1914 period and the export staple which underpinned the burgeoning trade and shipping interests of Cardiff, Newcastle and the other coal ports.[41] More generally, the dearth of strategic raw materials largely explains the South West's comparatively diminutive, and shrinking, industrial base which further depressed its trade and shipping needs in relation to those of other regions.

31

Such disadvantageous resource endowments were inextricably linked to the capital deficiencies which increasingly afflicted the South West's sea transport and fishing industries from the third quarter of the nineteenth century. It was at this time, of course, that the growing preponderance of the steam-driven vessel was transforming Britain's shipping, shipbuilding, port and, from the 1880s, fishing industries. Such vessels, merchant steamships and steam trawlers alike, were the fount of productivity gain and increased earning capacity. Against this, the steamer was considerably more expensive to build, operate and accommodate in port than the wooden sailing vessel. Therefore, to exploit the profitable potential of steam power and metal hulls, substantial quantities of capital were required. It was in this respect that the South West's paucity of primary and manufactured export staples proved critical. For it was in the ports which served the coalfields and the industrial regions, and in the fishing stations close to the productive North Sea grounds, that cargoes and catches abounded. Accordingly, it was in places like Cardiff, Glasgow, Liverpool, London, Hull and Grimsby that the dynamic process of capital generation, accumulation and investment was increasingly located.

Once these centripetal tendencies were set in motion, the shipping and trading fortunes of peripheral regions like the West Country inevitably declined. Though in the steamship enterprises of Hain of St Ives, Chellew of Truro, Bellamy of Plymouth, Holmans of Topsham and others there were instances of successful local adaptations to the changing market,[42] these were very much the exceptions which proved the rule. In general, south-western shipowners, shipbuilders and fishermen were unable to generate the capital necessary to modernise their capital stock. The construction and operation of relatively small wooden sailing vessels—merchant schooners and fishing smacks predominated—entailed low earnings, tight margins and inadequate surpluses for investment in larger sailing vessels, let alone steamships. At the same time, these traits were hardly likely to attract funds from outside the region when more profitable opportunities for investment in steam shipping were readily available elsewhere. Indeed, the very opposite occurred in the late nineteenth century as the South West's limited supplies of maritime capital were further depleted by the haemorrhage of locally generated funds to Cardiff, London, Liverpool or the east coast fishing ports.

As if to emphasise the role of capital in the South West's maritime economy, the sea-related activities which expanded in the region during the 1850–1914 period either relied to some degree on extra-regional sources of funding or else required relatively modest levels of investment. Thus, the maritime defence industry, the largest and most dynamic of the South West's sea-related activities, was sustained almost entirely by state funding. The region's port industry also depended to a certain extent on capital 'imports', for the major developments of the period, which were mainly located at Plymouth, were financed by railway companies—the Great Western Railway at Millbay, the London and South Western at Sutton Harbour and Cattedown.[43] In the other growth area, coastal leisure, capital requirements were comparatively small. The South West's seaside resorts generally evolved within, or as an adjunct to, established coastal communities, an important attribute of many being the very small-scale, 'unspoilt' character which low levels of investment entailed. Similarly, recreational sailing developed within the existing order of things, for the construction of yachts and cruisers entailed little expansion in the capacity of the merchant shipbuilding industry, while the accommodation of such craft exerted little additional pressure on the South West's port and harbour facilities.

The supply of capital, local resource endowments and technological change were the key factors which interacted to redefine the South West's relationship with the sea in the 1870–1914 era. While the maritime sector grew in a regional context, it underwent a transitional process in which maritime defence and, to a lesser degree, coastal leisure increasingly superseded the sea transport and fishing industries as the central strands of the region's maritime economy. In this, it might be argued that the South West's experience in the late nineteenth century signalled the changes which have transformed Britain's maritime interests since the mid-twentieth century.

NOTES

The author gratefully acknowledges the financial support provided by the Leverhulme Trust for the preparation of this paper.

1. See F. Broeze, 'From the Periphery to the Mainstream: The Challenge of Australia's Maritime History', *Great Circle*, 11 (1989), 1–13.
2. Employment in the coastal leisure industry is particularly difficult to measure using the occupational breakdown of the census. While there are few indications as to the numbers employed in the recreational sailing business, the largely seasonal and casual nature of work in

seaside resorts renders any quantification of employment in this industry an approximation. See J.K. Walton, *The English Seaside Resort: A Social History 1750–1914* (Leicester, 1983), 45–8. For the general problems of census analysis, see C.D. Lee, *British Regional Employment Statistics 1841–1971* (Cambridge, 1979), 3–46; and E. Higgs, *Making Sense of the Census: The Manuscript Returns for England and Wales* (London, 1989).

3. British Parliamentary Papers (BPP), 1918, XIII. Report of the Departmental Committee on Shipping and Shipbuilding.

4. J. Th. Thor, *British Trawlers and Iceland, 1919–1976* (Esbjerg, 1995), 45–50.

5. See Michael Duffy *et al.*, (eds), *The New Maritime History of Devon: Volume 1, From Early Times to the Late Eighteenth Century* (London, 1992).

6. P. Hilditch, 'Devon and Naval Strategy since 1815', and J. Coad, 'Architecture and Development of Devonport Naval Base, 1815–1982', in M. Duffy *et al.*, (eds), *The New Maritime History of Devon: Volume II, From the Late Eighteenth Century to the Present Day* (hereafter *NMHD: II*) (London, 1994), chapters 15 and 16; K.V. Burns, *The Devonport Dockyard Story* (Liskeard, 1984).

7. See J.F. Travis, *The Rise of the Devon Seaside Resorts, 1750–1900* (Exeter, 1993); and Walton, *English Seaside Resort*, 53, 65.

8. N.J. Morgan, 'Perceptions, Patterns and Policies of Tourism: The Development of the Devon Seaside Resorts during the Twentieth Century with Special Reference to Torquay and Ilfracombe' (unpublished PhD thesis, University of Exeter, 1991), I, 62.

9. I am grateful to Janet Cusack for the data presented in this paragraph.

10. Accounts and Papers (BPP, 1887, LXXV, 93; 1908, XIII, 155; 1912–13, XXVI, 465; 1914, XXX, 1217). Statistical Tables and Memorandum relating to the Sea Fisheries of the United Kingdom.

11. E. Vale, *The Harveys of Hayle: Engine Builders, Shipwrights and Merchants of Cornwall* (Truro, 1966).

12. C. Gill, *Sutton Harbour* (Plymouth, 1970); M. Langley and E. Small, *Millbay Docks* (Exeter, 1987).

13. D.J. Starkey, 'The Ports, Seaborne Trade and Shipping Industry of South Devon, 1786–1914', in *NMHD: II*, chapter 3.

14. Starkey, 'Ports, Seaborne Trade'.

15. D.J. Starkey, 'The Shipbuilding Industry of Southwest England, 1790–1913', in S. Ville (ed.), *Shipbuilding in the United Kingdom in the Nineteenth Century: A Regional Approach* (St John's, Newfoundland, 1993), 91–2.

16. See S. Pollard, *Peaceful Conquest: The Industrialization of Europe 1760–1970* (Oxford, 1981).

17. See M.A. Havinden, 'The South West: A Case of De-Industrialization?', in M. Palmer (ed.), *The Onset of Industrialization* (Nottingham, 1977); E.L. Jones, *De-Industrialization as Economic*

Adjustment: The Case of South-West England (Melbourne, 1987); S. Fisher and M.A. Havinden, 'The Long-Term Evolution of the Economy of South West England: From Autonomy to Dependence', in M.A. Havinden *et al.* (eds), *Centre and Periphery: Brittany and Cornwall & Devon Compared* (Exeter, 1991), 76–85.

18. A. Glyn-Jones, 'The Repopulation of the Countryside in Cornwall and Devon', in Havinden *et al.* (eds), *Centre and Periphery*, 132–5.

19. P. Hilditch, 'The Dockyard in the Local Economy', in *NMHD: II*, chapter 21.

20. Travis, *Devon Seaside Resorts*, 106.

21. Walton, *English Seaside Resort*, 68.

22. P. Payton, 'Naval Education and Training in Devon', in *NMHD: II*, chapter 19.

23. See K.J. O'Donoghue and H.S. Appleyard, *Hain of St Ives* (Kendal, 1986).

24. See D. Jenkins, 'The Chellew Steam Navigation Company Limited: A Note on Some Welsh Connections', *Maritime Wales*, 15 (1992), 82–4.

25. Starkey, 'Shipbuilding Industry', 100.

26. Walton, *English Seaside Resort*, 68.

27. Walton, *English Seaside Resort*, 71–2.

28. Payton, 'Naval Education', and Hilditch, 'Dockyard in the Local Economy', in *NMHD: II*, chapters 19, 21.

29. Travis, *Devon Seaside Resorts*; Morgan, 'Perceptions, Patterns'.

30. D.J. Starkey, 'The Industrial Background to the Development of the Steamship', in B. Greenhill (ed.), *The Advent of Steam: The Merchant Steamship Before 1900* (London, 1993), 127–35.

31. G. Jackson, 'The Ports' in M.J. Freeman and D.H. Aldcroft (eds), *Transport in Victorian Britain* (Manchester, 1988), 234–50.

32. A. Slaven, 'Shipbuilding', in J. Langton and R.J. Morris (eds), *Atlas of Industrializing Britain* (London, 1986), 132–5.

33. T. Lummis, *Occupation and Society: The East Anglian Fishermen 1880–1914* (Cambridge, 1985), 11–13.

34. Hilditch, 'Dockyard in the Local Economy'.

35. B. Greenhill, *The Merchant Schooners* (London, 1988); D.J. Starkey, 'Schooner Development in Britain', in B. Greenhill (ed.), *Sail's Last Century: The Merchant Sailing Ship 1830–1930* (London, 1993),133–47.

36. Starkey, 'Shipbuilding Industry', 83–4.

37. Starkey, 'Ports, Seaborne Trade'.

38. R. Craig, 'Steamship Enterprise in Devon, 1852–1920', in *NMHD: II*, chapter 8.

39. See E.A.G. Clark, *The Ports of the Exe Estuary, 1660–1860* (Exeter, 1960), 3–18.

40. Starkey, 'Shipbuilding Industry', 88–101.

41. See S. Palmer, 'The British Coal Export Trade, 1850–1913', in D. Alexander and R. Ommer (eds), *Volumes not Values: Canadian Ships and World Trades* (St John's, Newfoundland, 1979), 331–54

42.   Craig, 'Steamship Enterprise in Devon'.
43.   Gill, *Sutton Harbour*; Langley and Small, *Millbay Docks*.

CHAPTER 2

Climax and Climacteric: The British Coastal Trade, 1870–1930

John Armstrong

The period 1870–1930 saw the continued rise and precipitate decline of the British coastal trade. Coastal shipping had been a crucial component in industrialisation, transporting low-value, high-bulk goods such as coal, corn, bricks and slates, which were essential to the growth of towns and industry. In the early nineteenth century its volume increased steadily as the economy expanded and specialisation led to increased movement of goods from low cost areas to centres of consumption. The coastal trade continued to expand until the First World War, and in many ways was at its zenith just before that conflict. However, the Great War brought an abrupt end to this long period of expansion. In the 1920s, although there was growth from the very low wartime levels, the prewar volume of activity was never achieved and the interwar period saw the British coastal trade stagnate. This chapter will outline and explain the trends in each of these three sub-periods. In so doing the role and economics of the coastal ship will become apparent.

Apogee, 1870–1914

The period 1870–1914 saw the British coastal trade at an apogee. This high point can be demonstrated in a variety of ways. The number and tonnage of ships with cargoes entering the harbours of the UK in the coasting trade rose continuously between 1870 and 1913. A dense network of coastal liners had developed which linked virtually all major ports with regular, fast and scheduled services. The coastal collier was moving an increasing quantity of coal from the producing regions, especially the north-east of England and South Wales, to the consuming areas, particularly London and south-east England. In addition the screw collier took on the

37

competition offered by the railways and from the 1890s regained the lion's share of the coal trade to London, carrying more than the railway companies each year save two from then until the First World War. In the last years of the nineteenth century and the early years of the twentieth the coaster was performing about as much work as the railway system as a whole if measured in ton-miles. Finally the coaster was extensively used for passenger traffic, both as a means of business and pleasure travel, and increasingly in the last decade or so of the nineteenth century as part of the nascent mass leisure industry.

There is much evidence to support these points. Firstly, the volume of coastal shipping activity grew steadily in the period 1870–1913. Contrary to the view implicit in some transport history textbooks, the nineteenth century did not see the inexorable rise of the railway juggernaut at the expense of all other forms of transport. Hoffman pointed out many years ago that 'coastal shipping expanded in a surprisingly steady manner right up to ... 1914'.[1] Reference to the figures for entries and clearances of ships in the coastal trade at British ports confirms this. In 1870, 142,000 ships entered UK ports carrying cargoes in the coastal trade. They comprised some 18.4 million registered tons. By 1892, halfway through our sub-period, this had increased to 206,000 ship entrances of a total of 29.1 million registered tons, and by 1913 the two figures were 169,000 ship entrances totalling 34.8 million tons.[2] The crude tonnage figures suggest a near doubling of activity in about 40 years to give a simple per annum growth figure of 2 per cent. If we allow for compound growth using an end point ratio, this comes down a little but is still more than 1.5 per cent per annum, suggesting that there was a steady if unspectacular growth in coastal shipping activity between 1870 and 1914.[3]

The second piece of evidence to attest to the vigour of the coastal trade was the dense network of coastal liner companies which operated regular, frequent and fast scheduled services between all the major cities and towns of the kingdom. No systematic study has been made of these businesses, but the number of companies and services was very large.[4] Down the east coast several firms, including the Aberdeen Steam Navigation Co., the Dundee, Perth and London Shipping Co., the Carron Co., the Tyne Tees Steam Navigation, and the General Steam Navigation Co., offered a liner service from many towns.[5] It was similar on the west coast where the Bacon, Hough, and Powell Lines competed in England, while firms like Burns, Laird and Sloan ran services between Scotland and England.[6] These companies operated fast, large, well-appointed ships which carried both passengers and general cargo. They avoided dangerous and anti-social goods such as dynamite, coal or raw hides and required no minimum quantity. They were fast by comparison to railway freight traffic, reliable and ran to a timetable. A glance at the advertisements in any local newspaper for a port town will indicate the range of routes served and the frequency of sailings.

Coal was the largest commodity carried by coastal ship in this period, and the quantity being shipped increased steadily. In 1870 about 10.9 million tons of coal were carried coastwise, a figure that had risen to 15 million by 1892 and 20.5 million by 1913.[7] Once again the amount of work performed by the coastal ship roughly doubled in just over four decades. This was bettered by the performance of the screw colliers operating to London. In 1870 about 3 million tons of coal were carried to London by ship, by 1892 that had roughly doubled to 5.8 million and by 1913 it was 9 million tons.[8] The coaster also improved its competitiveness. Whereas in the 1870s and 1880s the coaster brought about 38 per cent of all coal coming in to London, from the 1890s it provided the majority of coal to the capital and from 1898 to 1913 this averaged over 52 per cent.[9] The increased competitiveness of the coasters sprang from a market in which they had an economic advantage, namely the industrial segment of the coal market: those firms located near the sea or navigable rivers which needed large quantities of coal delivered regularly, such as gas works, electric power stations, stores of bunker coal, and large industrial users. The coastal colliers responded to this segment of the market by providing large ships which benefited from economies in crew and capital costs as their size increased.[10] The evidence from the coal trade confirms not merely that the coastal ship was increasing its level of activity in this area, but also that it was competing successfully with the railway system and recapturing market share from it.

There is further evidence to suggest that the coaster was playing a vital role in internal transport, in an analysis of the amount of work performed in 1910 by coastal ships in comparison to railways and canals.[11] This suggests that the railway system and coastal shipping performed about the same quantity of work if measured in ton miles, whereas the canal network did not approach the other two modes. However, the way in which the railways and coasters achieved their output was quite different. The coaster had a very large average haul, around 250 miles, whereas the railway's was only about 50 miles. The coaster carried a smaller tonnage than the railways but each ton was carried a much longer distance. This is explicable because the coaster benefited from economies of a long haul, as much of its costs were incurred as terminal charges, i.e. payments made at the ports at each end of its voyage, whereas once at sea its running costs were meagre. Compare this to the railway where the running costs were more proportional to the distance covered, as the railway owned the land it ran on, had to prepare and maintain the permanent way, provide signal box operatives, police and level crossing attendants. The coaster did not incur these costs. Hence the coaster was particularly suited to conveying large quantities long distances, such as coal from Newcastle to London and china clay from Cornwall to Runcorn.

The final dynamic aspect of the coaster's performance was its role as a passenger carrier in this period. In providing a regular, scheduled service between the main port cities of the country, the coastal liner companies offered passenger accommodation, often for several classes of traveller. The ships were large, fast and well appointed with grand saloons attended by stewards and stewardesses in pale imitation of the crack trans-oceanic liners. Such passenger traffic could be substantial: for example, the Aberdeen Steam Navigation Co. (ASN), took £7,236 in 1894, reportedly a poor year.[12] This was at a time when first class fares were 30s., and second 15s., implying that several thousand passengers were carried.[13] Part of the appeal of the coastal steamer lay in its speed and reliability. The ASN claimed to do the 300-mile journey in 36 hours in 1875.[14] Although slower than the best passenger trains, the coaster offered the advantages of a brief sea cruise with attendant bracing air and ozone. That this was a lure is borne out by the seasonal surge in passenger traffic and the complaints of the company that poor summers led to a fall in fare payers.[15]

In addition to this part-business, part-recreational travel, in the last decade of the nineteenth century there was a great growth in the pure leisure role of the coastal steamer. The holiday trips of the Clyde river and coastal steamboats—trips 'doon the watter' - are well known,[16] but in addition the Bristol Channel, the Solent, the north Welsh coast and the Scottish islands were suitable locations for day cruises or longer trips. A combination of bank holidays, slightly larger real incomes, the secularisation of Sundays, and the appreciation of the commercial possibilities of the desire of people to escape from the towns in search of diversion and scenery, led to a boom in recreational coastal sea travel in the late Victorian and Edwardian eras.

If it is accepted that the coaster was alive, well, and expanding its activities in the late nineteenth and early twentieth centuries, we need to explain the economic basis of its role and how it was able to compete against the apparently all-devouring railways. The first necessity is to cease talking about coastal shipping as though it was a homogenous entity. One of the secrets of the coaster's success was the provision of a range of services to suit different types of trade. It segmented the market and then provided appropriate services to each segment. At the top end of this range of services was the liner trade.[17] This offered speed, regularity and reliability, with no minimum quantity required. In return for this premium quality, the liner charged the highest freight rates of any coaster. These were still significantly less than those charged by the railways for long distance routes and the service offered by the coaster was not inferior. For manufactured goods, such as Bovril, bird seed, soap, cigars or pianos, whose value-to-bulk ratio was high and whose starting point and ultimate destination were close to the port, river or canal, this was the most appropriate method of transport. A crucial determinant was the final location, for land carriage by horse and cart was very expensive and shippers endeavoured to minimise this element. Thus, if either the despatching point or the final destination were closer to a railway goods yard than a wharf or quay the railway stood a good chance of gaining the traffic.

The second segment served by the coaster was those firms that needed regular deliveries of a bulky product sufficient to allow some firms to specialise in this trade and devote particular coasters to that trade exclusively. The clearest example of this is the coal trade to London with screw colliers built for that trade alone, not seeking a return cargo, but going in water ballast and maximising the number of coal-carrying journeys they could make.[18] By the 1890s and 1900s 50 or 60 return trips each year between the Thames and the Tyne was not unusual. Some of these vessels specialised to the extent that they had hinged funnels and masts to allow them to navigate under London's bridges and penetrate up river.[19] Other trades with a similar need for regular bulk deliveries were china clay from Cornwall to Runcorn for transhipment into canal barges for despatch to the Potteries, iron ore from Cumberland to South Wales for smelting, followed by a cargo of Welsh coal to a port on the east coast of Ireland from whence pit timber could be picked up for the iron ore mines. These 'regular traders' offered a reliable

41

service for firms which needed a steady flow of raw materials or fuels. They kept prices low by speedy turnaround and suiting the ship to the trade.

Below this segment was that which needed bulky cargoes moved but less frequently and where reliability and regularity was less important. For this the coastal steamer provided a tramp service. It could be reasonably fast once at sea as it travelled steadily at nine knots or so. It required a reasonably full load to be profitable which meant matching the ship to the cargo, and hence the goods might have to wait until a suitable vessel became available. Its freight rates were lower than those charged by the coastal liner. Thus, non-perishable, bulk commodities whose despatch did not have to be instantaneous, such as iron and steel products, bags of grain, barrels of oil and hogsheads of sugar, were despatched in steam tramps.

Finally, there was the sailing ship. Even in 1870 it made up less than half the total tonnage of entries in the coastwise trade and it was declining. By 1900 it comprised only one-eighth.[20] It was unreliable, depending on wind strength and direction and affected by currents and tides. It could make a fast passage if the weather was with it, but it could also spend days skulking in port. Its main economic advantage lay in its provision of a very cheap form of bulk transport—a floating warehouse, cheaper than other forms of coaster and all modes of land transport. Schooners of 100 registered tons could carry about 160 tons of goods with a crew of three. Improvements in rig design and the use of winches and self-furling gear increased labour productivity and reduced crew size. Brigs and brigantines had largely been superseded by schooners and ketches because the shift from square rigging to fore and aft not only reduced labour requirements but also made the ship easier to handle when wind conditions were adverse.[21] Thus for bulky goods whose unit value was low, which did not deteriorate and which were not needed at a particular date, the sailing coaster offered the cheapest form of transport. Thus sand, stone, ballast, manure and grains were normal cargoes. In addition those goods which required careful and therefore lengthy loading usually went by sailing ship, for the demurrage costs were much lower on a sailer than a steamer because the latter's original capital cost was so much greater. Thus in the early twentieth century, goods like slates which cracked easily, bricks which were prone to chipping, and tiles and fireclay products which were frangible tended to be transported in sailing coasters.[22]

Thus one of the explanations of the success of the coaster was its ability to provide a range of services at a range of prices, so catering for a number of types of commodity and trade. A second reason is technological change. The coaster was not a technologically static mode of transport, and while the developments of the first three-quarters of the nineteenth century may be better known—the application of steam to propulsion, the use of iron for hulls, the paddle being superseded by the propeller, the use of water ballast—there were also a number of changes in the last quarter of the century. The use of steel for hulls, boiler pressures exceeding 100 lbs per square inch, the water tube boiler, triple expansion steam engines, and the turbine, first fitted commercially in 1901 to the *King Edward*,[23] were all important innovations which offered strength, economy and speed. Moreover, all were pioneered on coastal craft. The diffusion of these innovations took time and had a lasting effect upon improving the efficiency of the coastal fleet. In addition coastal ships were becoming larger in most trades and this brought economies in crew numbers and costs,[24] because crew size did not need to rise proportionately to ship size. We have already mentioned that there were improvements in the sailing ship, partially spurred by the need to keep costs down in order to undercut the rates charged by steam tramps. Also the shift from sail to steam in itself resulted in productivity gains, for the steam sailor was nearly four times as productive as the crew member of a sailing ship.[25] Hence shifting tonnage from sail to steam reduced labour requirements and increased labour productivity. Thus in a multitude of ways the coaster increased its efficiency and productivity in this period.

The third point to stress when explaining the coaster's ability to expand is the economics of operations. The coaster's main competitor, the railway, had a totally different cost structure. The coaster normally owned no wharf or quay, needed no land or fixed capital other than the ship itself, and had to pay the wages only of the crew which was relatively small in number when compared to the tonnage the ship could carry. Once the coaster was at sea its costs were minimal—the crew's wages and fuel for steamers. For the sailing ship the latter was avoided and although there might be wear and tear on the sails and ropes, repairing them and maintaining the ship was a normal part of the sailor's duties. Some sailing ships also passed on to the crew members the uncertainty of wind and weather by paying them piece rates by trip rather than regular weekly wages.[26] This method acted as an incentive to mariners to speed up their voyage and not fritter away time in port, since they earned the same whether the voyage took three days or three weeks. Most of the operating costs of a coaster were incurred as terminal costs, that is at the beginning and end of a voyage when entering or leaving port.[27] Then, port or harbour dues became payable, there might be pilotage charges, and fees for towage for sailing ships, though many coastal skippers took it as a matter of pride—as well as of pocket—to avoid these by expert handling and navigation. Also costs for unloading and loading might be incurred, though for most sailing ships and some steam tramps this was the responsibility of the crew members, and possibly trimming fees if it was a bulk cargo capable of shifting. In addition there were often other incidental expenses consequent upon obtaining a cargo such as the agent's fee, telegrams back to the home port, and odd running expenses. Hence a high proportion of costs other than fuel and labour were incurred at the ports and these charges were levied irrespective of the length of the preceding or subsequent voyage. Thus their cost per ton mile declined as the journey length increased and hence coasters had cost advantages on long hauls. The depreciation of coasters was also relatively low. Providing they did not meet an untimely end via a collision, stranding or freak storm, coastal ships could and did last for 20–25 years and even longer.[28] Thus their rate of depreciation was 4 or 5 per cent per annum. In addition some of the ravages of time and weather could be kept at bay by the regular maintenance which was part of the normal duties of the crew. Thus servicing the capital was not too onerous.

Compare this to the cost structure of the railways. The railways needed to buy expensive land not just for the tracks but also stations, goods yards, sidings and marshalling yards, some of it in prime locations such as city centres where costs were at their highest. The stories of landowners extorting huge sums for small strips of territory essential to a railway route are apocryphal but contain elements of truth. In addition to this outlay on fixed capital, the engineering works consuming bricks for viaducts and bridges, blasting tunnels, and digging cuttings were titanic and expensive. Then there was further capital cost in terms of rails, sleepers, points, signal boxes, and stations, plus, of course, the rolling stock, another large outlay on locomotives, waggons, carriages, and goods vans. As a result the capital cost of a short railway ran into millions of pounds before a bag of cotton had been carried. Compare this to £20,000 for a large coastal liner in the 1870s. Worse was to follow. Once the railway had laid down all this capital it needed an army of workers to operate it. Not just the drivers, firemen and guards on the train, but those who operated signals and level crossing gates, and police to guard the lines, station staff and workshop staff to fettle, repair and build the complex rolling stock. In 1898 in the UK over half a million people were employed on the railways,[29] whereas in 1896 there were slightly less than 30,000 mariners employed in the British coasting trade and even if those engaged in the 'Home Trade' are included the figure is less than 37,000.[30] If it is borne in mind that it has been estimated that in 1910 the railways and coasters performed about the same amount of work in moving goods when measured in ton miles,[31] the difference in labour force involved is enormous. It might be objected that the railways also carried passengers, and many more than the coasters, and hence the railway labour force was also catering for this type of traffic. This is fair comment. However, passenger traffic generated less than half of all railway revenue in 1900 while freight traffic contributed 54 per cent (£51.7 million out of a total of £95.1 million).[32] If we assign 54 per cent of the railway labour force to the goods traffic this gives 288,400 employees, somewhere between eight and nine times as many as the coastal fleet. The rates of pay of the average mariner, the able seaman or fireman, and railway employee were not greatly different. The skipper and first engineer of a steam coaster were paid more than the drivers of locomotives, but only double, not eight or nine times, and therefore the total wages bill of the railway system assigned to freight carriage must have been many times greater than that of the coastal fleet. Hence, these operating costs, as well as the charges to service the huge capital outlays, were much larger on the railway than on the coaster; these are disparities which explain why railway freight charges were so much higher than those on the coaster.

This section has attempted to explain some of the more important aspects of coaster operations and economics, which in turn help us to understand why its charges were lower than those of the railway and why the coaster was able to carry an increasing amount of freight. We now need to turn to a much gloomier period, that of the First World War.

Climateric, 1914–1918

The First World War was a climacteric for British coastal shipping. Not only did it have short-term deleterious effects but it initiated a 40-year depression in the industry, inasmuch as the registered tonnage of entries and clearances with cargoes in the coastal trade achieved in 1913 were not surpassed until 1952.[33]

Firstly let us look at the short-term effects during the period of conflict. The war caused the volume of coastal shipping activity to fall to less than half its prewar volume. Whereas in 1913 approximately 35 million registered tons of coastal shipping with cargoes entered British ports, in 1918 the equivalent figure was less than 17 million.[34] The contraction is not too surprising, for enemy action was directed at all of Britain's maritime trades and accounted for about 40 per cent of her total fleet. Coastal shipping was no exception, with numerous coasters falling victim to mines, shell fire, torpedoes and bombs. Heroism and tragedy co-existed in the coastal as much as in the deep water trades. In addition to destruction, the coastal fleet was subject to the depredations of the government. It requisitioned coasters to carry troops, munitions and coal for the war effort, and in some cases armed them and used them as Q ships, minesweepers, and escorts, further reducing the tonnage available for commercial activities. To cite one instance, Supple estimates that 'the Admiralty commandeered eighty percent of the colliers normally used to ship coal between the north-east and the south'.[35] In addition the government encouraged the redirection of some larger coasters into the foreign trade to help the hard-pressed deep water fleet.[36]

For those ships that continued to work in the coastal trade there were a number of additional difficulties. Firstly, there was the problem of waiting while convoys were formed and escorts provided, which slowed down turnaround times and reduced the amount of work performed in a given period. The latter was compounded by the deterioration in port facilities as more ships endeavoured to use the same ports whose equipment suffered from a lack of repair, replacement and renewal.[37] Secondly, the costs of operation increased drastically. Insurance premiums rose in view of the additional war risks, and wages climbed, partly to compensate sailors for the additional hazards they faced, partly because the general price level rose as aggregate demand exceeded aggregate supply. As a result the coaster's costs rose and it had to adjust its freight rates upward to compensate. Isserlis calculated that for all tramp ships, coastal and blue water, the freight rates charged in 1918 were about ten times those charged in 1913.[38] This is an extraordinary rise and more of a problem for coastal than overseas shipping, for the former faced competition from another mode, namely the railways. While 'the coasting trade ... remained free until the last year of war when a loose form of control was instituted',[39] the railways were taken at an early date into direct government control. This had two significant effects. Firstly the government directed some traffic which had previously been carried by coaster onto the railways because the risk of enemy action on the railways was tiny compared to sea-borne trade. Secondly the rates of carriage on the railways remained frozen at their 1914 level throughout the war. The government guaranteed to railway shareholders a return at least equivalent to that received before the war, so in effect the government was paying an immense subsidy to the users of the railway. Against this the coasters found it increasingly difficult to compete. Whereas before the war the freight rates by sea were much cheaper than by rail, especially for long distances, Aldcroft estimates that 'by the end of the war ... coastal rates were from fifty to two hundred percent in excess of the comparable railway rates'.[40] Thus coastal shipping firms found it very difficult to compete with the railways, especially when it is borne in mind that the railways had a whole plethora of 'exceptional rates' which were even lower than the published rates. Thus many routes which the coaster operated became unprofitable and hence the economic rationale compounded the direct effects of hostilities to reduce the amount of work performed by the coastal ship.

Stagnation, 1918–1930

If the war had a deleterious effect on the coastal trade, it might be thought that once hostilities ceased and the abnormal circumstances were reversed, the coastal trade would bounce back to its prewar position. This was not the case, as Table 2.1 shows.

Although entrances of coasters carrying cargoes rose from 16.8 million tons in 1918 to 24.2 million tons in 1920, they then dipped in 1921, recovered in 1922 to a little above the 1920 level, and then for the rest of the 1920s stayed well below the 1922 peak. This was at best a miserable performance but it is even worse when it is appreciated that the peak year of the 1920s, 1922, saw a level of coastal activity which was less than three-quarters of that achieved in 1913. Thus the coastal trade throughout the 1920s, and indeed in the 1930s also, never regained the position it had held in 1913. The interwar period was one of stagnation for the coastal trade. If the average tonnage of entrances for 1909–13, 32.5 million tons, is compared to that for 1919–30, 22 million tons, a reduction of about one-third is indicated, roughly 10.5 million tons.

Table 2.1: Net Registered Tonnage of Ships Entering UK Ports in the
Coasting Trade with Cargoes, 1913–1930 (million tons)

	Net Registered Tonnage
1913	34.759
1914	36.001
1915	27.468
1916	22.360
1917	19.201
1918	16.780
1919	19.901
1920	24.176
1921	20.949
1922	25.680
1923	21.407
1924	20.576
1925	20.627
1926	16.197
1927	22.160
1928	23.038
1929	24.021
1930	24.394

Source: British Parliamentary Papers, Trade and Navigation Accounts

Various explanations as to why the coaster did not regain its prewar position in the internal transport system of Britain have been advanced. One cause cited by a number of shipowners and captains can be dismissed fairly quickly. That is the complaint that foreign competition was forcing British ships and mariners out of the trade. In particular the Dutch motor coaster was blamed. For instance Jim Uglow, skipper of a sailing barge throughout the interwar period, complained that 'by 1930 the Dutch motor coasters were a real menace on the British coast',[41] while Hervey Benham, immensely knowledgeable on the activities of small ships, claimed that 'the Dutchmen were the barges' chief competitors up to the Second World War'.[42] However, this is unlikely to explain the stagnation of coastal shipping. The figures of entrances include foreign-owned ships and if the Dutch captured a large market share this would still be included in the entrances and clearances. As it was, foreign ships played only a small part in the British coastal trade. In the period 1920–30 their average share of the market was 0.7 per cent, and the peak year, 1920, recorded only 1.3 per cent.[43] Thus although the Dutch coaster may have been prominent in some trades it was not a significant player, and seeking government help to reserve the coastal trade to British ships was unlikely to have had much effect. It might be that the Dutch coaster had an indirect effect upon the British coastal trade, in that it pushed freight rates so low that they became unremunerative. If this were so one would have expected the Dutch to have captured a large share of the market, which was patently not the case.

The second argument that can be dealt with equally summarily is that the coaster had started a terminal decline from which it could not recover. The facts do not fit this interpretation. Although the coastal trade stagnated throughout the interwar period and declined even further in the Second World War, after the close of these hostilities it demonstrated rapid growth. In 1949 entrances exceeded those of the best interwar year, 1937, and in 1953 they passed the previous highest level achieved in 1914. The graph continued to climb at least until the 1960s when it was 25 per cent above the level of 1914.[44] Thus the coastal trade grew steadily after the 1939–45 war, which suggests that there were peculiar circumstances operating in the interwar period which caused it to stagnate.

Before 1914 the single most important commodity carried by the coaster was coal. As we have seen, in 1913 about 22.8 million tons were carried coastwise of which about 9 million went into London. Any reduction in coal consumption was likely to have an adverse effect upon the coastal trade. The coal industry was severely depressed for most of the interwar period,[45] with output never reaching the 1913 peak, and average output for 1920–9 at about 230 million tons per annum compared to 270 million in 1909–13, that is a reduction of around 15 per cent.[46] Admittedly 1921 and 1926 were hard hit by major strikes, especially the latter when the coal strike lasted more than nine months even if the General Strike was over in ten days, but this did not augur well for the coastal trade. However, another conventional truth of the decline in coal output between the wars is that much of it was attributable to a reduction in export demand. Whereas in 1909–13 the average quantity of coal exported was 65 million tons per annum, between 1920 and 1929 it averaged 49 million, a reduction of about one-quarter.[47] However, given that the output figures show a reduction of about 40 million tons per annum and the export demand was down by about 16 million, there is still plenty of reduction to account for.

Turning to coal carried coastwise, it is evident that whereas in the five years 1909–13 on average 21 million tons of coal were conveyed as cargo plus 2.4 million tons for bunkers in the coasting trade, a total of about 23.5 million tons,[48] in 1923–30 these figures respectively were 15 million tons and 1.4 million tons to give a total of 16.4 million tons.[49] Accordingly, there was a decrease of about 7 million tons, equivalent to 30 per cent. In other words the reduction in the amount of coal carried by coastal ship was proportionately greater than the fall in export demand, a fact that has hardly ever been mentioned. The absolute reduction, averaging 7 million tons of coal, could account for nearly as much shipping, say about 5 million registered tons, which was approximately half of the reduction previously noted in the activity level of coastal shipping in the interwar period compared to prewar. This decline in the coastal coal trade might have resulted from increased competition from the railways and the diversion of coastal coal traffic to the rail system. However, the railways did not increase the amount of coal they carried in the 1920s compared to prewar. Indeed they carried less coal than previously, down by about 21 million tons per annum.[50] So it was not that the railways gained at the coaster's expense. Rather, the reduction in coal traffic experienced by the railways, at about 10 per cent, was much less than that experienced by the coaster. So the overall market was in decline but the railway was retaining its market share to a greater extent than the coaster.

One symptom of the decline in demand for coastal shipping was the low level of remuneration earned. Many shipowners and masters bewailed the ruinously low freight rates which were being offered. Certainly there was a very rapid reduction in freight rates following the cessation of hostilities and the collapse of the postwar shipping boom. The average freight rate in 1920 was about half that in the last war year, and that for 1921 was less than one-quarter of the 1918 rate.[51] However, there is some dispute as to how low freight rates sunk thereafter. Isserlis suggests that in the period 1919–30 the rate was always above that obtained in 1913 and even in the worst year, 1930, it was about 37 per cent above the 1913 level.[52] Capie and Collins, basing their figures on *The Economist*, disagree. They suggest that for 1928–30 the average freight rate was below that of 1913, in 1930 some 20 per cent less.[53] These differences are quite important. For the average of the Isserlis rates for 1921–30 is 80 per cent above that of 1913, whereas *The Economist* series suggests only 10 per cent. This is a large discrepancy. However, these rates are all composites of a number of routes, mostly in the overseas trade. It would be preferable to use an index based solely on coastal routes, but, to the best of my knowledge, none exists.[54] We do know that the freight rates on coal from the Tyne area to London fell drastically in the postwar slump. Between 1918 and 1921 they plunged from about 17s. 3d. to 6s. 6d. per ton, registering a fall in each year of at least 25 per cent.[55] Then from 1921 to 1923, they dropped more slowly to about 4s. per ton. The course of coastal freights thereafter is less clear. Despite this uncertainty, it seems likely that rates in the mid-1920s were little more than the prewar level in money terms, where the average for 1911–13 was about 3s. 7d. and by the late 1920s the rates were below the prewar levels at, for instance, 3s. 2d. in 1927 and 2s. 8d. in 1930.[56]

At the same time most of the coaster's costs had risen, including wages and fuel. For example, the average cost of coal in 1921–30 was nearly half as much again as in 1909–13.[57] Whereas the able seamen and firemen on coastal colliers prewar were earning about 30s. per week,[58] in the 1920s it was more like 56s., a rise of over 80 per cent.[59] It is therefore clear that the freight rates earned by the coaster did not keep pace with increasing costs and, as a result, coasting became less remunerative. These low rates forced some owners to switch to overseas trade, or even abandon shipping, leaving vessels rusting at anchor. Thus, a low level of demand and excessive supply of coasters, especially in the non-liner trades, forced freight rates down to a barely remunerative level. This in turn forced some players out of the industry, prevented the renewal and modernisation of the fleet and made it less efficient.

Of course the coaster was not trading in a vacuum. Quite the contrary; as well as facing competition from the railways, the coaster faced potential competition from the upstart road transport industry. Motor lorries had made great strides in the First World War under the imperative of moving troops and munitions.[60] In theory road haulage could have impinged on demand for the coaster's services. In fact its impact in the 1920s was slight. Initially lorries and vans were used for short distance deliveries, from the railway station to the factory or from the port to the industrial estate, replacing horse-drawn carts and waggons.[61] In this role they complemented coasters rather than competing with them. In the 1920s the largest lorries were only rated at four tons, and although regularly overloaded were nowhere near the capacity of the coaster.[62] Similarly they were perceived as economical over relatively short distances by the coaster's standards, maybe up to 60 miles. Roads were not constructed for motor traffic, signposting was poor,[63] and as a result journey times were slow: road haulage consequently posed no real threat to the coaster because the types of traffic it served were quite different. The same cannot be said of the railways.

The railways represented a very real threat to the coaster and indeed shipowners and captains believed an unfair one. In the immediate postwar years the railways remained under government control while 'most of the limited control which had been exercised over coastal shipping was abandoned' in December 1918.[64] As a result, freight charges on the railways remained at the 1913 level until January 1920.[65] For this period the railway had a prodigious advantage over the coaster, whose costs had escalated by at least 200 per cent, and its freight rates were largely uncompetitive against the government-subsidised railway rates. Even when the government raised rates on the railways—three times in 1920 alone[66]—and eventually restored them to private ownership, albeit now in four regional monopolies, the complaints from coastal owners did not cease. They objected to the habit of the railways charging 'exceptional rates' which were below those officially quoted and never published or publicised. Some shipowners believed the railways made no profits on such rates and cross-subsidised them with higher charges on routes where competition from coastal ships was not possible.[67] In 1928 it was estimated that two-thirds of all goods were carried at exceptional rates[68] and the proportion was probably not much less in the earlier 1920s. Certainly coastal shipowners perceived them as a significant problem.

The other complaint voiced by shipowners concerned charges levied by railways on short haul traffic at the beginning and end of each voyage. It was very difficult for shipowners to avoid this cost, except by employing road haulage, which was used later in this period. The shipowners felt that the railways held the whip hand in this traffic, being able to enforce high charges because no alternative existed.[69] As a result the rate per ton mile on these short hauls could be three or four times as great as long hauls of the same commodity.[70] The railways might well retort that the realities of railway economics were such that there were economies in long hauls and diseconomies in short, but to the shipowner the charges seemed discriminatory and unfair. This was bolstered by their perception of the railway network after the 1921 re-organisation as being an oligopoly and, worse still, effectively a collection of regional monopolies. Thus the railways seemed to be in a very strong competitive position and the shipowners, despite various attempts, could not assail this.

Another cause of stagnation in the coastal trade of the 1920s, according to the shipowners, was the poor condition of port facilities. They argued that where there was limited capital available for improving berths and unloading equipment it went first to the overseas traders, leaving the coastal trade with obsolete, inadequate and inefficient facilities.[71] The result was that coasters often had to wait to get onto a berth, reducing revenue-earning time. When at a quay they were given low priority when labour was allocated. Docks were often tidal, lacked electricity, did not work at night, and did not have adequate storage space.[72] The shipowners were also concerned because they smelt the whiff of unfair competition. They pointed out that over 50 British ports were owned by the railway companies and that in these, facilities for coasters deteriorated while those for overseas trade were modernised.[73] They felt that this was deliberate policy on the part of the railways to disadvantage the coastal trade and so encourage the diversion of freight onto the railways. Certainly the coastal shipowners placed considerable blame on the poor quality of port provision. This was a common complaint, for there was always a tension between shipowner and port authority. The former wished the most expensive facilities for the least cost, the latter to provide the cheapest facilities for the largest dues. It remains unclear how far the shipowners' accusations against port authorities and railway companies were designed to divert blame from their own failings.

The picture painted so far has been gloomy. However, there were some aspects which were outside the control of the coaster owner and even the British government, such as the establishment of the Irish Free State, with the reclassification of some trade as foreign, and the worsening relationship between the two governments culminating in the 'economic war'.[74] Moreover, the coastal trade was not passive in this period. The coastal liner continued to offer a reliable service, so much so that it was used in 1919 to carry copies of Keynes's *Economic Consequences of the Peace* from the printers R. & R. Clark of Edinburgh to the publishers Macmillan in London.[75]

One of the longer-term effects of the war on the railway industry was to bring about the mergers which created four regional monopolies. The logic of this was that during the war, when the government had operated the railway system as an integrated whole, it believed it to have run at a significantly higher level of efficiency. This view is endorsed by Peter Cain who believed the average haul increased significantly and that further operating economies were extracted through the amalgamation of companies.[76] In this way the railway companies entered the 1920s with a more appropriate structure which made them more efficient. The coastal liner trade followed this precedent and that of many other industries and was subject to a significant degree of mergers and amalgamations between the wars. In 1917 Coast Lines Ltd was established, which was an amalgamation of three liner firms. In the next three years it absorbed a further ten liner companies and in the 1920s another ten coastal shipping businesses were merged into the firm, by which time it had a large share of such trade.[77] Coast Lines itself was taken over by the Royal Mail Steam Packet Group in 1917 and the advantages that should have flowed from being part of a large group may well have been negated by the difficulties which the group faced and which culminated in its crash and dismemberment in the early 1930s.[78] Thus the merger mania may have brought some economies to the coastal liners and, external to the individual firm, there continued to be a series of conferences and other agreements, both between coastal liner companies and between them and the railway companies. These aimed to restrict the excesses of competition and seek co-operation on freight rates, frequencies of sailings, etc. Thus, just as the railways had become four regional monopolies, the coasters endeavoured to gain greater control of their market. The extent to which they achieved this still needs investigation, as does the relative degree of efficiency gain in the two modes of transport, but it seems likely that the railways gained more from this exercise than did coastal shipping.

The coastal fleet in the 1920s also demonstrated technical improvements. The number and tonnage of sailing ships continued to decline and there was growth in both the number and tonnage of diesel ships and of coastal tankers. The latter, for instance, may have mustered 800 registered tons in 1914; by 1929 it was about 5,000.[79] The criticism that can be levelled against the British coastal fleet is not that it did not innovate but that it did so too slowly. However, with low freight rates, excess capacity and poor rates of return it is not surprising that the firms were not eager to invest larger sums.

NOTES

1. W.G. Hoffman, *British Industry 1770–1950* (Oxford, 1955), 47.
2. British Parliamentary Papers (BPP), Trade and Navigation Accounts, annually.
3. It should be stressed that these figures are for the registered tonnage of the ships entering not the cargoes they carried. However, they exclude ships in ballast and the likelihood of ships running consistently lightly loaded in the long run is very low. Hence they offer a reasonable guide to activity. Admittedly there were one or two changes to the basis on which the figures were collected and so the statistics are not strictly comparable. Overall, however, these changes may have balanced each other out, as of the two major alterations one was to include vessels previously excluded, the other was to exclude some which had until then counted. The fall in numbers of ships entering in the coastal trade between 1892 and 1913 was essentially a function of the decline of the sailing ship fleet and the fact that the average steam coaster was much larger than the average sailing coaster. See P.S. Bagwell and J. Armstrong, 'Coastal Shipping' in M.J. Freeman and D.H. Aldcroft (eds), *Transport in Victorian Britain* (Manchester, 1988), 171–217.
4. J.R. Cowper, 'British Coasting Trade and its National Importance', *Journal of the Institute of Transport*, 15 (1934), 223–32, suggests there were 308 services 'not including services to the western islands of Scotland' in 1931. The number pre-1914 would have been much greater.
5. C.H. Lee, 'Some Aspects of the Coastal Shipping Trade: The Aberdeen Steam Navigation Company 1835–1880', *Journal of Transport History*, 2nd series, 3 (1975), 94–107; G. Jackson, 'Operational Problems of the Transfer to Steam: Dundee, Perth and London Shipping Co., c.1820–1845', in T.C. Smout (ed.), *Scotland and the Sea* (Edinburgh, 1992), 154–81; I. Bowman, 'The Carron Line', *Transport History*, 10 (1979), 143–70 and 195–213; A.M. Northway, 'The Tyne Steam Shipping Co. : A Late-Nineteenth Century Shipping Line', *Maritime History*, 2 (1972), 69–88.
6. J. Armstrong, 'Freight Pricing Policy in Coastal Liner Companies Before the First World War', *Journal of Transport History*, 3rd series, 10 (1989), 180–97; G.E. Langmuir and G.H. Somner, *William Sloan & Co. Ltd., Glasgow 1825–1968* (World Ship Society, 1987).
7. BPP, Annual Report on Mines and Quarries, Part III.
8. B.R. Mitchell and P. Deane, *Abstract of British Historical Statistics* (Cambridge, 1962), 113; BPP, Annual Report on Mines and Quarries, Part III; London Bills of Entry, Coal Table Supplements, annually.
9. *Coal Merchant and Shipper*, 26 (1913), p.111.
10. J. Armstrong, 'Late Nineteenth-Century Freight Rates Revisited: Some Evidence from the British Coastal Coal Trade', *International Journal of Maritime History*, 6 (1994), 45–81.

11.   J. Armstrong, 'The Role of Coastal Shipping in UK Transport: An Estimate of Comparative Traffic Movements in 1910', *Journal of Transport History*, 3rd series, 8 (1987), 164–78.

12.   Aberdeen University Library (AUL), Ms. 2479/17, Directors' Report 1894.

13.   AUL, Ms 2479/29, Handbill.

14.   AUL, Ms 2479/29, Handbill.

15.   'the cold and wet weather which prevailed during August and September, always the best passenger months, told adversely on this branch of the company's business', AUL, Ms 2479/17, Directors' Report, 1896.

16.   A. M'Queen, *Clyde River Steamers, 1872–1922* (Stevenage, 1990); A.J.S. Paterson, *The Golden Years of the Clyde Steamers 1889–1914* (Newton Abbot, 1969); J. Williamson, *The Clyde Passenger Steamer* (1987).

17.   Based on Armstrong, 'Freight Pricing Policy'.

18.   Based on Armstrong, 'Late-Nineteenth Century'.

19.   J.A. MacRae and C.V. Waine, *The Steam Collier Fleets* (Wolverhampton, 1990), 54.

20.   C.I. Savage, *Inland Transport* (London, 1957).

21.   B. Greenhill, *The Merchant Schooners* (London, 1988).

22.   Public Record Office (PRO), RAIL 226/110.

23.   J.G. Bruce, 'The Contribution of Cross-Channel and Coastal Vessels to Developments in Marine Practice', *Journal of Transport History*, 1st series, 4 (1959), 65–80.

24.   Armstrong, 'Late-Nineteenth Century'.

25.   BPP, Trade and Navigation Accounts.

26.   PRO, BT 99/2569.

27.   See for example W.G. Rickman, *The Shipowners' Register of Port Charges* (London, 1924).

28.   M. Elis-Williams, 'The Sloop *Jenny* 1787–1919', *Maritime Wales*, 10 (1986), 138–41, gives an even longer-lived example.

29.   D.L. Munby, *Inland Transport Statistics. Great Britain 1900–1970* (Oxford, 1978), 46–7.

30.   BPP, 1897, LXXVIII, p.407.

31.   Armstrong, 'The Role of Coastal Shipping'.

32.   Munby, *Inland Water Statistics*, 22.

33.   BPP, Trade and Navigation Accounts.

34.   BPP, Trade and Navigation Accounts.

35.   B.E. Supple, *The History of the British Coal Industry. Volume 4 : 1913–1946 The Political Economy of Decline* (Oxford, 1987), 48.

36.   D.H. Aldcroft, 'The Eclipse of British Coastal Shipping 1913–1921', *Journal of Transport History*, 1st series, 6 (1963), 25.

37.   D.H. Aldcroft, *British Transport since 1914. An Economic History* (Newton Abbot, 1975), p.18.

38.   Mitchell and Deane, *Abstract*, 224.

39.   Aldcroft, *British Transport*, 16.

40. Aldcroft, 'The Eclipse', 28; Aldcroft, *British Transport*, 19.
41. J. Uglow, *Sailorman. A Barge Master's Story* (London, 1975), 84.
42. H. Benham, *Last Stronghold of Sail* (London, 1948), 178.
43. BPP, Trade and Navigation Accounts.
44. BPP, Trade and Navigation Accounts.
45. The sub-title of Supple's book on the interwar coal industry makes it clear: *The Political Economy of Decline*.
46. Mitchell and Deane, *Abstract*, 116.
47. Mitchell and Deane, *Abstract*, 121.
48. BPP, Annual Reports on Mines and Quarries.
49. Chamber of Shipping, Annual Reports, Statistical Tables.
50. Munby, *Inland Transport Statistics*, p.83.
51. Mitchell and Deane, *Abstract*, 224.
52. Mitchell and Deane, *Abstract*, 224.
53. F. Capie and M. Collins, *The Inter-War British Economy: A Statistical Abstract* (Manchester, 1983), 84.
54. The only coastal freight rate used by Isserlis to construct his overall tramp shipping index, route 85, coal from the Tyne to London, is very suspect as he has it <u>falling</u> from 1914 to 1918, till in the latter year it is about half that of the former: L. Isserlis, 'Tramp Shipping Cargoes and Freights', *Journal of the Royal Statistical Society*, 101 (1938), 120. This also conflicts with the 'average' freights given for 1914–23 in D.W. Lloyd and F.C. Swallow, *The North Country and Yorkshire Coal Annual for 1924* (Cardiff, 1924), 64, which show a rise from 1914 to 1917 when it is nearly five times the 1914 figure.
55. Lloyd and Swallow, *North Country*, 64.
56. Based on an analysis of the freight rates appearing in the *Iron and Coal Trades Review* and *Coal Merchant and Shipper*.
57. Mitchell and Deane, *Abstract*, 483–4.
58. Armstrong, 'Late-Nineteenth Century'.
59. MacRae and Waine, *Steam Collier Fleets*, 138.
60. J.M. Laux, 'Trucks in the West during the First World War', *Journal of Transport History*, 3rd series, 6 (1985), 64–70.
61. T. Barker and D. Gerhold, *The Rise and Rise of Road Transport 1700–1990* (Basingstoke, 1993), 85.
62. Barker and Gerhold, *Rise and Rise*, 85–6; T.C. Barker, *The Transport Contractors of Rye* (London, 1982), 20.
63. Barker, *Transport Contractors*, 20–3; Barker and Gerhold, *Rise and Rise*, 86.
64. D.H. Aldcroft, 'The Decontrol of British Shipping and Railways after the First World War', *Journal of Transport History*, 1st series, 5 (1961), 97.
65. Aldcroft, 'The Eclipse', 28.
66. Aldcroft, 'The Decontrol', 93.
67. BPP, 1921, XV, 344–5.
68. Munby, *Inland Transport Statistics*, 96.

69. BPP, 1921, XV, 344.
70. Savage, *Inland Transport* 26; BPP, 1929–30, XVI, 365.
71. Anon, *The Coastwise Trade of the UK Past and Present and its Possibilities* (London, 1925), p.64; Cowper, 'British Coasting Trade', 230.
72. P.S. Bagwell, *The Transport Revolution since 1770* (London, 1974), 281.
73. Savage, *Inland Transport*, 28.
74. Savage, *Inland Transport*, 26.
75. R. Skidelsky, *John Maynard Keynes: Hopes Betrayed 1883–1920* (London, 1983), 381, 393.
76. P.J. Cain, 'Private Enterprise or Public Utility? Output, Pricing and Investment on English and Welsh Railways, 1870–1914', *Journal of Transport History*, 3rd series, 1 (1980), 12,13, 20.
77. P. Mathias and A.W. Pearsall, *Shipping: A Survey of Historical Records* (Newton Abbot, 1971), 37–9.
78. E. Green and M. Moss, *A Business of National Importance: The Royal Mail Shipping Group, 1902–1937* (London, 1982).
79. Isserlis, 'Tramp Shipping Cargoes', 96–7.

CHAPTER 3

The End of the Line: Oswald Sanderson, Sir John Ellerman and the Wilsons of Hull

Brian Dyson

In the half century before the First World War, shipowners operated in a highly advantageous business environment. With the distribution of goods expanding at a rate ten times that of the growth of world output, the demand for shipping services increased rapidly. At the same time, technological developments in hull construction and marine engines led to major efficiency gains in the supply of such services.[1] That Britain was not only the world's leading trading nation, but also the fount of most of the technological innovations in shipping, meant that it was British shipowners, above all others, who exploited, and benefited from, these highly propitious conditions. Accordingly, it was estimated that on the eve of the First World War British shipping carried 'about 52 percent of the total sea-borne trade of the world, including 92 per cent of the Inter-Imperial trade, 63 per cent of the trade between the Empire and foreign countries, and 30 per cent of the trade between foreign countries'.[2]

The institutional structure of the British shipping industry was also conducive to growth. Evolving within a favourable legal framework, which permitted a degree of limited liability before such a facility became a statutory right, and unencumbered by restrictive state policies, shipowners were able to develop business structures in the first half of the nineteenth century which were sufficiently flexible to accommodate the dynamic growth in the scope, scale and cost of operations that occurred after 1870. Confidence, borne of repeat contracting, control over information flows and the exploitation of family and port-based networks, was at the heart of this business growth.[3] While proprietorships and partnerships increasingly gave way to joint-stock and holding companies from

59

the 1870s onwards, family firms remained a feature of the industry, even as large-scale enterprises developed apace in the late Victorian and Edwardian eras.[4] This chapter is concerned with the largest of these family companies, the Hull firm of Thos Wilson Sons and Co. (TWSC). In focusing on the management and eventual sale of the enterprise in 1916, it demonstrates that while the family firm, as a business unit, was not inimical to rapid and large-scale growth, its performance relied on uncertain factors such as individual ability and interpersonal relations. Such weaknesses might be countered by various strategies, one of which, the appointment of a manager from outside the family, but from within the firm's commercial networks, was resorted to by the principals of TWSC, Charles and Arthur Wilson. This chapter, in charting the recruitment and career of Oswald Sanderson, the Managing Director selected by the Wilsons, therefore sheds some light on the business policies of large-scale shipping enterprises in the first quarter of the twentieth century.

Managing the World's Largest Privately Owned Shipping Firm

The firm which became TWSC had its origins in a partnership founded by four merchants in Hull in 1825. Thomas Wilson and his partners, John Beckington, Thomas Hudson and John Hudson (no relation), were principally concerned in the importation and distribution of Swedish iron ore, investing in their first ship, the *Thomas & Ann*, in 1825. Wilson was always the active and dominant partner, and by 1841, with the withdrawal of the Hudsons, had full control of the firm, now renamed Thos Wilson Son & Co, having taken his eldest son David (1817–93) as his new partner. David was joined in about 1850 by the two youngest sons, Charles Henry (1833–1907) and Arthur (1836–1909), and the 'Son' of the title was pluralised. When Thomas Wilson died on 21 June 1869, aged 77, his firm owned over 20 ships, all registered in Hull. By now, TWSC was being run by Charles Henry (36) and Arthur (33), under whose astute and purposeful management the firm enjoyed swift and profitable growth. In the 1860s and 1870s services were expanded to the Adriatic, Sicily, the Black Sea and India, and in 1875 to New York via Newcastle. In 1885 the Wilsons entered the London–New York trade. Partnerships were established with other lines for these services, such as the Wilson-Hill Line. Following the purchase for £300,000 of the 23 vessels of the Bailey & Leetham Line in 1903, the Wilson Line reached its peak, owning more than 100 vessels, aggregating over 190,000 grt.

3.1 Charles Henry Wellesley Wilson, second Lord Nunburnholme, in 1910 (from *Transit*, vol. VI, no. 10, October 1910)

In 1891 the Company was registered as a private limited company, the entire share capital of £2,000,000, made up of 20,000 ordinary shares of £100 each, being owned by members of the Wilson family, with Charles nominated as Chairman, and Arthur as Deputy Chairman. With wealth, of course, went social position and political influence. Charles Wilson married Florence Jane Helen Wellesley, daughter of Colonel W.H.C. Wellesley, a descendant of the Duke of Wellington, in 1871. In 1878 he bought Warter Priory (with 300 acres) from Lord Muncaster, and by the turn of the century owned nearly 8,000 acres, with an estate near Balmoral, a chalet in Nice, and a London home at 41 Grosvenor Square. He was also Liberal MP for Hull between 1874 and 1906. Arthur Wilson, too, established himself as an important society figure in the region. He bought land at Tranby, near Hull, and built a mansion, Tranby Croft, completed in 1876. He eventually owned 3,000 acres in the region, was Master of the Holderness Hunt, Sheriff of Hull in 1888–89, and High Sheriff of Yorkshire in 1891, despite the celebrated 'Baccarat Scandal' which occurred as a result of alleged cheating by a member of the Prince of Wales's party which was staying at Tranby Croft for the Doncaster St Leger races in September 1890.[5]

Despite outward appearances, it is evident that by the late nineteenth century all was not well within the Wilson dynasty, and that the sons of Charles and Arthur were not made of the same stuff as their illustrious fathers and grandfather. Someone else was needed to manage TWSC if the firm was to continue to enjoy long-term success as an independent venture. Accordingly, from the mid-1890s, the Wilson brothers were looking for a manager, preferably an individual from within their own commercial network whom they could trust to run and preserve the family's shipping empire. Such was the tenor of an interview which Liverpool shipping agent Harold Sanderson had with Charles Wilson in March 1896: 'Mr Wilson seemed very discouraged that neither his nor Mr Arthur Wilson's sons seemed likely to take the management off their hands. He says they are badly in need of someone, but he does not know which way to turn as their business is a complicated one.'[6]

Harold Sanderson regularly communicated such information to his younger brother, Oswald, then living in New York. In one such report, dated 5 December 1898, Harold recorded: 'C[harles] W[ilson] was very friendly—he would I think be glad to have you in Hull—he seems to fear however your position would be intolerable by reason of A[rthur] W[ilson]'s peculiarities, and opposition in the office. His idea is that you should have £4000 if you come over.'[7] In early 1899 Charles Wilson duly wrote to Oswald Sanderson, a former employee and distant relative by marriage, offering him a management position within the firm. Known as 'Count' to his intimates, Oswald Sanderson was born on 3 January 1863, and had begun his commercial career in the offices of the Wilson Line before joining his father in the firm of Sanderson & Co. in New York, Boston and Chicago, which acted as agents for the Wilson Line and others. He eventually became senior partner and owner of the firm.

Sanderson responded positively to Charles Wilson's approach but, knowing of the awe in which his prospective bosses were held, and heeding his brother's advice, he was clearly determined to establish the nature of his proposed position in the firm. He insisted on being called Manager, on having a directorship, and on confirmation that his proposed starting salary of £4,000 a year would progress to a higher level.[8] Sanderson also expressed his concern to his brother that unless he had a guaranteed senior position at Hull he would be better off where he was: 'to leave here & go there as a Managing Clerk is stretching loyalty to a great length'.[9] Sanderson's demands, however, appear to have put Charles Wilson off, and on 22 February 1899 he shelved the proposal.[10]

A year later Sanderson offered to visit Hull to discuss terms personally with the Wilsons.[11] This apparently happened in the summer of 1900, and on 26 July, back in New York, Sanderson wrote to them again outlining his terms. He was to be Manager, 'with authority second to yours only, the object being to relieve you both, as much as possible of the details of management'. He still expressed his wish to be a Director, 'thus reducing to a minimum any possibility of friction'. His remuneration was to be £4,000 in the first year, and £5,000 per year for the following three years, and he would maintain his controlling interest in his New York company.[12] In reply, Charles Wilson again refused to consider a directorship for Sanderson, but agreed the matter could be reconsidered at a later stage. He also quibbled over the salary, claiming both that trade was bad, and that Sanderson's continuing income from the New York business (about £500 per year) could be deducted from his TWSC salary, so that ultimately he would be paid £4,500.[13] Sanderson duly dropped his demands for a directorship, provided he was guaranteed 'an equivalent authority'. He looked forward to having good relations with 'Kenneth, Tommie and Clive, so that we all shall work together harmoniously and unselfishly for the good of Thomas Wilson Sons & Co. Ltd'.[14] Finally, on 10 October, he also dropped his claim for a higher salary, being prepared to trust to the Wilsons' fairness. Sanderson left for Hull with his family via Liverpool on 29 December 1900, so that his wife, Beatrice, could spend Christmas at home in her native New York.[15] He started work at Hull in January 1901.

Sanderson's work evidently proved satisfactory. He was elected to the Board of Directors of TWSC on 20 August 1902, and in 1905 he was appointed Managing Director with effect from 11 August for a period of 15 years at £6,000 per year, plus a share in the profits of the firm.[16] For a time, though, he was very much the man in the middle as Charles and Arthur Wilson argued over various business matters, notably over the decision to purchase Earle's Shipbuilding and Engineering Company of Hull, which Arthur very much opposed.[17] Charles Henry Wilson was created Baron Nunburnholme of Kingston-upon-Hull in 1906, but died suddenly at Warter Priory on 27 October 1907, after having survived a heart attack two weeks before. He left three sons and four daughters. He was succeeded as Chairman of TWSC by Arthur Wilson.

Business had continued to prosper in the latter years of Charles's and Arthur's reign. An agency agreement was established with Det Forenede Dampskibs-Selskab (the United Steamship Company of Copenhagen) to operate joint services from London to St Petersburg, Riga and Copenhagen through the newly formed United Shipping Company based in London. And in 1906 TWSC joined with the North Eastern Railway to operate services from Hull to Hamburg, Antwerp, Ghent and Dunkirk through the Wilson's & North-Eastern Railway Shipping Company (WNERSC). After the death of 'Mr Arthur' from cancer in October 1909 the chairmanship passed to his son, E. Kenneth Wilson (aged 39), while Charles Henry Wellesley Wilson, 2nd Lord Nunburnholme (aged 34), became Deputy Chairman. The rest of the Board comprised Oswald Sanderson, Arthur's brother, Clive H.A. Wilson, and the Hon. Guy Wilson MP, Lord Nunburnholme's brother. Between the appointment of Guy Wilson to the Board in June 1908 and the traumatic events of 1916, there were to be no further boardroom changes.

A Family at War

At the outbreak of the First World War there were still 92 vessels in the Wilson fleet, of which three were tugs and seven were operated by WNERSC. The effects of the war on trading results were dramatic, but it was some time before this became clear. To begin with, some 16 Wilson ships were interned in the Baltic, where 13 remained in April 1915. Compilation of the accounts was further delayed by the shortage of personnel, with over 100 Wilson office staff in Hull quickly joining the armed forces.

Nevertheless, the gross profit for 1914 was some £250,000, reducing to about £130,000 after allowing for depreciation. Sanderson described these results as 'discouraging'.[18] Profits quickly recovered, however, and returns for 1916 showed a surplus of £1,321,026 3s. 10d. before allowing for depreciation and excess profits duty.[19] Despite this, within 18 months the entire operation was sold to Sir John Reeves Ellerman. The disposal of the firm, which surprised the shipping interest and shocked the city of Hull, was due neither to a dearth of successors, the official reason,[20] nor to the desire of the Wilsons to divest when profits were high. Rather, the largest privately owned shipping company in the world was sold because of that fundamental weakness of family firms, interpersonal rivalries between principals. In this case, the crisis was triggered by the strained relationship between Oswald Sanderson, the Manager recruited in 1900 to relieve the Wilsons of the day-to-day operations of the firm, and the son of Charles Henry Wilson, 'Tommy' Wilson, the 2nd Lord Nunburnholme.

Sanderson's correspondence clearly shows that he remained on excellent terms with the Dowager Lady Nunburnholme, Mrs Arthur Wilson, and with Kenneth, Clive and Guy Wilson. The problem for all of them appears to have been Tommy, the 2nd Lord Nunburnholme. Charles Henry Wellesley Wilson was born in 1875. He eventually became a Major in the East Yorkshire Regiment, serving with distinction in the Boer War, where he gained a DSO in 1900. However, he does not appear to have ever been particularly popular. On the ennoblement of his father in 1906, he did succeed him as Liberal MP for West Hull, but only after Lord Nunburnholme personally intervened to ensure his adoption at a selection meeting of the local party, which was not persuaded of the son's merits. He made no impact at all at Westminster, where his sojourn was cut short by his father's death. Nunburnholme did not do very well out of his father's demise, causing Arthur Wilson to suggest to Sanderson that his nephew had been 'most abominably treated under this most recent Will'.[21] He was on bad terms with his mother, the Dowager Lady Nunburnholme, and appears to have been extremely jealous of Sanderson, whose public role grew while Nunburnholme appears to have made little impact on public or even regional life, although he was Sheriff of Hull in 1910, and later Lord Lieutenant of the East Riding and President of the Territorial Force

Association. Sanderson, however, was Chairman of WNERSC, President of the Humber Conservancy Commission, a Director of the United Shipping Company and of Earle's, a Director of Lloyd's Bank Ltd, a British member of the Council of Administration of the Suez Canal Company, and a Director of the North Eastern Railway Company. Furthermore, it was Nunburnholme's cousin, Kenneth, who was considered to be more suitable as new Chairman of the firm, with Nunburnholme himself having to be content with the Deputy's position. That he did not like this is clear from his extraordinary behaviour during 1916.

On 16 March 1916, the President of the Board of Trade, Walter Runciman, invited Sanderson to join a small Departmental Committee to consider the position of the shipping and shipbuilding industries after the war.[22] After consulting his Chairman, Sanderson agreed to join. When Nunburnholme heard of this, he vehemently objected: 'I certainly cannot agree to your serving on Runciman's Committee as you are on too many other things, which take you away from Hull, & further I should strongly object to discussing our policy with anybody after the War'.[23] In case Sanderson had not got the message, Nunburnholme later added: 'These questions of high policy are a matter for Kenneth & myself, & we do not take the same view or look upon the matter from the same point of view as yourself'.[24] Sanderson was duly shocked by this attitude: 'Your concluding paragraph astonishes me, & if you correctly convey the Proprietors [sic] views in it, I must reconsider my whole position with the Company.'[25] Henceforth, Sanderson had his correspondence with the Deputy Chairman copied, and circulated to the other directors. Kenneth Wilson came down strongly in support of Sanderson:

> Words can't describe my annoyance at the letter that Tommy has written to you. It is just like him writing to you, what he doesn't say to your face. I may say at once I don't agree to that last paragraph, and I shall ask him to withdraw it ... It is all absolute jealousy. Instead of this, he ought to be proud of having a representative on such a committee, and everyone else except him thinks the same.[26]

Three days later the Chairman added: 'He fears the committee may induce you to ask us to spend a great deal of our accumulated money (a great deal of which goes back to the Government) in building unnecessary ships'. In a postscript he added: 'It is no good fuming over Tommy, the only thing is to treat him as a joke!!'.[27] A frequent exchange of letters ensued. Kenneth Wilson, writing to Sanderson from Invershin on 19 July, expressed his exasperation: 'personally I am getting very fed up with these letters. It is very disconcerting. If he wants to get out, let's sell the whole thing lock stock & barrel, & not sell it piece meal.'[28] This is the first intimation in the surviving correspondence of what was shortly to happen.

Many years later, the shadowy figure of Ernest Olivier emerged to shed some light over subsequent events. Olivier appears at one time to have been a shipping agent in the eastern Mediterranean, who worked for the Wilsons and others in various places, including Alexandria and Smyrna. In a letter to a later Managing Director of the Wilson Line, written in 1947, Olivier claimed that in July 1916 he spent a week at Londesborough Park with Lord Nunburnholme, who asked Olivier to sound out Sir John Ellerman, the shipping, brewing and newspaper magnate,[29] regarding the possible purchase of the Wilson Line. Olivier broached the subject with Ellerman and Captain John Westcott (Managing Director of the Westcott & Laurance Line, another Ellerman operation) at his Windsor home, then reported back to Nunburnholme in Hull, with negotiations thereafter conducted by Sanderson.[30] Sanderson in fact knew Ellerman already, and the latter had evidently formed a high opinion of him. Indeed, in September 1899 Ellerman had attempted to persuade Sanderson to become agent for his Leyland Line in New York during his visit to the city.[31]

But before much progress in the negotiations to purchase the Wilson Line had been made, another argument erupted between the Wilson directors. This was over a newly built vessel, the 5793-ton *Oswego*. In early July the three principal Wilson directors had agreed, at Nunburnholme's pressing, to sell the vessel if a buyer could be found at the right price (although there was disagreement over what that should be). It seems that all three were concerned about shipping losses, but Wilson and Sanderson had slightly different concerns from Nunburnholme. TWSC's fleet had declined to some 68 ships after the loss of 26 due to enemy action, of which the latest was the *Aaro*. With no immediate buyer, and not wishing to waste the services of a valuable ship at the height of war, Sanderson and his Chairman had the *Oswego* prepared for sea trials and ordered stores to be purchased. Indeed, Sanderson questioned Nunburnholme's motives: 'It looks as though some dread miserly spirit has got hold of him & almost warped his mind entirely into one idea Gold, Gold & always Gold. Everything that we can sell profitably he seems to want to let go & hive the money away, the business seems a second consideration just now.' Nunburnholme's strategy, he said, appeared to be to sell off the ships individually, replacing them later when the market dropped.[32]

Thwarted, Nunburnholme demanded a Board meeting to vote on the matter and told Sanderson: 'I have to think of the future of my Family and am more interested in the matter than any member of the Firm'.[33] Writing to Kenneth Wilson he confirmed: 'I do wish to go out of business. We have, after paying E[xcess] P[rofits] T[ax] about £3,000,000 and 68 ships, worth another £6,000,000 and we get more by selling them singly than by any other way, as no company could finance such high figures ...'. He was prepared to consider an offer of £250,000 or even £225,000 for the *Oswego*, which was considerably less than Sanderson and Wilson were prepared to do.[34] He further upset Sanderson by suggesting that the Managing Director was more interested in his commission (or share of the profits) than the interests of the firm. Told of this, Kenneth Wilson, writing from his Roehampton home on 2 August, again expressed his support for Sanderson: 'It is unpardonable, & a thing that nobody in his position ought to have dreamt of saying. If he hasn't already apologised, I do so myself on behalf of the Firm. These sort of things make one think more than ever, we had better be out of the business.'[35] Wilson, still at Roehampton, forwarded to Sanderson the next missive from Nunburnholme at Londesborough which warned bluntly: 'You had better not interfere between Oswald & myself; we have no quarrel, but you seem likely to bring one about'.[36] In his covering letter to Sanderson, Wilson wrote: 'I am absolutely disgusted, & cannot conceive how any man in his senses dare hold up a ship which is worth £400 a day for a month. It is not fair on the Firm, or the Country.'[37] Writing to Sanderson again on the next day, Wilson concluded: 'I really think the best thing for you to do to bring matters to a crisis would be to resign, but we can talk this over next week'.[38]

Sanderson remained convinced that a much better price could be obtained for the *Oswego* later, and that the needs of the country at the height of a great war were paramount.[39] Nunburnholme, getting even more frantic, repeated that he was prepared to sell the vessel for £250,000, and that he was calling an Extraordinary General Meeting for 15 August.[40] He followed this up by sending identical letters to Sanderson and Wilson complaining about their behaviour: 'I hold that your action is detrimental to the interests of the Shareholders of the Company'.[41] Sanderson was indignant. Promptly replying to this letter, and a telephone conversation, he wrote:

I am sorry that you still disagree with your brother Directors' view that the *Oswego* should not lie idle pending a purchaser at an agreed price being found. The suggestion that a valuable ship in these times of utmost need shall be kept from employment pending a buyer being forthcoming is one that the remainder of your Colleagues cannot assent to, & we have therefore ordered the ship to be coaled & ballasted as any further delay means her lying idle & consequent loss to the Shareholders of the Company.

He further pointed out that Kenneth Wilson thought the price should be nearer £275,000. 'I hope on reconsideration you will not maintain the unfortunate position you have chosen to adopt, & arrange for all to continue to work as we have until recently harmoniously together'.[42]

In the face of such opposition , Nunburnholme was forced to climb down and on 8 August wrote to Sanderson from Londesborough: 'I have made my protest, and have disclaimed all responsibility—So the matter is at an end'. [43] On the same day, Kenneth Wilson asked Sanderson for the return of his letters 'to keep as a record. I have no doubt he is a bit mad, especially when money comes into the question'.[44] Fortunately, from an historical viewpoint, Sanderson appears not to have complied. Furthermore, the matter was far from over.

Evidently very upset by what he regarded as undue interference in managerial affairs, Sanderson sought to clarify the situation by writing to Nunburnholme on 16 August and outlining future procedures following the latter's 'recent action':

No direct orders are to be given to the Managers by you which conflict with those already given by the Managing Director, and any desires you have in this connection you will first consult with the Managing Director, or, if he is away, any other Director present, and act in agreement with them.

In the event of your not being in agreement with your colleagues in matters of high policy, you will give way without recriminations later, whether the policy proves to be right or wrong; that you will be good enough not to attend meetings with Directors of other big Companies without the consent of your colleagues.

I hope you will not think this letter stiff—it is not intended to be so but is purely a matter of business. Personally I hope we shall always be the best of friends as we are, I believe, at present.[45]

Sanderson believed that Nunburnholme had already agreed to these conditions in conversation with Kenneth Wilson. But Nunburnholme was again irate. He telephoned Sanderson from London, demanding the withdrawal of the letter. Sanderson explained what then happened to the Dowager Lady Nunburnholme on 17 August: 'He asked me to sound you as to your willingness to sell out. I told him I had & gathered if all the others were willing & a fair price obtainable you would agree. With this danger of friction still present, but I hope stilled, you might consider & let me have your views.'[46]

Sanderson's negotiations with Ellerman in London now began in earnest, while Kenneth Wilson organised things in Hull, apparently doing his utmost to keep Nunburnholme out of the discussions. He explained to Sanderson on 20 August: 'I told the Dow [sic] I declined to go & see Ellerman with Tommy. If he insists on going, I shall say it must be done by letter.'[47] A subsequent family meeting was held, probably on the morning of Friday 25 August, with Kenneth and Clive Wilson, Nunburnholme and the Dowager Lady Nunburnholme present, to agree terms: again with Nunburnholme isolated and wanting to sell at any price (as low as £180 or even £170 a share).[48] Writing again to Sanderson (probably on the morning of Monday 28 August), Wilson said he had received 'a very strong letter from the Dowager saying that if he [i.e. Nunburnholme] interferes, we are immediately to exercise our option of buying him out'.[49]

Sanderson met Ellerman in London on 29 August. He telephoned the result to Wilson, who was unable to follow most of what was said owing to a bad connection.[50] Sanderson therefore wrote to his Chairman about the meeting to confirm things. He had, he said, told Ellerman that both branches of the Wilson family 'thought that considering the few male members of the family to come on, the time had arrived to get out if a satisfactory price could be obtained'. Ellerman offered £3.6 million for the shares and £0.5 million for the debentures, a total of £4.1 million. He also expressed his concern about the effects of excess profits tax, the need to replace vessels lost, and the foreshortening of the war should Romania enter. Ellerman emphasised that he wished Sanderson to continue as Managing Director. Sanderson therefore asked not to be directly included in the negotiations in future.[51] Following their telephone conversation, Kenneth Wilson replied on the same day and suggested that Ellerman's offer was about £800,000 short of what the family wanted. He thought that, as a precaution, perhaps other potential buyers could be sounded out. In any case, he advised Sanderson to go on his planned holiday to Falmouth.[52]

Having thought about it, Kenneth Wilson interrupted Sanderson's holiday by announcing on 1 September that he was prepared to accept an offer from Ellerman of £210 for each of the ordinary shares, but would go down to £200 if necessary, plus the 10 per cent dividend already declared. He thought the Dowager would agree, while 'Tommy was keen to get out at any price...'. He arranged to meet Ellerman on the following Wednesday (6 September) at 3 p.m. in London, and invited Sanderson to attend.[53] No deal appears to have been struck, however, and the negotiations dragged on. By 8 October the offer had reached its final level of about £190 a share, or a total price of some £4.3 million.[54] At the last meeting of the old Board held in Hull on 8 November, Ellerman, Edward Lloyd and Captain John Richard Westcott were made nominal shareholders.[55] The formal transfer of ownership was eventually concluded on 13 November. The Board met at 11 a.m. that day at Ellerman's London offices at 12 Moorgate, attended by Kenneth Wilson, Lord Nunburnholme, Oswald Sanderson, Clive Wilson, Ellerman, Westcott and Lloyd. During the initial stages the meeting was chaired by Sanderson. Nunburnholme and the two Wilsons announced their resignations; Ellerman, Lloyd and Westcott were elected to the Board, and Ellerman was then elected Chairman. Sanderson was confirmed as Managing Director. Some 19,860 of TWSC's ordinary £100 shares were duly transferred from the various Wilson family members and trustees to Ellerman and Ellerman Lines, while Sanderson continued to hold his 110 shares.[56] The purchase comprised 75 Wilson vessels (including seven WNERSC).

The Wilsons do not appear to have been particularly saddened by the great change. Writing to his eldest son Oswald on 7 December 1916, Sanderson observed:

> The transfer of the Wilsons and their small Companies is completed ... I have not seen my colleagues since the sale. To put it tersely having got their money they spent the time investing it. You will be amused to hear the transfer was effected in a very short time, each participant getting his cheque and securities. The anxiety seemed to be to get the money in the Bank - no speeches - no regrets - nothing was said by any of them either to Sir John or myself. It would be a joke if it had not got its tragic side - after 38 years of close relationship. [57]

The last tranche of money—comprising £500,000 for the debentures—was duly paid at the end of December 1916.[58]

Disposal: 'A Heaven Sent Stroke of Luck'

The voluminous correspondence with Sanderson shows that Ellerman was effectively running TWSC from mid-October 1916. A little over a week after the completion of the deal, Ellerman confirmed that he intended to put Kenneth Wilson back on the Board, and that the name of the Company would soon be changed.[59] In public, Sanderson made assurances that the old name would be kept.[60] But the revised Memorandum & Article of Association passed at Extraordinary General Meetings on 11 and 29 January 1917 duly confirmed the new name of 'Ellerman's Wilson Line' (EWL). Kenneth Wilson was elected a Director on 22 March 1917. Meetings of the Board were subsequently held either at Hull or London.[61] The *Oswego* was started on the Atlantic run, but on 26 March Ellerman, with some irony, suggested to Sanderson that the vessel be sold— possibly for as much as £300,000.[62] Sanderson responded by cautioning against such a move, arguing that ships would be needed after the war, and that such a high figure would be difficult to obtain.[63]

Sanderson remained on friendly terms with most of the Wilson clan, and even Nunburnholme's attitude towards his former Managing Director appears to have mellowed. As early as 12 September he had suggested that if Sanderson was unable to reach terms with 'our friend', 'three or four of us' might consider starting a tramp company, with each putting up £100,000 and buying ships at the bottom of the market.[64] Sanderson was not tempted. His relations with the rest of the family appear to have been more valued, particularly Guy Wilson, whose East Riding Yeomanry regiment included his second son, Lloyd Sanderson. Writing to Guy Wilson on 23 May 1917, Sanderson noted the great personal break for himself after 38 years with the Wilson family. As for the new situation: 'Sir John Ellerman is leaving me practically in entire charge here, he has not even been down to Hull yet. The new Directors are really so in name only, as the full responsibility rests with the Chairman & myself. Kenneth rejoined the Board at Ellerman's request, I think he rather wanted to sever his connection completely ...'. He noted how bad things were, with the government having taken over the British mercantile marine for the rest of the war at comparatively low rates of charter hire and that, with enormously increased costs, particularly insurance, shipping

ELLERMAN'S WILSON LINE LIMITED.

INTENDED SAILINGS FROM HULL.

To ARCHANGEL (During open Navigation)	Fortnightly	To ALEXANDRIA PORT SAID and SUEZ	Fortnightly	
To AALESUND BERGEN CHRISTIANSUND STAVANGER TRONDHJEM (DRONTHEIM)	Weekly	ADELAIDE MELBOURNE and SYDNEY	Monthly	
		BOMBAY and KURRACHEE	Fortnightly	
CHRISTIANIA CHRISTIANSAND	Weekly	BOSTON, U.S.A.	Fortnightly	
		CONSTANTINOPLE	Suspended	
To GOTHENBURG	Twice Weekly (Cargo only)	GENOA. LEGHORN, MARSEILLES, NAPLES, PALERMO, MESSINA, CATANIA	About every 10 days	
STOCKHOLM NORRKOPPING KALMAR	Suspended	LIVERPOOL	Suspended	
		NEWCASTLE	Weekly	
To COPENHAGEN	Twice weekly	NEW YORK	Weekly	
(NEWCASTLE to COPENHAGEN, Weekly)		NOVOROSSISK and ODESSA	Suspended	
To LIBAU RIGA REVAL PETROGRAD	Suspended do. do. do.	ROUEN	Fortnightly	
		TRIESTE, FIUME and VENICE	Suspended	

From GRIMSBY.

To GOTHENBURG MALMO and HALMSTAD	Suspended Weekly	To CHRISTIANIA and SKIEN	Fortnightly	

For Freight and further particulars apply **ELLERMAN'S WILSON LINE, LTD., HULL**
Marine Risks taken at Current Rates of Premium

WILSONS & NORTH EASTERN RAILWAY SHIPPING CO., LIMITED.

INTENDED SAILINGS FROM HULL.

To DUNKIRK, Twice Weekly   From DUNKIRK to HULL, Twice Weekly
SAILINGS TO ANTWERP, GHENT, AND HAMBURG SUSPENDED.

WILSONS & NORTH EASTERN RAILWAY SHIPPING CO., Ltd., HULL.
Telegrams—"WILSONS, HULL."

FROM HULL TO IRISH PORTS.

Port.	Owners.	Agents.	Sailings.
BELFAST(via Liverpool)	Ellerman's Wilson Line, Ltd.	W. H. Stott & Co., Ltd., Liverpool / Jas. Little & Co., Belfast	Suspended.
CORK (via Liverpool)	Ellerman's Wilson Line, Ltd.	W. H. Stott & Co., Ltd., Liverpool	Suspended.
DUBLIN (via Liverpool)	Ellerman's Wilson Line, Ltd.	W. H. Stott & Co., Ltd., Liverpool	Suspended.
DROGHEDA (via Liverpool)	Ellerman's Wilson Line, Ltd.	W. H. Stott & Co., Ltd., Liverpool	Suspended.
LIMERICK (via Liverpool)	Ellerman's Wilson Line, Ltd.	W. H. Stott & Co., Ltd., Liverpool	Suspended.
LONDONDERRY (via Liverpool)	Ellerman's Wilson Line, Ltd.	W. H. Stott & Co., Ltd., Liverpool	Suspended.
WATERFORD (via Liverpool)	Ellerman's Wilson Line, Ltd.	W. H. Stott & Co., Ltd., Liverpool	Suspended.

Printed for the Proprietor, H. E. C. NEWHAM, Hull, by KNIGHT & FORSTER LTD., Leeds.

3.2 One of the first Wilson Line advertisements to appear after the takeover by Ellerman (from *Hull Trade and Transit*, vol. XIII, no. 4, February 1917) companies were making little or nothing. 'You can therefore judge what a heaven sent stroke of luck it was selling the business when you did & my finding a purchaser able to pay in cash; you at the same time found the market for Investment at good rates of interest.'[65]

Guy Wilson duly replied, saying that he in fact knew very little about what had happened in relation to the sale. Sanderson responded:

> It was a most fortunate thing you got out when you did, I do not think you could do so now. Matters had reached a climax with Tommy, who wished to sell everything in the way of ships & trust to Wilson's goodwill to go back into their Trades when, if ever, steamers got cheap & I finally told them all that I thought the best thing that could be done under the circumstances was to realise if they could do so for cash. I saw the Dowager Lady Nunburnholme & Mrs Arthur Wilson, also the boys & they decided that if I could get a cash offer perhaps it would be best as there were so few Wilson boys coming on; the rest you know. Kenneth rather hankered to remain on as I think he liked to have some Directorships of importance, but so far as the management of the business is concerned, it is understood that the Directors do not interfere, it is left in my hands under the control of Sir John Ellerman. I am very glad to have him in the Office, it is nice to see old faces under the altered conditions.[66]

The acquisition of TWSC made Ellerman the biggest shipowner in Britain with over 200 vessels. However, EWL lost 49 ships between 1914 and 1918 through enemy action, and was badly hit by the Russian Revolution, although the effects were partly offset by increasing trade with Poland. In the early 1920s, however, trade was very bad, and shipping suffered. By the end of 1922 Ellerman was asking his staff, including Sanderson, to take large cuts in salary. Sanderson wrote, but appears not to have sent, a letter virtually offering his resignation if his own salary were cut by as much as was threatened (from £8,000 to £7,500). He offered to remain as a Director 'in the capacity of inactivity such as Kenneth is'.[67] Sanderson's own position, and that of EWL, became increasingly uncomfortable. He wrote about the problem, and his proposed solution, to his son Lloyd, Vice-President of EWL New York Incorporated, on 9 April 1925:

> For your private information, I have asked Sir John to make an alteration in my status here on the grounds that I want to be free

from the details of management of my Headquarters in Hull. I have suggested my being appointed Deputy-Chairman, no Managing Director to be appointed in my place, but the office to be managed as at present, I having, of course, always control of any important negotiations, as at present, and to make London my Headquarters. I shall be in close consultation with Sir John and come to Hull as often as is thought necessary ... Really for a man of my activities, the position is rather cramped here. I am writing this quite confidentially and am not saying a word about it to anyone. Nothing has been arranged yet, and Sir John is thinking it over. I can tell you all about it when you come over.[68]

Nothing appears to have come of this move. In the following year, Oswald Sanderson went into a Leeds nursing home for a gall bladder operation to be performed by Sir Berkeley Moynihan on Saturday 18 December. He wrote to Ellerman from there two days earlier to explain that, though the operation was fairly minor, it was necessary to prevent the onset of cancer. Unfortunately, complications set in and he died on Christmas Day, officially from cirrhosis of the liver. He was aged 63.[69]

For the previous 26 years, Oswald Sanderson had managed TWSC and its successor, EWL. He had been recruited by the principals of a major family firm, whose business acumen had propelled the company into the first rank of British shipping concerns in an age when large-scale enterprise had begun to dominate the industry. Though Sanderson's function on appointment was to ease the workload of the ageing Wilson brothers, he was increasingly responsible for maintaining the profitability and independence of TWSC in an ever more competitive environment. That the firm remained viable and family-owned down to 1916—even if its performance was 'steady-state' rather than dynamic[70]—attests to the managerial skills of Oswald Sanderson and the wise recruitment policy of his employers.

Once TWSC became part of a much bigger business empire, its fortunes began to falter. As Sanderson told his son in 1925:

Between ourselves, [Sir John's] Liverpool, Glasgow and London interests are shackling Wilson's development, and I am a little restive under it, because with the Russian Trade practically non-existent, we must get further afield. In endeavouring to do so, however, we invariably clash with Sir John's other interests.[71]

This situation prevailed down to the Second World War, when EWL suffered great losses to the enemy. Despite a good recovery during the 1950s, the firm then faded gradually and was left with just three ships in the early 1970s. It was latterly known as EWL—the Transport Division of Ellerman Lines. Operations in Hull ceased in 1981. But in the opinion of many people in that city, the end of the Line really occurred in 1916.

NOTES

I am grateful to my colleagues Professor Barbara English and Dr David J Starkey for their comments on earlier drafts of this chapter.

1. See Gordon H. Boyce, *Information, Mediation and Institutional Development: The Rise of Large-Scale Enterprise in British Shipping, 1870–1919* (Manchester, 1995).
2. British Parliamentary Papers, 1918, XIII. Report of the Departmental Committee on Shipping and Shipbuilding.
3. Boyce, *Information*, 3-4.
4. David J. Starkey, 'Ownership Structures in the British Shipping Industry: The Case of Hull, 1820–1916', *International Journal of Maritime History*, 8:2 (1996), 71–95.
5. For a history of the Wilson Line see James Taylor, *Ellerman's: A Wealth of Shipping* (London, 1976), ch. 7; Arthur G. Credland and Michael Thompson, *The Wilson Line of Hull, 1831–1981* (Beverley, 1994); *The Times Shipping Number*, 13 December 1912. For the Wilson family, see Gertrude M. Attwood, *The Wilsons of Tranby Croft* (Cherry Burton, 1988), and Rhoda Lamb, 'The Life and Times of Charles Henry Wilson, First Baron Nunburnholme' (Diploma in Social Studies dissertation, University of Hull, 1974). Much has been written about the baccarat scandal, including Sir Michael Havers, Edward Grayson and Peter Shankland, *The Royal Baccarat Scandal* (London, 1977), W. Teignmouth Shore, (ed.), *The Baccarat Case* (Edinburgh, 1932), and Attwood, *Wilsons*, 85-118. There is also a large file of general historical material in the Brynmor Jones Library, University of Hull, Wilson Line Archive (hereafter, DEW).
6. DEW/4/10. Note of letter from Harold A. Sanderson to Oswald Sanderson, 7 March 1896.
7. DEW/4/10. Harold to Oswald Sanderson, 5 December 1898.
8. Charles Wilson's letter has not survived, but a copy of Oswald Sanderson's reply, addressed to Charles and Arthur Wilson, and dated 7 February 1899, is to be found in DEW(2)/14/2.
9. DEW/4/10. Copy. Sanderson to Harold Sanderson, 7 February 1899.
10. DEW/4/10. Charles Wilson to Sanderson, 22 February 1899.
11. DEW/4/10. Copy. Sanderson to Charles Wilson, 7 January 1900.

12. DEW/4/10. Copy. Sanderson to Charles and Arthur Wilson, 26 July 1900.
13. DEW/4/10. Charles Wilson to Sanderson, 9 August 1900.
14. DEW/4/10. Copy. Sanderson to Charles Wilson, 31 August 1900. 'Tommie' (usually spelt 'Tommy') was the family name for Charles Henry Wellesley Wilson, son of Charles Henry Wilson; Kenneth and Clive were sons of Arthur Wilson.
15. DEW/4/10. Copy. Sanderson to Charles Wilson, 10 October 1900.
16. DEW(2)/14/4. Copy. Agreement appointing Sanderson Managing Director of TWSC, August 1905.
17. DEW/4/10. Arthur Wilson to Sanderson, 1 March 1904.
18. DEW(2)/14/14. Copy. Oswald Sanderson to Guy Wilson, 20 April 1915.
19. DEW(2)/3/50. Financial statements and reports, 1916.
20. This, at any rate, was the line adopted by Sanderson in negotiations to sell the Company. DEW/4/1, Sanderson to Kenneth Wilson, 29 August 1916.
21. DEW/4/10. Arthur Wilson to Sanderson, 4 December 1907.
22. DEW(2)/14/15. Copy. Runciman to Sanderson, 16 March 1916.
23. DEW(2)/14/15. Typed extract from Nunburnholme to Sanderson, 19 March 1916.
24. DEW(2)/14/15. Copy. Nunburnholme to Sanderson, 22 March 1916.
25. DEW(2)/14/15. Copy. Sanderson to Nunburnholme, 23 March 1916.
26. DEW(2)/14/15. Wilson to Sanderson, 24 March 1916.
27. DEW(2)/14/15. Wilson to Sanderson, 27 March 1916.
28. DEW(2)/14/15. Wilson to Sanderson, 19 July 1916.
29. For short biographies of both Ellerman, and his son and heir, also John Reeves Ellerman, see David J. Jeremy, (ed.), *The Dictionary of Business Biography* (London, 1984), II, 248–64; and Taylor, *Wealth of Shipping*.
30. DEW/4/1. E. Olivier to J.W. Bayley, 28 March 1947.
31. DEW/4/10. Record of interview between Sanderson and Ellerman in New York, 6 September 1899.
32. DEW(2)/14/15. Copy. Sanderson to Kenneth Wilson, 20 July 1916.
33. DEW(2)/14/14. Nunburnholme to Sanderson, 27 July 1916.
34. DEW/4/1. Nunburnholme to Kenneth Wilson, 31 July 1916.
35. DEW(2)/14/15. Kenneth Wilson to Sanderson, 2 August 1916.
36. DEW(2)/14/15. Nunburnholme to Kenneth Wilson, 4 August 1916.
37. DEW(2)/14/15. Kenneth Wilson to Sanderson, 4 August 1916.
38. DEW(2)/14/15. Wilson to Sanderson, 5 August 1916.
39. DEW(2)/14/14. Copy. Sanderson to Clive Wilson, 5 August 1916.
40. DEW(2)/14/15. Nunburnholme to Kenneth Wilson, 5 August 1916.
41. DEW(2)/14/14. Nunburnholme to Sanderson, 6 August 1916; DEW(2)/14/15. Nunburnholme to Kenneth Wilson.
42. DEW(2)/14/14. Copy. Sanderson to Nunburnholme, 7 August 1916.
43. DEW(2)/14/15. Nunburnholme to Sanderson, 8 August 1916,

44. DEW(2)/14/15. Kenneth Wilson to Nunburnholme, 8 August 1916.
45. DEW(2)/14/15. Copy. Sanderson to Nunburnholme, 16 August 1916.
46. DEW(2)/14/15. Copy. Sanderson to the Dowager Lady Nunburnholme, 17 August 1916.
47. DEW/4/1. Nunburnholme to Sanderson, 20 August 1916.
48. DEW/4/1. Kenneth Wilson to Sanderson, 26 August 1916.
49. DEW/4/1. Kenneth Wilson to Sanderson, 'Monday' undated (but probably 28 August 1916).
50. DEW(2)/14/15. Telegram Kenneth Wilson to Sanderson, 29 August 1916.
51. DEW/4/1. Copy. Sanderson to Kenneth Wilson, 29 August 1916.
52. DEW/4/1. Kenneth Wilson to Sanderson, 29 August 1916.
53. DEW/4/1. Kenneth Wilson to Sanderson, 1 September 1916.
54. DEW/4/1. Kenneth Wilson to Sanderson, 8 October 1916.
55. DEW(2)/2/2 Directors' Minute Book, 8 November 1916.
56 DEW(2)/2/2 Directors' Minute Book, 13 November 1916.
57. DEW/4/10. Copy extract. Sanderson to Oswald B. Sanderson, 7 December 1916.
58. DEW(2)/5/2. Copy. Sanderson to Ellerman, 29 December 1916.
59. DEW(2)/5/2. Ellerman to Sanderson, 22 November 1916, there were thousands more letters from Ellerman over the next 17 years, beginning 12 October 1916.
60. Interview with Sanderson in the *Eastern Morning News*, 14 October 1916.
61. DEW(2)/2/2. Minute Book.
62. DEW(2)/5/2. Ellerman to Sanderson, 26 March 1917.
63. DEW(2)/5/2. Copy. Sanderson to Ellerman, 28 March 1917.
64. DEW/4/1. Nunburnholme to Sanderson, 12 September 1916.
65. DEW/4/1. Copy. Sanderson to Guy Wilson, 23 May 1917.
66. DEW/4/1. Copy. Sanderson to Guy Wilson, 29 August 1917.
67. DEW/4/10. Sanderson to Ellerman, 9 November 1922.
68. DEW/4/10. Sanderson to E. Lloyd Sanderson, 9 April 1925.
69. Sanderson's funeral at Hessle on 30 December 1926 was conducted by the Archbishop of York and attended by representatives from many shipping lines, as well as the Dowager Lady Nunburnholme, Stanley Wilson, Guy Wilson, Kenneth Wilson and H.S. Holden (his successor at EWL). Apart from his wife, Beatrice, he left three sons and a daughter, and an estate of £124,577 net. Obituary and funeral report in *The Times*, 28 and 30 December 1926; copy of death certificate in DEW(2)/9/26(o); report of will in *The Times*, 5 March 1927. Nunburnholme had died in 1924, also in a Leeds nursing home after an operation. Ellerman had a mild stroke in early 1933 and a more serious one at Dieppe on 16 July 1933, from which he did not recover. His fortune was estimated at between £37 and £40 million.
70. Starkey, 'Ownership Structures'.
71. DEW/4/10. Sanderson to E. Lloyd Sanderson, 9 April 1925.

CHAPTER 4

An Inevitable Decline? Britain's Shipping and Shipbuilding Industries since 1930

Alan G. Jamieson

In 1930 the British merchant fleet was the largest in the world and the British shipbuilding industry, despite its serious problems, was still the world's most productive. In the late 1990s neither shipping nor shipbuilding can rate even one whole percentage point when their shares of world tonnage and output are calculated (see Tables 4.1 and 4.2). It is the purpose of this chapter to give an overview of the decline of the British shipping and shipbuilding industries between 1930 and the late 1990s, and to consider if that decline was inevitable.

For present purposes the years since 1930 may be divided into the following four periods:

1. 1930–45: A period of depression and war which, despite some revisionist views, must still be seen as having inflicted serious damage on Britain's maritime industries.
2. 1945–57: The twelve good years, when British shipping and shipbuilding enjoyed a prosperity unknown since before the First World War. However, this successful period was largely due to the collapse or withdrawal of rivals. In their new-found and short-lived prosperity, British shipowners and shipbuilders still looked back into the past rather than forward into the future, neglecting new trading opportunities and new ship types.
3. 1958–73: A period of growing crisis across the whole range of British maritime industries, including shipping, shipbuilding, fishing, and the ports. The steady stream of official inquiries into the problems of those industries reveals the increasing anxiety about the condition of the maritime pillars on which

the British economy—and British power—had rested for several centuries.

4.   Since 1973, and despite such new openings as the offshore oil and gas industry in the North Sea, the traditional British maritime industries have declined rapidly. However, as with de-industrialisation in general, Britain has gone first on a path down which other mature economies have followed. The decline of British shipping and shipbuilding has been matched by similar contractions in other maritime nations of Western Europe.

Table 4.1: Tonnage of UK Registered Merchant Fleet and Its Percentage of World Tonnage 1930–1993

Year	UK Fleet (million) gross tons)	As % of world tonnage
1930	20.3	29.9
1939	17.9	26.1
1948	18.0	22.4
1958	20.3	17.2
1968	21.9	11.3
1978	30.9	7.6
1988	8.3	2.0
1993	4.1	0.9

Source: *Lloyd's Register of Shipping.*

Such is the outline of the period under review. At its outset, in 1930, the British shipping and shipbuilding industries were still struggling to adjust to the new, less favourable business environment of the post-1918 era. While recognising the largely negative impact of the Great War on British maritime industries, many business leaders took the blow in their stride. They were used to the often violent swing from boom to bust in the sea transport sector and, encouraged by the short postwar boom of 1919–20, they hoped that the prewar prosperity of their business could be restored during the 1920s.

However, it was obvious even in the 1920s that fundamental changes had taken place which threatened the prosperity of Britain's maritime industries. World trade had barely been restored to its 1913 level, in volume terms, even by 1930, so there was a shortage of cargoes at a time when the growth of non-British merchant fleets meant there was more shipping available than ever before. Other problems were evident: the steady fall in British coal exports after

1918 was a hard blow to Britain's tramp shipping; British coastal shipping had begun a long-term decline; and, in the worst condition of all, the British shipbuilding industry was steadily worn down by world-wide over-capacity and a fall in orders.[1]

Such negative developments were greatly exacerbated when the world depression began to affect Britain in 1930. In response to the growing economic crisis, the British government was forced to carry through economic policy changes of a far-reaching nature, changes that marked a clear turning point in the long-term development of Britain's shipping and shipbuilding interests. Accordingly, by 1932 Britain had turned away from free trade and embraced the protectionism that was sweeping the globe. The cosmopolitan, free trade world economy that had helped to foster the success of Britain's shipowners and shipbuilders in the period 1870–1914 was to a large extent at an end.[2]

One facet of British shipping that had recovered to some extent in the 1920s was the liner sector. Although transatlantic services had been hit by the decline in the emigrant trade, liner services to other parts of the world had prospered. Then, in 1930, came the collapse of Lord Kylsant's Royal Mail group, which had been one of the 'Big Five' liner shipping groups in 1914. Public confidence in shipping as an investment was seriously shaken. While it was true that most shipping companies still relied chiefly on self-finance for capital investment, the larger firms had offered shares to the public. The Royal Mail collapse was to be long remembered and helped to discourage investment in shipping in the post-1945 period.[3]

Table 4.2: Output of UK Shipyards and Its Percentage of World Shipbuilding Output 1930–1993

Year	UK Output (million gross tons)	As % of world output
1930	1.5	51.2
1938	1.0	34.0
1948	1.2	51.1
1956	1.4	20.7
1966	1.1	7.7
1976	1.3	4.2
1986	0.2	1.3
1993	0.2	1.0

Source: *Lloyd's Register of Shipping.*

With the government turning away from free trade, the liner sector of shipping in disarray, and world trade falling to ever lower levels, the period 1930–35 was perhaps the most depressed that British shipowners and shipbuilders had ever known. The sectors already in difficulty before 1930—shipbuilding, tramp shipping, and coastal shipping—could only fall to new depths. As shipyards closed and lay-up berths became crowded with redundant ships, the government came under increasing pressure to give aid to the maritime industries. Finally, by the Shipping Assistance Act of 1935, the government helped shipbuilding through the scrap and build scheme and provided an operational subsidy under certain conditions for tramp shipping. The trade recovery of 1937 proved short-lived, and in 1939, partly due to strategic concerns, the government was ready to give more aid to shipbuilding and to provide financial support to liner shipping as well as tramps. However, passage of the Shipping Assistance Bill of 1939 was interrupted by the outbreak of the Second World War, a conflict which soon brought all the British maritime industries under government control.[4]

There have been attempts to refute the view that the British maritime industries were already showing serious signs of decline in the interwar period. These revisionist works have stressed that whatever their difficulties, such industries retained their position of pre-eminence in relation to Britain's rivals.[5] The two leading challengers in the 1920s, the USA and Japan, were both hit hard by the Great Depression and their shipping and shipbuilding industries began to falter in the 1930s. The great pre-1914 rival, Germany, recovered from the First World War, but her maritime challenge in the interwar period was weak in comparison with that made before the war.

On balance, however, one may question this revisionist point of view. Even if Britain was still stronger than her maritime rivals, that margin of superiority was being constantly eroded. In 1914 the UK merchant fleet had represented 41 per cent of world tonnage; by 1919 it was 34 per cent; and by 1939 it was only 27 per cent. Moreover, British shipowners were too intent on defending old areas of superiority and neglected new areas of growth. This is shown by the slow British response to the development of the motorship and the failure to develop a substantial number of independent tanker companies. In 1914 Britain had owned half the world's tankers; in 1939 she owned only a quarter. In both years the vast majority of British tankers were owned by oil companies.[6]

Perhaps the British response to motorships and tankers was due to the power of the coal lobby. As already noted, British tramp shipowners had previously been very dependent on the coal export trade. Indeed many shipowners had close links with the coal industry. Equipping with marine diesel engines and carrying oil might have seemed like treason. Whatever the motivation, British shipowners ignored what appear in retrospect as golden opportunities.

In 1926 the Anglo-Saxon Oil Company (now Shell) had offered 37 of its tankers for sale with ten-year charters back to the company. Some 26 were bought by Norwegians; only half a dozen went to British owners and one of those was later sold on to Norwegians. Thus were born the Norwegian independent tanker companies, while British owners, with exceptions such as Hunting, preferred to remain with dry cargo tramps.[7]

The weaknesses of the British shipping and shipbuilding were soon exposed by the Second World War. In some ways the conflict resembled its predecessor, with heavy losses in ships and crews, but in other ways it was different. One difference was that the government made greater efforts than in the Great War to control the profits made by shipowners, a circumstance the latter would later cite as causing a lack of resources for investment in new ships after the war.

The main difference between the two conflicts, however, was that in the Second World War Britain simply did not have the same maritime resources to deploy as in the Great War. In 1914–18, Britain had sufficient shipping not only to support her own war efforts without outside help, but also to give assistance to her allies as well. This was not the case in the Second World War. Between 1939 and 1941 Britain needed the aid of ships from other European maritime nations, first as neutrals, then as allies. For example, a quarter of the oil brought to Britain came in Norwegian tankers. Between 1942 and 1945 Britain became even more dependent on the maritime resources of the United States for shipping assistance. In 1939 the USA's share of world tonnage had been 14 per cent; by the end of the war it was 56 per cent. In the same period the British share of world tonnage fell from 27 to 18 per cent.[8]

Although Britain emerged victorious from the Second World War and her maritime industries had played a vital part in securing that victory, great damage had been inflicted upon those industries during the period 1930–45 as a whole. Then, after 1945, the British shipowners and shipbuilders were given what appeared to be a chance to reverse decline and revive their fortunes. Potentially the USA could control world shipping in 1945, but it soon became clear that she had no desire to do so, at least in the sphere of merchant shipping and shipbuilding. US shipping policy had always been protectionist, closely tailored to American needs, and with little interest in providing the 'common carrier' function that had brought British shipping such world-wide profits in the past. In any case the war-ravaged world did not have the dollars to hire American ships or to have vessels constructed in the USA. Without regret, the USA sold off part of her war-built merchant fleet and then laid up some 14 million tons of the rest as a reserve fleet to meet any future emergencies.[9]

With American withdrawal, Britain was given a unique opportunity since all her other maritime rivals were little immediate threat, with their fleets depleted and their shipyards wrecked. For twelve years British shipping and shipbuilding prospered. The creation of the inoperative US reserve fleet meant that by 1948 Britain had 27 per cent of world tonnage, the same share as in 1939. In 1949 British shipyards produced 43 per cent of world shipbuilding output, a proportion that had not been approached for years.[10]

However, as in the 1920s, the British seemed more intent on rebuilding the old maritime world than on seizing new opportunities. After 1951 foreign buyers began to desert British shipbuilders in search of cheaper and more modern ships from the reviving shipyards abroad. British shipowners remained conservative in their choice of ship designs, few tramp operators showing much interest at first in the new bulk carriers. Similarly, British shipowners were slow to meet the need for bigger oil tankers caused by the ever-increasing world demand for oil.

In the early 1950s oil companies had lucrative long-term charters available to anybody ready to build suitable tankers. While the British hesitated, men like Onassis and Niarchos seized the opportunity. British shipyards were perfectly capable of building the new bigger tankers—Vickers at Barrow built two 32,000 dwt tankers for Niarchos in 1951 and 1952—but British owners were slow to respond. When they did, from the mid-1950s onwards, with P&O's subsidiary, Trident Tankers, leading the way, they were just in time to be caught up in the worst shipping depression since the 1930s.[11]

Nor were British liner companies any more innovative. They continued with a large commitment to oceanic passenger trades;

indeed, in 1959 just over half of all the vessels engaged in those trades were British. However, it was becoming increasingly clear that air travel would mean the end of the passenger liner. In 1959 more people crossed the Atlantic by air than by sea for the first time. Between 1949 and 1956 the tonnage of the British merchant fleet grew by 7 per cent but world tonnage increased by 28 per cent in the same period, indicating that Britain's maritime rivals were beginning to re-assert themselves.[12]

Perhaps the mental rigidity displayed by many business leaders in British shipping and shipbuilding was a reflection of the lack of new blood in those industries. New shipbuilding companies were rare after 1914, while liner shipping was too expensive for most new entrants even by the time of the First World War. Later entrants were often the shipping arms of already powerful businesses, such as Blue Star Line formed by the Vesteys and the Palm Line set up by Unilever. However, the real entry level, the point where new blood entered the industry, was tramp shipping. A number of new tramp companies were set up in the boom of 1919–20, but after then only a handful were formed and they were often short-lived. Thus by the 1950s, most British shipping companies were mature firms, often closely linked with equally old-established shipbuilding companies.[13] However, even if shipowners had wished to innovate, rising costs put pressure on their traditional method of self-finance, while an appeal for outside funds, whether to banks or investors, might get a poor response since rates of return on shipping investments were low compared to investments in other British industries in the post-1945 period.[14]

By the late 1950s the good years for the British shipping and shipbuilding industries were drawing to a close. Foreign rivals, above all Japan and West Germany, were beginning to re-assert themselves. Their impact was most immediately obvious in shipbuilding. By 1958 British shipbuilding output was only 16 per cent of the world total, yet it had been over 40 per cent in 1950. In 1956 Japan replaced Britain as the leading shipbuilding nation.[15] British shipowners began to suffer as well, especially after a world shipping depression began in 1958. For the first time since the 1930s the British government was forced to consider giving financial aid to the shipping and shipbuilding industries.

The prospect of such renewed state support was but one symptom of the mounting problems facing the different components of Britain's maritime economy in the late 1950s. British merchant shipping was increasingly losing its share of world trade, not just to old rivals such as Japan, but also to the new flag of convenience fleets and to ex-colonies that insisted on establishing their own merchant fleets.[16] British shipbuilding was damaged by bad labour relations and competition from more modern shipyards abroad. The fishing industry was hampered by a lack of new investment and the efforts of countries such as Iceland to drive it out of distant fishing grounds by extending fishing limits. British ports, hit by bad labour relations and low investment, were increasingly seen as old-fashioned and inefficient.[17]

Such crises spawned a series of parliamentary and other inquiries during the 1960s. First came the Fleck Report of 1960 on the fishing industry, then the Rochdale Report of 1962 on major British ports, followed by the Devlin Report of 1965 on dock labour. The Geddes Report on the shipbuilding industry appeared in 1966, the Pearson Report on seamen in 1967, and finally the Rochdale Report on the shipping industry in 1970.[18] No other sector of the British economy came under such intense scrutiny in these years. At a time when the British economy in general was experiencing considerable growth, the maritime industries were making slow progress, stagnating, or going into definite decline.

Reluctantly British governments during the 1960s felt compelled to give some assistance to the maritime sector. Port authorities and fishing companies received support for capital investment but the two areas which were to absorb most government money for the next 20 years or so were the dock labour problem and above all the shipbuilding industry.[19] Merchant shipping received less support because from the mid-1960s trading conditions began to improve. Between 1968 and 1973 there was the so-called supertanker boom and this was largely responsible for boosting the British merchant fleet to its tonnage peak of 33 million gross tons in 1975. Even then, however, the British fleet was barely 10 per cent of total world tonnage.

But the maritime industries had to do more than try to hold on to their old positions with government assistance, since by 1973 they were facing three new, revolutionary changes. Firstly, there was a revolution in cargo handling caused by the spread of containerisation and roll on-roll off traffic during the 1960s, changes which allowed more cargo to be moved by fewer ships with much less dock labour. Secondly, there was an increasing concentration of British trade on continental Europe. This change was crowned by British entry into the Common Market in 1973, but the trend had been growing since the early 1960s. In 1961 a third of British trade had been with Western Europe, but by the mid-1970s the proportion had risen to a half. This change had profound implications for British oceanic shipping and for British ports. Thirdly, the rise of the offshore oil and gas industry in the North Sea seemed to offer a new and lucrative field for maritime enterprise, with a need for yards to build rigs, ports to serve as bases and terminals, and new fleets of vessels to support offshore operations.

With regard to the cargo-handling revolution, British shipping and ports largely adapted well, if rather slowly, partly due to labour problems. Heavy capital costs were involved and while the ports were assisted by government loans, British ocean shipping lines largely containerised by forming consortia such as OCL and ACT to share the cost of new ships and to rationalise services.[20]

As already noted, the shift of British trade patterns towards a concentration on Europe had begun in the 1960s, but after Britain's entry into the Common Market it became more pronounced. Britain's deep sea trade only grew by 6 per cent between 1966 and 1977, but total British overseas trade grew by 25 per cent in that period, most of the increase being on short sea routes to Europe.[21] This shift in trade patterns brought increased importance to ports on the south and east coasts of Britain. By 1984 three-quarters of UK sea borne trade was carried on short sea routes, mostly to Europe.

North Sea oil and gas failed to produce the boost for the British maritime industries that some had expected. The drilling rigs were overwhelmingly American, Norwegian or Dutch, and the same went for the supply vessels. Many of the production platforms were built in Britain, although only two of the main platform yards were British-owned, and the pipelines came from Japan. Relatively few supply vessels were built in Britain and hopes that trawlers made redundant by the collapse of the British deep sea fishing industry in the mid-1970s might find employment in other capacities in the North Sea were only partially fulfilled. North Sea oil and gas gave a massive boost to the British economy as a whole, but were of much less assistance to the British maritime industries themselves.[22]

The year 1973 was important not just for Britain's entry into the Common Market, but also for the large rise in oil prices which ended the supertanker boom. For the next two decades the world shipping and shipbuilding industries would be in varying states of depression largely as a result of the oil crisis. Excess tonnage and excess shipbuilding capacity meant hard times for all maritime nations, but Britain suffered particularly badly. After holding out during the 1970s, many British shipping companies could not cope with the continuation of depressed conditions during the 1980s. Some firms collapsed, such as Reardon Smith and Lyle Shipping; some firms gave up shipping altogether, such as British & Commonwealth and Ocean Transport & Trading; and others, such as Shell and BP, began to flag out their ships to reduce crew and other costs. The last government support for shipping ended in 1984 and by 1988 the UK fleet was down to 5.6 million tons, just over 1 per cent of world tonnage. Nationalisation was seen as the cure for the problems of the British shipyards in 1977, but was not. Privatisation of the remaining shipyards in the 1980s was all too often just a prelude to their final closure.[23]

In the 1990s Britain's maritime industries are mere shadows of their former selves. Britain still has world-class shipping companies, such as P&O, but oceanic services are now less important than short sea routes to Europe. Some British shipping companies, such as the Blue Star Line, do not own any British flag vessels, which makes it increasingly hard to define what 'British shipping' is.[24] It is now best seen as British participation in an international shipping industry in which fewer and fewer vessels can be easily tied to one nation whatever their nominal flag. In March 1995 Britain had just five merchant shipyards, of which only two were building vessels of over 30,000 gross tons.[25] Britain's port industry, although increasingly concentrated on a handful of major ports, seems to be largely efficient. The British fishing industry is now much reduced and circumscribed by European Union fishing policy. North Sea oil production is past its peak and the problem now is to get rid of the platforms, not to build or supply them.

In part the decline of British shipping and shipbuilding was just the working of economic forces, with comparative advantage shifting to other nations as they showed themselves more efficient in building and operating ships.[26] However, one cannot escape the view that much of the success of British shipping was linked to Empire, whether formal or informal.[27] Although the British shipping industry made great play of its commitment to free trade and stressed that much of its profits came from its role as a 'common carrier' in the cross trades, it is clear that particularly for liner shipping the imperial connection was vital.

A sort of informal protectionism operated and British merchants abroad would never use a foreign ship to carry their cargo if a British one was available. This British dominance of the long-haul routes binding the Empire—and the world—together was institutionalised in the conference system.[28] It was this that permitted British shipping companies to retain a powerful hold on, for example, Indian trade for several decades after India became independent, and this led to ex-colonies denouncing shipping conferences as neo-imperialism. By 1970 many such ex-colonies had merchant fleets of their own, had joined the conferences, and were squeezing the British companies out.

The story of the decline of once great industries must encourage feelings of regret. Clearly the maritime dimension of the British economy is no longer as important as it was in 1958, let alone 1914. In the past the British maritime industries provided vital services not just to Britain and her empire but also to the wider world. Since 1945 the end of Empire, the entry into Europe, and the rise of new maritime nations have made it inevitable that Britain's maritime industries would be reduced. It is certainly true that an obsession with the past by shipowners and shipbuilders caused new opportunities to be missed. However, it seems unlikely that the British shipping and shipbuilding industries could have preserved anything like their former dominance, although some may question the wisdom in allowing them to decline to quite such low levels as we see today.

NOTES

1. C.E. Fayle, *A Short History of the World's Shipping Industry* (London, 1933), 292–310; P.J. Cain and A.G. Hopkins, *British Imperialism: Crisis and Deconstruction, 1914–1990* (London, 1993), 31–48; D.H. Aldcroft, *Studies in British Transport History, 1870–1970* (Newton Abbot, 1974), 144–168; L. Jones, *Shipbuilding in Britain: Mainly Between the Two World Wars* (Cardiff, 1957).
2. Cain and Hopkins, *British Imperialism: Crisis and Deconstruction*, 76–93.
3. E. Green and M. Moss, *A Business of National Importance: The Royal Mail Shipping Group, 1902–37* (London, 1982). The other four big liner shipping groups in 1914 were P&O, Cunard, Ellerman, and Furness Withy.
4. M. Davies, *Belief in the Sea: State Encouragement of British Merchant Shipping and Shipbuilding* (London, 1992), 119–136. See also articles on shipping (by L. Isserlis) and shipbuilding (by H.M. Hallsworth) in British Association for the Advancement of Science, *Britain in Depression: A Record of British Industries since 1929* (London, 1935), 235–58.
5. For example, G.C. Kennedy, 'Great Britain's Maritime Strength and the British Merchant Marine, 1922–1935', *Mariner's Mirror*, 80 (1994), 66–76.

6. S.G. Sturmey, *British Shipping and World Competition* (London, 1962), 74–81 and 82–5; M.E. Fletcher, 'From Coal to Oil in British Shipping', *Journal of Transport History*, 3 (1975), 1–19; G. Henning and K. Trace, 'Britain and the Motor Ship: A Case of the Delayed Adoption of a New Technology?', *Journal of Economic History*, 35 (1975), 353–85; A.J. Robertson, 'Backward British Businessmen and the Motor Ship, 1918–39: The Critique Reviewed', *Journal of Transport History*, 9 (1988), 190–7; D. Griffiths, 'British Shipping and the Diesel Engine: The Early Years', *Mariner's Mirror*, 81 (1995), 313–31; M. Ratcliffe, *Liquid Gold Ships: A History of the Tanker, 1859–1984* (London, 1985), 62–72.

7. Sturmey, *British Shipping and World Competition*, 75–6; P. Hunting (ed.), *The Hunting History: Hunting plc since 1874* (London, 1991), 41–62.

8. For British shipping in the Second World War see C.B.A. Behrens, *Merchant Shipping and the Demands of War* (London, 1955) for passenger liners and dry cargo shipping; D.J. Payton-Smith, *Oil* (London, 1971) for tankers; and C.I. Savage, *Inland Transport* (London, 1957) for coastal shipping. For wartime shipbuilding see M.M. Postan, *British War Production* (London, 1952), 290–303; and C. Barnett, *The Audit of War* (London, 1986), 107–24. For Anglo-American shipping relations see J.J. Safford, 'Anglo-American Maritime Relations During the Two World Wars: A Comparative Analysis', *American Neptune*, 41 (1981), 262–79.

9. R. Hope, *A New History of British Shipping* (London, 1990), 394–5; A.W. Cafruny, *Ruling the Waves: The Political Economy of International Shipping* (Berkeley, USA, 1987), 74–88.

10. A. Slaven, 'Modern British Shipbuilding, 1800–1990', in L.A. Ritchie (ed.), *The Shipbuilding Industry: A Guide to Historical Records* (Manchester, 1992), 14–15. See also E.H. Lorenz, *Economic Decline in Britain: The Shipbuilding Industry, 1890–1970* (Oxford, 1991).

11. G. Harlaftis, *Greek Shipowners and Greece, 1945–75* (London, 1993), 41–5; and *A History of Greek-Owned Shipping* (London, 1996), 262, 264; Ratcliffe, *Liquid Gold Ships, 119–135*; N. Harris (ed.), *Portrait of a Shipbuilder: Barrow-Built Vessels from 1873* (St Michael's-on-Wyre, Lancs, 1989), 40–2; D. Howarth and S. Howarth, *The Story of P&O* (revised edition, London, 1994), 156–7; I. Denholm, 'The Decline of British Shipping: A Personal View', *Maritime Policy and Management*, 17 (1991), 1–2.

12. Report of Lord Rochdale's Committee of Inquiry into Shipping (Cmnd. 4337) (London, 1970), 84–96; Sturmey, *British Shipping and World Competition*, 163–5.

13. Denholm, 'Decline of British Shipping', 1–2. Cardiff was the greatest tramp shipping port, and of the 36 shipping companies covered in J.G. Jenkins and D. Jenkins, *Cardiff Shipowners* (Cardiff, 1986) only three were set up after 1920—two in the 1920s and one in the 1930s.

See also M. Kajimoto, *Cardiff Shipping Between the Wars* (Tezukayama University, Nara, Japan, 1996).

14. Rochdale Report on Shipping (1970), 333–5.

15. G.C. Allen, *British Industries and their Organisation* (5th edition, London, 1970), 133–4.

16. For flags of convenience see Cafruny, *Ruling the Waves*, 89–114; Sturmey, *British Shipping and World Competition*, 210–33; B.N. Metaxas, *Flags of Convenience* (Aldershot, 1985). For the rise of third world fleets, see A.G. Jamieson, 'Facing the Rising Tide: British Attitudes to Asian National Shipping Lines, 1959–1964', *International Journal of Maritime History*, 7:2 (1995), 135–48.

17. For ports see A.G. Jamieson, '"Not More Ports, But Better Ports": The Development of British Ports since 1945', *Northern Mariner*, 7:1 (1996), 29–34.

18. Report of the Committee of Inquiry into the Fishing Industry [Fleck Report] (Cmnd. 1266), British Parliamentary Papers (BPP) 1960 1, Vol. XV; Report of the Committee of Inquiry into the Major Ports of Great Britain [Rochdale Report] (Cmnd. 1824), BPP 1961–2, Vol. XX; Final Report of the Committee of Inquiry into Certain Matters Concerning the Port Transport Industry [Devlin Report] (Comnd. 2734), BPP 1964–5, Vol. XXI; Report of the Shipbuilding Inquiry Committee [Geddes Report] (Cmnd. 2937), BPP 1965–6, Vol. VII; Final Report of the Committee of Inquiry into Certain Matters Concerning the Shipping Industry [Pearson Report] (Cmnd. 3211), BPP 1966–7, Vol. XXXVI; Report of the Committee of Inquiry into Shipping [Rochdale Report] (Cmnd. 4337), BPP 1969–70, Vol. XXVII.

19. Davies, *Belief in the Sea*, 203 65. See also B.W. Hogwood, *Government and Shipbuilding: The Politics of Industrial Change* (Farnborough, 1979). For dock labour see P. Turnbull, C. Woolfson and J. Kelly, *Dock Strike: Conflict and Restructuring in Britain's Ports* (Aldershot, 1992).

20. Rochdale Report on Shipping (1970), 105–113; Turnbull, Woolfson and Kelly, *Dock Strike*, chapter 2; C. van den Burg, *Containerization and Other Unit Transport* (revised edition, London, 1975).

21. Annual Report of the National Ports Council 1979.

22. C. Harvie, *Fool's Gold: The Story of North Sea Oil* (London, 1994), 144–7. For a more favourable view of the involvement of British maritime industries with the North Sea see Central Office of Information, *Britain's Offshore Equipment and Services Industry* (London, 1982). For government efforts to secure North Sea work for British industry see M. Jenkin, *British Industry and the North Sea: State Intervention in a Developing Industrial Sector* (London, 1981).

23. Davies, *Belief in the Sea*, 267–350; Hope, *New History of British Shipping*, 444–69; Slaven, 'Modern British Shipbuilding', 17–22; R.M. Stopford and J.R. Barton, 'Economic Problems of Shipbuilding and the State', *Maritime Policy and Management*, 13 (1986), 27–44. See also D. Todd, *The World Shipbuilding Industry* (London, 1985).

24. D. Hornsby, *Ocean Ships* (Shepperton, 1994), 44. At the time of publication most Blue Star ships were registered in the Bahamas; others were registered at Gibraltar, Liberia, Panama, Singapore, and on the Norwegian international register.
25. Clarkson Research Studies Ltd., *World Shipyard Monitor*, 2:3 (1995).
26. R.O. Goss, 'The Decline of British Shipping: A Case for Action? A Comment ...', *Maritime Policy and Management*, 20 (1993), 93–4.
27. Rochdale Inquiry into Shipping (1970), 16.
28. Sturmey, *British Shipping and World Competition*, 322–58; Rochdale Inquiry into Shipping (1970), 116–36; B.M. Deakin, *Shipping Conferences* (Cambridge, 1973).

CHAPTER 5

Shipping and the British Economy since 1870: A Retrospective View

Sidney Pollard

Any review of the British economy over the past century or so has had to start with the overriding impression of decline. In *absolute* terms, indeed, the economy expanded at an unprecedented rate in that period, as it did in the rest of the Western world, and the population's standard of living has probably risen about fourfold since 1870. It is in *relative* terms, by comparison with the preceding economic growth rate of the mid-Victorian period, or, in other words, measured against what was presumably a potential growth rate, that the observer is haunted by a sense of failure and missed opportunity.

It is necessary to keep a sense of proportion about this. If we choose our starting point around the 1860s, when Britain produced half the world's steel, more than half of the world's ships, and a similar proportion of coal, it is clear that such a position could not be held for ever by a medium-sized country with limited natural resources: some inroads into that lead, a catching up by other countries, would appear to be inevitable. During the catching-up process, the growth rates abroad would necessarily be higher than the rate for Britain, and the question then becomes whether, or when, catching-up turned into overtaking and leaving the British economy behind.

As always in any long-term series of annual statistical data, it is not always easy to discern such a turning point, if any: where it is set depends on criteria chosen arbitrarily beforehand. Using benchmarks which are themselves arbitrary, and choosing as our standard real gross domestic product (GDP) per worker, we get annual growth rates of 1.32 per cent for the Victorian high noon of 1856–73; a drop to 0.9 per cent in 1873–82; a rise to 1.43 per cent in

1882–99; and a serious falling off to 0.31 per cent to 1913,[1] but with the proviso that the last few years of this phase saw a renewed acceleration. What are we to make of this, and where, in this series, did the downturn begin? It is not surprising that several different critical points, when the decline was thought to have set in, have been put forward by past observers. Thus Coppock opted for the 1870s, taking the view that Britain never fully recovered from the effects of the depression of that decade, which affected all of the advanced countries; Phelps Brown and Handfield Jones opted for the 1890s; while McCloskey saw no sign of real decline until the turn of the twentieth century.[2]

There is no doubt that in the last quarter of the nineteenth century Britain lost ground to some other countries. Thus, her share of world exports fell from around 20 per cent in 1870 to 14 per cent in 1913, and her share of manufacturing exports, perhaps a more significant indicator, declined from 38 per cent in 1881–5, to 27.5 per cent in 1911–13. But these were still remarkably high figures. In terms of productivity, only the USA, with her enormously greater resource base and more favourable population structure, had overtaken the UK. Even Germany, Europe's industrial giant, still had a long way to go to catch up with Britain. Thus, taking the American manufacturing output per head as equal to 100, the position for 1913 was as follows:[3]

UK	90
Belgium	73
Germany	64
Switzerland	64
France	46

Other countries were therefore a good deal further behind, and it has to be remembered that the British lead in terms of income per head was greater still. Other signs, such as the rapid expansion of higher and technical education, also point to the remarkable strength of the British economy right up to 1914.

One reason for the greater British lead in incomes than in manufacturing output is to be sought largely in the fact that British superiority over continental countries and the rest of the world in other sectors, such as agriculture and the service trades, was even more marked than in manufacturing. Prominent among the service trades was the shipping industry. In that sector Britain's position was truly astonishing. Her share of the world's tonnage in 1910 was no less than 33.37 per cent, almost exactly the same as in 1870, so that there had been no decline; but her share of the world's steam tonnage, the more modern and far more productive part of the world's fleet, was a good deal higher still, standing at 41.5 per cent. In terms of work done, ships under the British flag enjoyed an even greater superiority, carrying no less than 52 per cent of the world's traffic before the First World War.[4]

This dominant position is all the more remarkable since shipping services were wholly open to international competition, transport costs—which frequently provide a certain measure of national protection in other industries—being negligible in this case. Moreover, after the repeal of the Navigation Acts, British ships, unlike some others, enjoyed no preference or protection in home ports; and while there were some subsidies for certain types of British vessels for postal services and as potential carriers in wartime, these were for services rendered or to be rendered, and were generally below those paid by other countries for their own shipping. Additionally, safety regulations were more strict in Britain, and British wages were a good deal above those of her rivals, apart from those paid to American sailors. How was it done? Where are we to seek the causes of this competitive edge?

Some credit must go to associated activities. British owners were able to have close and often durable relations with British shipbuilders, at the time much the most efficient in the world, forming, incidentally, another reason for doubting the overall British decline before 1914. Credit was cheaper in the UK, insurance companies more efficient and reliable, and there may have been some advantage in having *Lloyd's Register*, which determined a ship's classification for insurance purposes, close at hand. Yet these are surely minor advantages. Many of them were equally accessible to competitors abroad.

Can we then find the answer within the shipping industry itself? It is not altogether easy to establish the nature of such an advantage. British ships may have been better, perhaps more up-to-date and more efficient: some of the most active competitors, such as Norway and Greece, worked largely with second-hand British tonnage. Yet British yards also built for foreigners. British officers were probably better trained or of higher quality altogether in some sense, though the oft-repeated assertion that Britain used cheap foreign labour was only partially correct. The maximum proportion of foreign manpower was 28 per cent, in 1903; it usually stood at around 15 per cent, with a similar proportion of lascars.[5] In any case, foreign shipowners might have gained the same advantages, had they so wished. If it existed, British superiority in this regard would therefore be difficult to define; but it is possible that the greater sense of responsibility, the greater care for property, the better understanding of machinery, and the firmer traditions of discipline, which distinguished British society in general at the time from those of less advanced economies, may have been material factors. In the last resort, the advanced nature of the whole economy would have favoured British shipowners. These factors may also help to account for the relative strength of some of the most powerful competitors, such as the United States, France or Germany, compared with less advanced countries.

In these respects, then, British shipping benefited from being part of a rich, mature economy. There were other advantages derived from that fact. Among them was the relatively low cost of capital and the efficiency of the financial sector in general. British ships may have got better insurance terms because they were better known. There was also the matter of better company organisation. While there were still many tramp and cargo ships in single ownership, much of the British tonnage was in the hands of large companies, enjoying the benefits of size in terms of purchasing, advertising and public esteem in the passenger trade, and the ability to carry losses more easily. Yet size alone was no guarantee of success, as the ill-fated International Mercantile Marine of 1902 clearly showed. A long-established lead also had other advantages, beside prestige in the eyes of the public: thus, British companies stood to benefit most from the cartelised shipping conferences of the time.

Beyond all these factors, which were flattering to Britons engaged in the shipping industry, was the geographical reality, the 'luck' of being an island kingdom in the right place. It clearly helped to determine the character of Britain as a maritime nation in the generation before the First World War, one based more than any other major economy on shipping and maritime trade, though it should be stressed that the need of the British economy for a large shipping tonnage did not necessarily imply that it had to be provided by British owners: others might have muscled in, had they been competitive enough.

Nevertheless, just as, in the Middle Ages, the centrality of Mediterranean trade had favoured the Italian city states, and the proximity to Africa and Atlantic coastline favoured Portugal and later Spain, the shift to the North Atlantic helped to ensure Dutch and later British maritime superiority. At the same time, the progress of these countries helped to raise the significance of the sea routes which favoured them, so that cause and effect did by no means work in only one direction. Britain was favoured by lying across what became the world's most important sea routes; she was favoured by possessing excellent natural harbours and a long coastline, so that an exceptionally large part of her population was inured to the sea, by fishing and local sea traffic as well as by long-distance trading out of British ports. There was also the specific advantage of large coal exports from Britain, providing a welcome cargo for outward bound ships which otherwise would have had to sail in ballast within the typical pattern of bulky imports and lightweight exports. Given these preconditions, but also given the skill and enterprise of British seafarers and an economy and society supporting them, Britain had captured much of the world's maritime trade, conquered and opened up much of the accessible overseas territory, and built up the world's most powerful navy to protect all this, before our era began. It was, in turn, this combination of geographical opportunity with a favourable social structure and personal skill and enterprise which then sent British ships to establish trading links with Asiatic ports, Pacific islands and Central and South American coasts within and outside the Empire where frequently no Europeans had ventured before.

How far trade and robbery, settlement and slavery in these overseas territories had helped the British economy to grow and take the lead in industrialisation in past centuries is a hotly debated issue. What is significant for our period is that, together with her early industrialisation and her geographical location, they thrust the British economy into a unique role within the advanced world by the late nineteenth century, a role as a maritime economy. Thus Britain carried much of the emigrant traffic out of Europe; she acted as entrepôt for colonial product imports into the whole of Europe; and even the form taken by her industrialisation, the real backbone of her economic growth, showed an exceptional emphasis on working up materials derived from overseas, such as cotton, tobacco, or palm oil for the use of European customers, rather than working on European materials. This was borne out remarkably clearly by the fact that while the industrial strength of other leading economies lay in mining, metals and engineering, Britain's most successful firms were to be found among the transformation manufactures. A recent listing of the world's largest industrial companies in 1912 may be divided as follows among Britain and the rest, distinguishing the mining/metallurgical sector, oil companies, and other manufacturing companies (see Table 5.1).

Table 5.1: The World's Largest Industrial Companies in 1912

	Manufacture	Oil	Mining/ Metallurgy	Total
Largest 20 companies				
UK	3	-	1	4
Rest of world	3	1	12	16
Largest 100 companies				
UK	7	2	5	*14
Rest of world	14	11	62	**87

Notes: * Two of these were mining overseas.
          ** The total comes to 101 because one (Anglo-Dutch) company appears in both lists.
Source: Based on data in C. Schmidt, 'The World's Largest Industrial Companies of 1912', *Business History*, 37 (1995), 85–96.

The difference between Britain and the rest is striking. Possibly greater still is the difference in attitude to agriculture between Britain and the continental countries. While the latter attempted to remain self-sufficient in food, Britain had early on seen herself as specialising in manufacturing, relying on her mercantile marine to bring in a large share of her basic foodstuff needs from abroad in exchange. Thus while in Britain in 1870 only 20.4 per cent of the male labour force still worked in agriculture, the proportion in Germany in 1900 (then at about the same level of income per head as Britain in 1870) was 35.7 per cent, in France (1910) it was 40.3 per cent, and even in Belgium (1890) it was still 32.1 per cent.[6] Cheap food, brought by the sea, also helps to explain the relatively high level of real incomes in Britain before 1914 as well as Britain's superiority over Germany in feeding her population during the 1914–18 war.[7]

Between the wars, Britain's share of world manufacturing output continued to decline, though slowly, and the same might be said about her merchant marine. Thus the share of the world's manufactured exports provided by the UK fell from 27.5 per cent in 1911–13 to 18.6 per cent in 1936–8, and her share of the world's shipping fell from 38 per cent to 27.9 per cent. But, considering the expected catching up by other countries, this did not seem unduly alarming. Certainly, while Britain did worse than most advanced countries in the 1920s, she suffered less in the slump and regained some ground in the 1930s.

It was in the years after the Second World War that signs of a serious relative decline, no longer to be explained by the catching up of others, and indicating a falling below the levels of other more advanced countries, began to multiply. As far as shipping was concerned, the proportion of tonnage under the British flag dropped from 20.2 per cent in 1950 to 9.6 per cent in 1975. By 1993, the UK was rated 26th among the world's leading shipping nations, with 4.1 million gross registered tons (grt); ten years earlier the figure had stood at 17.2 million grt, ranking sixth in the world. The 1993 value represented no more than 1 per cent of the world's total. This startling collapse was, of course, due in large measure to the shift to flags of convenience: Panama and Liberia, with 57.6 million and 53.9 million grt respectively in 1993, were among the leading nominal owners. Yet there was also a genuine, possibly catastrophic, decline in the competitive position of British shipping services in this period. Leaving aside the confusing registration of shipping, which resulted in only 19 per cent of British maritime trade being carried in vessels registered in Britain in 1993, net earnings on shipping account offer a reasonable indication of the true position. In recent years the overwhelmingly positive balance has turned into a scarcely credible negative balance (see Table 5.2).

Table 5.2: UK Balance of Shipping Earnings, 1935–1993 (£ million)

	1935–1938	1963	1983	1993
Debits	79.25	242	4,099	4,301
Credits	102.75	376	3,023	3,843
Net	+23.50	+134	-1,076	-458

Source: J. Foreman-Peck, 'Trade and the Balance of Payments', in N.F.R. Crafts and N. Woodward (eds). *The British Economy since 1945* (Oxford, 1991), 157; and *Annual Abstract of Statistics.*

This loss has to be seen against a background of a revolution in the economic role of shipping in the preceding half-century. Passenger traffic by sea had almost entirely disappeared, except for cruise liners and car and other ferries, while among cargo carriers, oil tankers of enormous size had come to dominate the tonnage underway on the high seas. Overall, however, the world's tonnage was still increasing rather than declining, and the question arises why the British were doing so relatively badly within these totals.

As in the case of pre-1914 success, we might begin by making the quality of officers and crews responsible. But just as in the earlier period, it would be difficult to back such a judgement with any evidence. It is possible, picking on individual events, such as the capsizing of the *Herald of Free Enterprise*, to accuse some British crews of laxness, but a number of other spectacular accidents, particularly involving supertankers, have shown a degree of incompetence and negligence among foreign masters and sailors which would certainly not be met with in Britain. There is, in fact, no evidence to show that it was failings among the personnel which were responsible for the relative British decline.

If, following our previous method, we turn to the locational factor as affecting the British Isles under the changed modern conditions, it is clear that some of the earlier advantages have been lost. The significance of the bulk carriage of colonial goods has declined, coal exports have all but ceased, and in the carriage of oil the British, having their own supply, create no particularly large home demand, though there is some inward and outward carriage of oil in order to mix qualities. As against that, the main weight of British trade has shifted from overseas to nearby European shores, reducing the length of the typical voyage and correspondingly the need for tonnage. Thus while 35 per cent of British trade was with Western Europe in 1890 and 26 per cent in 1938, by 1991 this had risen to 64 per cent, the relative share of long-distance trade having declined *pari passu*. For the ferry trade and for luxury cruises Britain still offers a large market, but these do not make up for the passenger trade of the past across the Atlantic and to the former colonies. But, as noted above, ships are not bound to touch their own shores only. As before 1914, much British shipping was engaged in trade between third countries, so the relative decline of Britain as a home market for shipping services does not by itself furnish an adequate reason for the decline of her mercantile fleet.

We are left with the third possibility: the relative decline of the British economy as a whole having its effect on the shipping industry in particular. Of that decline in relation to Europe, let alone the Far East, there can be no doubt. In terms of the world export of manufactures, the UK share fell from the typical prewar level of 22.4 per cent in 1937 to 9.1 per cent in 1971 and 8.3 per cent in 1988.[8] In terms of output per head, the British level has fallen from a postwar position, even after the immediate postwar rehabilitation, of well above Western Europe to having been overtaken to a serious extent (see Table 5.3). Moreover, even at its slower growth rate, British economic growth was subject to repeated and destructive crises and 'stops'.

Table 5.3: GDP Per Capita and Per Worker (UK = 100)

| | Per Capita | | Per Worker |
	1950	1987	1992
France	70.5	103.2	130.4
Germany	60.1	108.6	120.1
Sweden	93.5	112.5	-
Japan	26.8	106.3	102.8
Italy	55.7	98.3	125.3

Source: N.F.R. Crafts and N. Woodward, 'The British Economy since 1945: Introduction and Overview'. In N.F.R. Crafts and N. Woodward (eds), *The British Economy since 1945* (Oxford, 1991), 9: and *National Institute Economic Review* (1994, Part II), 56.

In spite of the oil bonanza and the great efforts made in recent years to create an 'enterprise economy', the latest data show that Britain continues to lag. Thus taking the equation 1987 = 100, GDP for 1994 compared as follows:[9]

France	115.6
Germany	133.5
Japan	123.4
UK	111.6

Innumerable explanations have been offered for that disappointing performance. Without attempting to be comprehensive, they may be classified under several headings. There was, first of all, the temporary postwar effect, when the British population, having been on the winning side in a country which, moreover, had suffered only relatively light destruction, expected a rapid rise in their standards of living, and exerted great pressure for higher incomes which, in the end, could be granted only at the expense of necessary investment. A low rate of investment was, in fact, one of the most obvious permanent causes of slow British growth. The population of continental countries (and Japan), by contrast, knew that in view of the destruction and losses suffered, rising incomes would have to wait, and that investments had to take a high priority. Another consequence of the victorious war was the continuing illusion of grandeur, the taking on of military responsibilities, colonial and other wars, and the protection of the sterling area and the pound sterling as a lead currency, which overtaxed the economic strength of the country.

Further cause for concern was the poor provision of technical and commercial education at all levels. Student numbers in institutions of higher education reading for technical and scientific subjects were lower than elsewhere, while apprenticeship, the traditional training for craftsmen, was in decline and the postwar school vocational training which was taking its place elsewhere lagged badly behind. Too much of the research and development that did take place was devoted to defence, leaving insufficient for industrial development. A long tradition of industrial leadership made British managers unwilling to learn from the experience of others, except the Americans, quite unlike the eager learners in Europe and the Far East. Britain was also said to have suffered from a lack of the 'industrial spirit', in the sense of devoting too many resources to non-productive sectors. Certainly, too many of the best brains went into the City rather than into provincial industry, and economic policy tended to favour finance rather than productive interests. Too many large firms were said to be run by their owner families rather than by professional management. Lastly, much blame has fallen on trade unions. Their old-fashioned organisation by craft, instead of by industry, led to restrictive practices and disputes. Altogether, their relative strength was said to have made them too strike-prone, and too hostile to innovation.

Not all of these explanations would find universal acceptance, nor is this a complete list of possible sources of weakness. Those selected here have been limited to causes which might affect the whole of the productive economy, omitting problems specific to individual sectors. Nor do we need to pursue the issue further here. Suffice it to say that just as, before 1914, the strength of Britain's economy contributed in a dozen ways to the success of her shipping industry, so now her relative decline is reflected also in the competitive weakness of that industry today. If and when the British economy as a whole finds itself on an upward path once more, shipping may again be expected to rise with it.

NOTES

1. R. Floud, 'Britain, 1860–1914: A Survey', in R. Floud and D. McCloskey (eds), *The Economic History of Britain since 1700, Volume. 2* (Cambridge, 1994), 15.
2. E.H. Phelps Brown and S.J. Handfield Jones, 'The Climacteric of the 1890s: A Study in the Expanding Economy', *Oxford Economic Papers*, 14 (1952), 266–307; D.J. Coppock, 'British Industrial Growth during the "Great Depression" (1873–96): A Pessimist's View', *Economic History Review*, 17 (1964), 389 96; D.N. McCloskey, 'Did Victorian Britain Fail?', *Economic History Review*, 23 (1970), 446–59.
3. S. Pollard, *Britain's Prime and Britain's Decline* (London, 1989), 13, 15.
4. There are some divergences in the published statistics, according to whether the (relatively small) tonnage of the rest of the Empire is included or not. See A.W. Kirkaldy, *British Shipping, its History, Organisation and Importance* (London, 1914), Appendix XVII.
5. C.E. Fayle, *A Short History of the World's Shipping Industry* (London, 1933), 289.
6. N.F.R. Crafts, *British Economic Growth during the Industrial Revolution* (Oxford, 1985), 59.
7. A. Offer, *The First World War: An Agrarian Interpretation* (Oxford, 1989).
8. S. Glynn and A. Booth, *Modern Britain: An Economic and Social History* (London, 1996), 226.
9. *National Institute Economic Review*.

CHAPTER 6

Naval Procurement and Shipbuilding Capacity, 1918-1939

Andrew Gordon

The cycle of war/peace/rearmament is classically one of boom/slump/boom for those engineering industries adaptable to military production; and the 20-year period between the two World Wars conforms to the model. The exceptional demand of wartime in 1914–18 had postponed (for the first time but not the last) the death from natural causes of creaking Victorian shipyards which, in the normal way of things, were in the process of being overtaken and made obsolete by foreign competition. They met the overriding needs of this war—as they would of the next—but they left a legacy of unprofitable surplus capacities which would blemish Britain's heavy-industrial landscape for most of the twentieth century, and which greatly exacerbated the shipbuilding depression of the interwar years.

The ups and downs of the famous names among naval building yards in the 1920s and 1930s are easy to trace. The records are mostly available and we know what ships they built and when. The graph of their profitability echoes (with a delay of a year or two) the temperature chart of international affairs and the ratification or ending of disarmament treaties. However, it should be emphasised that there are two kinds of building capacity which benefit from naval orders in wartime: the highly skilled 'cream', which produce thoroughbred warships, and the 'skimmed milk', which produce vessels constructed to simple mercantile standards to perform workhorse tasks for the duration of hostilities (escort sloops, minesweepers, A/S trawlers, boom-defence drifters, MFVs etc.)—ships which, in Jackie Fisher's typical hyperbole 'will last six months and can be driven by the man in the street'.[1] Generically, the 'skimmed-milk' naval businesses belong with the non-Admiralty commercial shipyards which in both World Wars were fully stretched replacing merchant tonnage lost to U-boats, though they tend to be at the smaller end of the slipway range.

A navy's prevalence in a war of endurance may depend on both kinds of capacity. But after peace has broken out, as in 1918, the 'skimmed-milk' yards have little or no further interface with the vagaries of naval demand, and those which have been nurtured or revived by recent war are left high and dry as absolutely surplus to normal commercial demand. Also, while they may or may not have benefited from the acquisition of capital assets at government expense, the efficiency of their working practices was not the factor which had brought them life-saving prosperity in the sellers' market of wartime. This last, of course, applies also to the 'cream'; but the point being made here is that in the grand war/peace cycle there are two areas of Admiralty–Industry interface: one which is continuous and obvious; and one which falls into abeyance in peacetime and whose legacies are scrambled up in the resumed drama of commercial boom/slump cycles.

Immediately after the war's end, British commercial shipbuilding seemed to be bouncing back, as international trade resumed and shipowners scrambled to replace war-worn stock. It was a false dawn and the ensuing slump was steep. While Britain's maritime effort had been focused so intently on the war and on the Western Approaches, her non-European trading partners had been building up their own national merchant fleets in their own new shipyards to fill the gaps caused by the temporary mass withdrawal and government control of British shipping. Some of the Red Ensign's traditional, staple, carrying markets would never be recovered. Thus while Britannia's increasingly obsolescent shipbuilding capacities had been artificially featherbedded—and even increased—by the war, her dominant share of the world's carrying trade had been prematurely and substantially diminished.

In these circumstances, the general health of British shipbuilding in the immediate postwar years rested, to a disproportionate degree, on the flow of substantial and regular orders from the Admiralty—which was unfortunate, for a configuration of three separate but associated reasons. Firstly, the country was bankrupt. The war had consumed colossal financial resources. Unlike Germany's fiscal managers, the Treasury had wisely exhausted taxation as a source of money supply, before resorting to loans, but the UK still emerged from the war with its national debt multiplied by a factor of 15. And from the over-taxed, heavily mortgaged British population, the government (of whatever political hue) had to find the money to support the welfare and social-reform expectations of the demobilised heroes and their families. Now, 'pensions, insurance, health, education, etc. [were] to be the most influential factor in the success and failure of governments',[2] not battleships—a far cry from the 'We Want Eight, and We Won't Wait' slogan in the prelude to war.

Secondly, the conscripted, muddied, bereaved and pocket-picked electorate was heartily sick of uniforms, deference and orders, and of being imposed upon by the officer classes. The Great War had been advertised as the 'War to End Wars' and 'public opinion swung for a time bitterly against the military establishments'.[3] It was now held that weapons were a cause of, rather than a defence against aggression, and 'all who doubted this new theory and tried to keep the sword still bright and the powder dry were dubbed "militarists"'.[4] Private arms manufacturers were vilified as profiteers who were probably plotting for a return to prewar military culture.

Thirdly, millions of people invested their hopes and ideals in the new League of Nations and in the experiment of collective security. After the slaughterhouse obscenity of trench warfare, nations MUST, surely, find a better way of settling their differences. 'The world was living in an era of dreams and would take ... [huge] doses of morphia'.[5] It was not foreseen that major powers might opt out of the new system or contribute little towards supporting it, and when Britain found herself thrust, largely by default, to the leadership of the League, it was immensely convenient for financial and diplomatic reasons to lead disarmament by example, as the men of vision demanded.

In the two years after the Great War the prospects were surprisingly bad for the 'Pax Britannica' status quo, and correspondingly good for naval construction yards. Japan and the United States—both wartime allies of Britain—were squaring up for irreconcilable differences in the Pacific. The American naval lobby affected to distrust the Anglo-Japanese Alliance (which had enabled the Royal Navy to concentrate its strength in home waters in 1914), and demanded its termination. It also called for the most powerful fleet in the world, for reasons which had more to do with prestige than with the USA's maritime defence commitments. If the Americans were building, so too must the Japanese; and it became clear that war-weary Britain must either stop the new naval race or win it, for otherwise she would find herself shoved from first to third among naval powers and her Empire a hostage to foreign seapower.

Winning the race was an unlikely proposition, given Britain's postwar financial straits, and, in truth, it is unlikely that any of the three competing powers would have had the will to see through their projected capital-ship programmes. Nevertheless, in 1921 the Admiralty obtained sanction for four 48,000-ton fast battleships (the 'G3' design) with 16 inch guns, and hinted at four more, with 18 inch armament.

Stopping the threatened race seemed a better idea; and when the Americans invited the main naval powers to meet in Washington in 1921, the British readily agreed. On the table had to be the alliance with Japan, and this placed Britain in an acutely difficult position. The specific circumstances which had made the alliance necessary—the German naval threat—had ceased to exist, but to imagine that that made it redundant was to assume that Britain could re-deploy permanently in the Far East the deterrent naval presence which the alliance had made dispensable. Unless it could be taken for granted that the currently idle naval yards of continental Europe would remain dormant for ever, logic pointed to a decisively powerful 'two-ocean' navy, which was the last thing the government wanted and would be a futile quest anyway with the threatened 'Pacific' building race. A fudged diplomatic solution, in the face of protests from Their Lordships, was inevitable.

The outcome of the Washington Conference—a palliative conjunction of leaps of faith and leaps of logic—is well enough known. As a means of averting the Pacific naval race in the short term, it was a success. As a lasting, post-alliance foundation for Britain's imperial security, it was a disaster. It was a disaster, too, for Britain's naval shipyards, with the vaunted capital-ship programme cancelled except for two stunted battleships of reduced tonnage (*Nelson* and *Rodney*) permitted as replacements for war-worn and obsolescent dreadnoughts. The cancellation of the other battleships 'was as severe a blow as the Clyde shipbuilders had experienced, coming as it did at a time when naval construction was at its lowest ebb and the heavy armament industry almost threatened with extinction.'[6] 'Barrow has been killed by the Washington agreement', the government was told when representatives of the town lobbied for investment.[7]

With the limited programmes of cruisers and lesser vessels allowed after Washington and, later, the 1930 Treaty of London, much capacity did become derelict and many thousands of skilled men were lost through redundancy, emigration, retirement or the finding of alternative work. The scope available to the Admiralty to provide life support in the circumstances of stringent economy of the 1920s was very limited. In 1924 a suggested addition to the Navy Estimate of £5 million to offset unemployment in shipbuilding was cut by the Treasury to £1.8 million and not repeated,[8] and in 1926 the Admiralty's guarantee of shipbuilding loans to major commercial firms had to be terminated.[9] The work of the Royal Dockyards was limited to refit and repair, and the construction of warships concentrated in private yards to maintain 'a war building potential'.[10] In 1929 Vickers-Armstrong's Barrow-in-Furness yard was awarded an effective monopoly of the private building of submarines in order 'to keep a unique industrial capacity in being'.[11]

Warship tonnage under construction in 1930 was a seventh of the 1913 level,[12] and the dearth of naval orders added to the pessimism engendered by the world-wide shipping depression. It did not 'require much research into the facts and figures to reach the conclusion that there is no prospect of the large additions to the country's shipbuilding facilities that were made under Government pressure during the war to meet the demand for both merchant vessels and warships ever being utilised'.[13]

Already, in the 1920s, 201 building berths had been broken by market forces.[14] Now, the nation's shipyards, hitherto in cut-throat competition, were belatedly compelled to take whatever measures they could 'to eliminate redundant productive capacity and secure economical costs by means of concentration'.[15] In 1929 they 'clubbed together to provide some financial compensation for yards which agreed to close'[16] by purchasing obsolete yards and selling the capital equipment for purposes other than shipbuilding. The scheme was known as National Shipbuilders Security (NSS) and 96 per cent of the industry joined it. Between 1930 and 1939 NSS bought up and liquidated 1¼ million tons of capacity, represented by a further 212 berths at 37 different yards. The damage to the active skilled labour force was far-reaching and irreparable. In 1930 unemployment on the Clyde and the Tyne reached 80 per cent.

The slump in naval orders was, of course, not the main cause of the shipbuilding depression, and hence of the need for NSS; but it was a major factor in the crippling rates of unemployment among skilled labourers in the major shipbuilding centres on the Clyde, the Tyne and the Mersey for the reason that, *per slipway*, warship construction demands very much larger amounts of skilled work than does normal mercantile construction. It was estimated, for example, that the labour bill for an 8,000-ton cruiser was equal to that of about 20 similar-sized cargo ships.[17] And some naval capacities became reluctant clients for NSS: Palmers of Jarrow, on Tyneside, being the most conspicuous example. This famous complex of shipyards, steelworks, engine-shops and dry docks boasted 'that they could produce an entire vessel from raw materials[18] —a claim which the recent battleship *Resolution* would appear to bear out. The steelworks had had to close in 1923, and, after delivering the cruiser *York* and four destroyers, the rest of the concern was bought out by NSS in 1932. It was eventually 'saved' by Vickers (predator or philanthropist, according to taste) in 1934 and committed to ship-repairing—which was considered to be a permissible interpretation of NSS rules. A similar episode had occurred over the even larger shipbuilding/armaments complex of Armstrong-Whitworth in 1927, although NSS was not involved as a 'middle man', and Armstrong's financial problems by no means stemmed mainly from its shipbuilding interests.

As indicated above, these events took place in a climate of pacifism and popular hostility towards arms manufacturers which no government could afford to ignore. While the Conservatives were free-market non-interventionists in principle, Labour had no mandate 'to soften the harsh realities of rationalisation by making comfortable gifts to bankers, creditors or shareholders'[19] and claimed to have nationalisation as their eventual aim. Both parties exacerbated the shipbuilders' predicament by placing obstructions in the way of export credit guarantees to foreign purchasers of armaments. However, by the time Vickers was rescuing the Palmers yard, the deep depression in naval orders was palpably lessening, and the general economy was beginning its long slow climb out of the doldrums. 1932 had been the worst year for most of the major indicators, and economists argue about whether the bottom of the slump occurred in August, September or October of that year.[20] The Japanese were expanding into mainland Asia, and within a few months Adolf Hitler had come to power in Germany.

The darkening clouds of the international climate meant that the second London Naval Conference in 1935 would be unlikely to obtain any meaningful projection of the 'Washington–London' building restrictions, although, as the leader of collective security, Britain would have to go through the motions of trying to keep the ball of disamament rolling. In the meantime the Admiralty obtained approval to make good some of the navy's deficiencies, within prevailing treaty limits. The first step was to abandon the small 6–

7,000-ton cruisers which other naval powers had not, as a rule, adopted, and succeed them with more substantial design.

The four small units of the 1933 programme (one Leander and three Arethusas) were exchanged on the drawing board for two Southamptons and an Arethusa. The total tonnage was the same as that of the original programme, but at a time when nine of Britain's fifteen 'naval' yards were still making a loss, the powerful 10,000-ton *Southampton* and *Newcastle* became symbols of a long-awaited, if tenuous, revival in Clydebank and Tyneside respectively;[21] indeed, *Newcastle* actually occasioned Vicker's reopening of Armstrong's dormant naval yard. They also represented, in their provision of armour plate, a reconciliation between the Royal Navy and sound, pre-Fisher cruiser design principles. Two other symbols of economic upturn were the commencement of the aircraft-carrier *Ark Royal* on Merseyside, and the government-subsidised liner *Queen Mary* in Clydebank. The ageing capital-ship inventory of the fleet, meanwhile, was still confined to refits and partial reconstructions, and only in a very few cases could such work be described as radical.

At the beginning of October 1935, Mussolini invaded Abyssinia. As a test of collective security, the crisis was not a success. Britain was expected to bear the brunt alone, and for several months hovered on the brink of war with Italy, on behalf of the League of Nations. A Treasury Emergency Expenditure Committee (TEEC) sanctioned a flood of procurement requests—mainly from the Admiralty—which in normal times would have been approved only after years of haggling. Most of the TEEC's business concerned stores, ammunition and equipment which could be purchased and deployed in the timescale of a few months at the most, but some of it went further. The 1933 and 1934 cruisers were accelerated. Overtime (almost a forgotten commodity) was authorised on the building of the 'G' class destroyer flotilla, and permission was given to start the 'Hs' as soon as they were launched.[22] Two old cruisers were taken in hand for conversion to anti-aircraft ships.[23] Four coastal motor boats were ordered by non-competitive contract,[24] and 20 trawlers were bought outright.[25]

It was the rise of the Nazi German threat, which very quickly followed on the heels of the Abyssinia crisis and only shortly preceded the expiry of the 'Washington' building constraints, which reconciled the National Government to rearmament and heralded a spasm of boom for the naval shipyards. Although Britain would continue to strive, with some short-term success, to mend fences with Italy, the 'Washington' assumption that the Royal Navy's 'main fleet' could always be spared from European waters in the event of trouble with Japan was no longer plausible. The naval response to the Rome–Berlin 'axis' was as much a matter of imperial security as of European power dynamics, and the issue which Washington had papered over—the logical need for a two-ocean navy—now confronted the Admiralty. The real breakthrough came with the third report of the Defence Requirements Committee (DRC) on 21 November 1935.[26] The committee's terms of reference had been aimed at 1939, but 'the situation of providing against a first class power in the West and East has never risen before',[27] and the Admiralty took the opportunity to plan for a new 'two-power' standard which, like the naval building plans of Germany (and soon Japan), could not be effected until 1942 because of the lengths of construction times. Post-treaty replacement, and rearmament, were becoming rolled into one massive programme of new construction.

The first instalment of the 'DRC Fleet' was presented to Parliament in a Supplementary Estimate in April 1936, after the main Estimates in March, in order not to be seen to prejudice the Second London Naval Conference and its thin hope of deferring renewed naval competition. It included the first two (*King George* V and *Prince of* Wales) of seven new battleships, an armoured aircraft-carrier (*Illustrious*), five cruisers, nine destroyers additional to previous projections, six sloops and four submarines. The British public, it should be mentioned, had not yet shaken off the hallucinogens of pacifism and disarmament—and would not do so entirely until after the Anschluss and the Munich crisis in 1938.

The 1936 programme did not go so far as to stretch the country's private naval shipyards. It is not irrefutably clear that any stage of rearmament did, for the issue of productive capacities—which of them are critical and which of them are not—at any given moment in a dynamic and snowballing rearmament programme, can be impenetrably complicated, and was certainly so in the late 1930s. Technologically complicated warships are really only *assembled* in shipyards: to have any meaning, capacity calculations would have to embrace the whole creative process, from the supply of raw materials and right through all the 'inland' naval industries of steel, gear-cutting, boiler-making, tubes, machinery, lubricants, armour, munitions, optics, cabling, switchgear, computing systems, and so on, before reaching the more obviously visible shipyards. At any stage in this complex critical-path matrix—in time of rearmament—'extraneous' delays can be imposed by capacity problems or priority clashes in the machine tool industries. Most of these technologies and capacities were shared with the wider commercial (even international) market. And at the end of it all, it should be remembered that the great majority of the sailors needed to run a warship take longer to be trained than the ship does to be built, and that there is no point in sending them to war unammunitioned, or if their resupply is not assured. In short, a huge range of stable 'supply' conditions would have to prevail (as they do on the normal peacetime procurement plateau) before one could clearly identify bottlenecks, or critical factors, in warship production.

Certainly the loss of skilled labourers in the late 1920s and early 1930s had been severe—terminally so (as it seemed at the time)—in the case of one or two shipyards. In October 1935 the inter-service supply committee responsible for overseeing shipbuilding capacities had warned, not for the first time, of a serious potential shortage of skilled labour within its province.[28] The position was actually worse than it appeared on paper, for some of the unemployed men registered as skilled had been out of work for so long that their skills had atrophied or they were too old and unfit for the rigorous work conditions in shipyards. And in 1937 it was estimated that the shipbuilding industry's labour reserves were now fully employed on the 1,125,426 gross tons of merchant ships and the 547,000 displacement tons of warships now building: which implied that 'the labour was sufficient to man the industry [only] to some 65 per cent of total capacity'.[29] Many slipways remained empty, therefore, even when naval and civilian production processes were both working at full stretch.

The Admiralty made an early and implausible attempt to get the Treasury to subsidise extensions to certain shipyards, but there is much evidence that the flow of new construction into the water, and thence the fleet, was never actually constrained by a shortfall in effective shipyard capacity: the bottlenecks in both the inland naval industries and the supply of machine tools were consistently greater.

These 'inland' naval bottlenecks occurred most acutely in the supply of gunmountings and armour-plate, and were themselves exacerbated by bottlenecks in the supply of the machine tools necessary to expand capacities for gunmountings and armour-plate. In all three fields (four, if one includes the supply of optical glass, which did not really delay the production of ships) these bottlenecks were overwhelmingly attributable to shortages of skilled labour. The machine-tool industry was hardly accessible to Admiralty influence, for the plant necessary to the production of one munition was often in demand for the manufacture of many others (even within the naval sphere, the lathes and the shaping and milling machines for producing marine engines were equally essential to gunmounting production). And with commercial domestic and export demand rising, Britain's few manufacturers of machine tools—whose total annual capacity had been valued at £8.5 million in 1936—were unable to meet the extra £12 million of orders demanded by rearmament over the next two and a half years.[30]

Even the first two (the 1936) battleships were delayed by gunmountings, athough this was partly because the Admiralty had changed the design of their 14-inch main-armament mountings at the eleventh hour. Only six months after ordering these vessels the Admiralty pressed the Treasury to be allowed to order the gunmountings for the next three (*Duke of York*, *Howe* and *Anson*) now, in advance of parliamentary approval, 'in order that [they] may be ready in time'.[31] A year later Their Lordships used the same argument to order the 16-inch mountings of *Lion* and *Temeraire* nine months before the ships themselves. These major constitutional and contracting irregularities were invariably accompanied by substantial awards of plant and machine tools, at government expense, to the manufacturers. The pattern was commonly repeated with the medium-calibre mountings for the same battleships and the carriers, cruisers and destroyers of the 'DRC Fleet'.

Meanwhile the Admiralty was warning the Treasury that if substantial awards of new plant were not made to the armour-plate producers, the third, fourth and fifth battleships were liable to be considerably delayed, and the same would go for *Illustrious* and her sister carriers, *Victorious*, *Formidable* and *Indomitable*. There was clearly an element of 'bottleneck fraud' in Their Lordships' petitionings: one might rationally suppose that if some alleged bottleneck is relieved, the supply of some finished product will increase. The country had no need of hulls, naval gunmountings, or armour-plate for their own sakes: it needed whole warships with no essential bits missing; but the Treasury was surprisingly disinclined to nail this particular jelly to the wall, and usually obliged, after more-or-less token shows of reluctance.[32]

Shipyard capacity may have been a 'barrier-in-waiting' which would have assumed the critical mantle had other barriers been less severe—indeed, with the systematic relief of other bottlenecks, it must have done so sooner or later. As it was, the shortage of Royal Dockyard space precluded the reconstruction of the 'R' class battleships,[33] and delimited plans for the anti-aircraft equipment of the fleet.[34] But we may say that, as rearmament happened, the critical factor in determining the scale of Britain's naval rearmament was neither slipway capacity nor the pool of skilled labour available to the shipyards (it was also not money, but that argument, perhaps, requires a slightly differently slanted article).

The Czechoslovakian crisis, in September–October 1938, introduced an unprecedented era into British defence preparations and the Admiralty's procurement practices: a hybrid era of measures characteristic of wartime, while peace still prevailed. As early as 1935 the Admiralty had prepared simple sketch designs for escorts and patrol vessels which could be constructed at short notice by 'skimmed-milk' capacities in emergency. The equipments of such ships were reduced to essentials, and the hulls so designed 'that the vessels can be built under the rules of Lloyd's Register or British Corporation, modified to suit Admiralty standards'.[35] In May 1938— four months before Munich—it had in addition been decided that up to 105 non-essential fittings and 35 trials could be omitted, further to reduce the time they would take to come into service. After Munich, the decision was taken to make a start on emergency (= wartime) construction immediately.

As already mentioned, the leading fleets of the 'post-treaty' world appeared to be gearing themselves towards a hypothetical showdown in 1942. And with the 'cream' of Britain's naval industries fully committed to the time-consuming production of the fleet units deemed necessary to meet the hypothesis of war with Japan in 1942 in defence of the Empire, the only means of increasing the output of naval hulls to meet a new, additional threat (that from Nazi Germany) was to resort to the 'skimmed-milk' capacities which had not been visited by the Royal Navy since 1918—capacities which were, anyway, appropriate to the sort of maritime war likely to be prosecuted by Germany (in contrast to that expected in the Far East). This may seem obvious, but it is worth remembering that, however essential they may have been to the defence of sea-lanes in wartime, the sorts of escorts, sloops, minesweepers, etc., which the smaller, semi-skilled, less labour-intensive civilian yards could produce had no legitimate role in the hardware establishment of the peacetime navy, and could probably not even have been manned from the pool of regular personnel.

Therefore, while the 'skimmed-milk' warships which the Admiralty took to ordering after Munich were hardly sufficiently numerous to have an identifiable impact on the British shipbuilding industry as a whole, they were remarkable, both for the reasons given above and because many of them were ordered without parliamentary consent.

The first off the drawing boards and onto the slipways were the Hunt class of escort-destroyers. The defined requirement was for 'a fast escort vessel capable of operating with fast transports and detached warships in addition to shipping convoys'.[36] In response to verbal instructions, the Constructor's department produced a design in which economy of weight was sacrificed to robustness and simplicity of construction. It was a staff specification that 'the hull should be capable of withstanding minor damage when handled by inexperienced personnel' and it was admitted that the ships were intended 'to meet requirements that arise only in war'.[37] Twenty Hunts were provided for in the 1939 programme, the first ten being ordered in November 1938,[38] a long way ahead of parliamentary approval. Early in 1939 the Admiralty began collaborating with Smiths Dock Ltd to convert an established whalecatcher design into a simple 'coastal escort', and 56 of what became Flower class corvettes—whose part in the Battle of the Atlantic was to be far from just coastal—were ordered before war began.

Added to the 32 thoroughbred anti-submarine sloops building from 1936 and the 36 old destroyers converting into convoy escorts from 1937, plus miscellaneous other vessels, these 76 utility warships brought the Royal Navy's total prewar 'escort' provision up to 150. This was a remarkable testament to the Admiralty's realism, given the likely war hypothesis by which the German U-boat force— which had, theoretically been non-existent in 1935— could gain access to the critical convoy focal-areas in the Western Approaches only from German bases via the long haul through the Scotland–Norway gap and round the north of the Shetlands.

NOTES

1. Attributed to Fisher in R. Baker *et al*, (eds), *Selected Papers on British Warship Design in World War II* (London, 1947), 120.
2. Gavin Kennedy, *The Economics of Defence* (London, 1975), 272.
3. Donald Cameron Watt, *Too Serious a Business: European Armed Forces and the Approach to the Second World War* (London, 1975), 31.
4. Lord Chatfield, *It Might Happen Again* (London, 1947), 7.
5. Chatfield, *It Might Happen Again*, 5.
6. Oscar Parkes, *British Battleships* (London, 1970), 657.
7. B. Swann and M. Turnbull, *Records of Interest to Social Scientists, 1919–1939, Employment and Unemployment* (London, 1978), 50.

8. Public Record Office (PRO), ADM 167/69. Admiralty Board Minutes 1792 and 1813, 18 January and 18 February 1924.

9. R. Higham, *Armed Forces In Peacetime: Britain, 1918–1940* (London, 1926), 194.

10. Chatfield, *It Might Happen Again*, 14.

11. J.D. Scott, *Vickers: A History* (London, 1963), 183.

12. *Fairplay*, 6 March 1930.

13. *Fairplay*, 6 March 1930.

14. *Shipbuilding and Shipping Record*, 3 March 1966.

15. *Fairplay*, 6 March 1930.

16. *Shipbuilding and Shipping Record*, 3 March 1966.

17. *Brassey's Naval Annual* (1934), 96.

18. H. Lyon in B. Ranft (ed.), *Technical Change and British Naval Policy, 1860–1939* (London, 1977), 24. See also Scott, *Vickers*, 218.

19. Swann and Turnbull, *Records of Interest*, 15.

20. H.W. Richardson, *Economic Recovery in Britain, 1932–39* (London, 1967), 21.

21. W. Ashworth, *Contracts and Finance* (London, 1953), 199.

22. PRO, T161/716/S40250/1, 1st and 2nd Treasury Emergency Expenditure Committee (TEEC), 16 and 17 September 1935; T161/716/S40250/3, 18th TEEC, 18 October 1935.

23. PRO, T161/716/S40250/1 and 2, 4th and 12th TEEC, 20 September and 4 October 1935.

24. PRO, T161/716/S40250/3, 19th TEEC, 21 October 1935.

25. PRO, T161/716/S40250/2 and 3, 15th and 16th TEEC, 11 and 14 October 1935.

26. PRO, CAB 16/112, Defence Requirements Committee (DRC) paper 37, 21 November 1935.

27. PRO, CAB 21/534, Meeting of Committee on 'Financial Aspects ...', 12 November 1937, 'Defence Expenditure 1937–39'.

28. PRO, CAB 60/4, 60th PSOC, 24 October 1935.

29. PRO, CAB 102/533, 'Execution of Naval New Construction Programme 1936–39'.

30. PRO, CAB 21/673, Meeting between PSOC leaders and the Machine Tool Trades Association, 28 October 1936.

31. PRO, CAB 16/123, Discussion on DRC 3rd Report, 21 November 1935.

32. For a full discussion of these issues see G.A.H. Gordon, *British Seapower and Procurement Between the Wars* (London, 1988), chapter 19.

33. PRO, ADM 167/100, Board Minute 3604, 15 December 1938.

34. PRO, ADM 167/99, Board Minute 3468, 5 May 1937.

35. PRO, ADM 1/9417, 'Escort Vessels etc. Special Designs for Rapid Construction', 1937.

36. PRO, ADM 1/9940, 'Escort Vessels of 1939 Programme, Sketch Design and Legend'.

37.   PRO, ADM 1/9940, 'Escort Vessels of 1939 Programme, Sketch Design and Legend'.
38.   PRO, T161/909/S36130/39, 'New Construction Programme, 1939'.

CHAPTER 7

British Naval Procurement and Shipbuilding, 1945–1964[1]

Anthony Gorst and Lewis Johnman

The decline of British naval power in the twentieth century has been the subject of considerable analysis. From differing perspectives and with differing emphases, Kennedy, Gordon and Grove have analysed the process of decline whereby Britain lost unrivalled command of the seas and became a second-class naval power.[2] The common theme in these works is the central role of the policy process and the attendant issues of strategic concerns and the influence of economic conditions. The period has also been analysed from the perspective of the Department of Naval Construction within the Admiralty by D.K. Brown.[3] This chapter seeks to build on these works and alter the perspective by examining the interaction between the naval procurement process and the British shipbuilding industry in the period 1945–64. In this period it became something of an article of faith between the Admiralty and the shipbuilders that neither naval power nor the shipbuilding industry should ever again face the traumas of the interwar years when a combination of disarmament, naval limitations treaties and the collapse of international trade had resulted in the near emasculation of the British shipbuilding industry with a range of related problems which were to surface in the rearmament period and the Second World War.[4]

The central theme of this paper is the attempt by all governments of the period, both Labour and Conservative, to use the mechanism of Admiralty orders to regulate conditions in the shipbuilding industry. In November 1945 the Cabinet, discussing the Revised New Construction Programme for 1945, outlined considerations that were to condition policy for the next twenty years: 'It was most important from the point of view of the

Government's employment policy that full weight should be given to the possibility of varying warship building in order to even out the slumps and booms of merchant building'.[5] The acknowledged aim throughout this period was to use naval shipbuilding in a *contra-cyclical* fashion to even out the building cycle within the shipyards: the boom/slump cycle, particularly of the interwar period, was recognised as having contributed to serious capacity and skill shortages, as well as heavy localised unemployment (Jarrow being the most famous example), in both the rearmament period and in the war itself. The two major reports on the industry's problems in the war highlighted what was termed 'the fossilisation of inefficiency', although given the industry's appalling profit record in the interwar period this was perhaps not surprising as little capital had been available for investment and modernisation.[6] The other factor that postwar governments wished to avoid was the industry's traditional response to downturns in the building cycle: the enforced reduction of capacity, managed by the industry itself, which was typified by the activities of National Shipbuilders Security (NSS) in the 1930s. By 1939 NSS had put over 180 berths, with an annual capacity of 1,350,000 gross tons, out of commission.[7]

There were, however, a number of flaws in the government's strategy for the postwar shipbuilding industry. In terms of international trade and its impact on shipbuilding, the post-Second World War period did not resemble the post-First World War period and therefore a strategy of contra-cyclical building proved extremely difficult to implement, as for the first postwar decade full order books for mercantile construction dominated the industry. This was compounded by uncertainties surrounding the Admiralty's construction requirements in terms of both numbers and types of vessels as it sought to develop a distinctive role in an unpredictable international environment, tried to come to terms with rapid technological change, and had to operate within a budgetary environment characterised by economic stringency. Further, the pattern of Admiralty requirements was difficult to fit into the glutted programme of mercantile building.

In March 1945 the Director of Plans presented to the Admiralty Board a report from the Future Building Committee for the 1945 New Construction Programme. This paper, which looked forward to the reconstruction of the postwar fleet after the exigencies of war, recognised the necessity of synchronising warship and mercantile building in the aftermath of hostilities. From the Admiralty's point of view:

7.1 An unidentified Second World War submarine refitting at Scotts of Greenock, date unknown (courtesy of the Keeper of the Records of Scotland)

When the replacement programmes for the Merchant Navy and the Royal Navy have been completed the demand in the shipyards is likely to require a reduction in capacity of the order of 40% which will call for a decline in the labour force to about a 100,000.

The Shipyards will thus be compelled either to turn over to other work or to discharge the men to other employment. In either case if mass unemployment is to be avoided the changeover must be effected gradually. To do this it is clearly necessary to have long-term ship construction programmes, with sufficient flexibility to allow for warship building to be most active in periods when merchant shipbuilding is low, and vice versa, assuming that considerations of defence, etc., permit this course.

After highlighting the difficulties of forecasting the timing of the reconstruction of the mercantile marine the Director of Plans concluded that:

The only satisfactory means of overcoming these difficulties is to have a longer-term naval programme than has previously been the custom sufficiently flexible to absorb specialised labour as it becomes surplus to merchant ship construction owing to fluctuations in demand; this conservation of labour would, in turn, permit of the acceleration of either naval or merchant programmes as necessary.[8]

Much of the premise upon which this paper was based was conditioned by the memory of the post-First World War experience of brief boom and long-term slump. In fact, the strength of international economic recovery from 1945 was probably beyond reasonable forecasting and the reconstruction of the mercantile marine was to last, sustained by the Korean War commodities boom, until the late 1950s.

Given the full and lengthening order books of British yards in the 1940s and 1950s, it was thus difficult to synchronise warship building with mercantile building. As the figures demonstrate, whether in absolute terms as in Figure 7.2, or log scaled as in Figure 7.3, the volume of naval building was not significant enough to make much impact in overall terms. Furthermore, the trend of warship building tended to follow that of the mercantile sector, rising when it rose and falling when it fell. Moreover, the Admiralty was unable to evolve the desired longer-term naval programme until the mid-1950s when a sustained frigate building programme

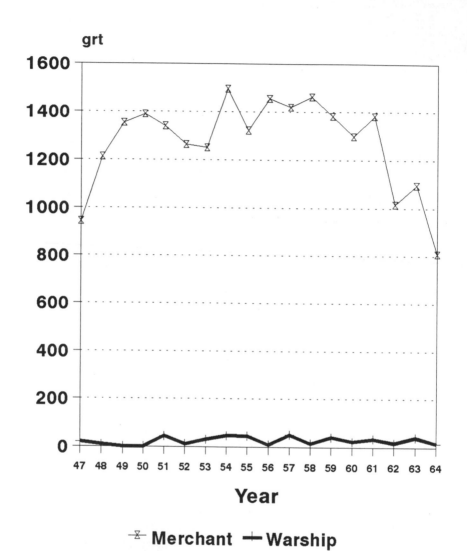

7.2 Merchant and Warship Construction in Great Britain, 1947–1964 (derived from *Lloyd's Register*, various dates, and Conways)

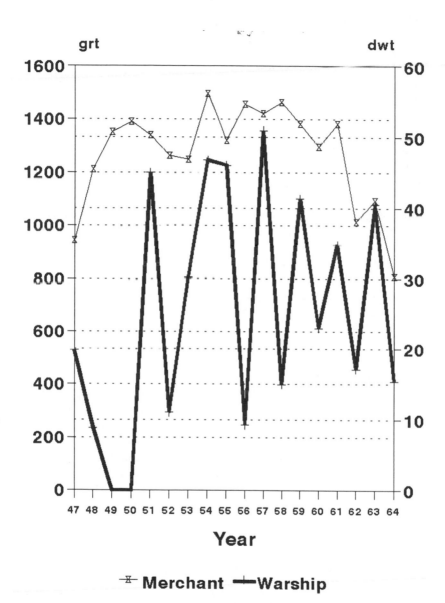

7.3 Merchant and Warship Construction in Great Britain, 1947–1964 (derived from *Lloyd's Register*, various dates, and Conways)

came into being: successive construction programmes in the 1950s were characterised by delay and uncertainty due to the inability of the defence policy-makers to arrive at a settled strategy that could be carried out within the confines of a finite defence budget.

Naval policy and strategy were traditionally the prerogative of the Board of Admiralty. However, with the postwar restructuring of the defence policy-making machinery, naval strategy and policy became the product of a number of influences: the creation of a Ministry of Defence, with a senior Cabinet minister at its head, together with the establishment of a standing Defence Committee, exposed the Admiralty to a wider range of debates. This was symbolised by the fact that from 1946 onwards the annual naval construction programme was submitted to the Defence Committee rather than to the full Cabinet (with the nostalgic exception of the Churchill government when there was a temporary return to prewar practice). Therefore naval policy and strategy evolved out of discussions on a wider defence policy conducted in a broader sphere and in a more sustained fashion than the Admiralty had been hitherto used. The Royal Navy and the Admiralty had to fight their corner in both strategic and economic terms against the competing demands of the Royal Air Force and the Army. Moreover, these debates took place not only in the Chiefs of Staff Committee but also in the new Defence Committee where the Admiralty had to justify both its role and its expenditure in front of an often unsympathetic ministerial audience, including the Chancellor of the Exchequer. The attitude of A.V. Alexander, the first Minister of Defence, who had previously been First Lord of the Admiralty, was untypical and should be contrasted with that of Duncan Sandys with his distinctly anti-naval (particularly carrier) tendencies. Within the Admiralty, strategy was the province of the Naval Staff, under the First Sea Lord, while procurement was the province of the materiel departments under the Third Sea Lord and Controller of the Navy. Close contact was maintained between these separate entities through normal bureaucratic channels and regular meetings of the Admiralty Board.

The procurement process was part of a complex equation that included overall defence expenditure and the share of this allocated to the navy, overall defence policy and the role of the navy, judgements by the Board of Admiralty as to the numbers and types of ship required and the timing of orders. It is little wonder that the annual naval construction programmes became the source of much anguish both within the Admiralty and within the wider defence policy-making sphere. As the Board noted in January 1955:

> The succession of Ministerial reviews of the rearmament programme ... has resulted in the plans for Naval New Construction in particular never having been stable for long enough to permit the preparation of detailed submissions. They have been progressively whittled down in step with our financial prospects ... the 1953–4 and 1954–5 programmes are the remnants of previous larger hopes, particularly so for frigates, and as they now stand cannot be regarded in themselves as the product of any conscious planning and indeed appear to be open to criticism in this regard.[9]

The major problem that the Royal Navy faced, in common with the other services, was arriving at a settled role within a firm strategy in an era of profound strategic and political change. The advent of the atomic bomb in 1945, followed by the hydrogen bomb in 1953, coupled with the attendant Cold War, transformed the traditional preoccupations of the navy. Was the Royal Navy to concentrate on preparing for 'Hot War' or for waging the 'Cold War'? Was it to concentrate on preparations for nuclear war, including 'broken-backed' warfare; to concentrate on 'limited' war on the Korean War model; or concentrate on waging the Cold War through an extension of previous imperial practice of 'showing the flag'?[10]

Each of these scenarios demanded a distinct strategy from the increasingly harassed planners and, moreover, emphasised different elements of the fleet with concomitant implications for the new construction programme. Conventional war demanded the maintenance of a nucleus active fleet plus a large reserve fleet, heavily weighted towards specialised anti-submarine frigates and minesweeping and minehunting forces. Nuclear war demanded a contribution to the maintenance of deterrent forces in being as well as the provision of convoy escort forces for the period of 'broken-backed' warfare. Limited war involved a concentration on high-quality forces in being including aircraft-carrier groups. Waging the Cold War meant an active fleet of imposing vessels including carrier groups, cruisers and general-purpose destroyers and frigates.[11]

For much of the postwar period the Admiralty had grave difficulty in arriving at a settled role for the navy within an agreed strategy. This was to have profound consequences for the hoped for 'longer-term' naval building programme. From 1945 to 1950 the Royal Navy was working on the basis of being ready for a large-

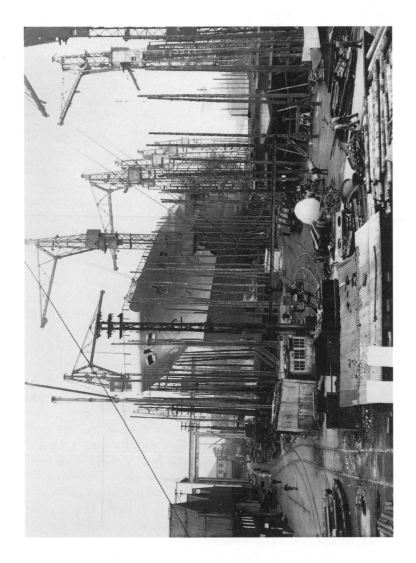

7.4 HMS *Ocean* just prior to launching, August 1945 at Stephen's Yard (courtesy of the Keeper of the Records of Scotland)

scale war with the Soviet Union from 1957. Although there was little in the way of genuine new construction in this period, it is clear from papers prepared by the Naval Staff that they were looking towards the eventual establishment of a balanced fleet containing battleships, carriers, cruisers and escorts of nearly 500 ships divided into active and reserve fleets sustained by a new construction programme that would provide modern high-quality replacements as the survivors of the Second World War navy wore out.[12] The developing 'war scare' that began with the events of 1948 came to the fore with the outbreak of the Korean War in the summer of 1950 and led to a reassessment of both the timescale and circumstances of a future war and of the role of the navy within this war. The result was that the new construction and modernisation programmes of 1951–2 focused on the provision of 23 escorts of various types and 80 minesweepers, to the exclusion of almost everything else beyond the modernisation of the aircraft-carriers and the conversion of wartime destroyers to anti-submarine frigates.[13]

The advent of the hydrogen bomb and the spiraling cost of the rearmament programme, however, soon forced the 'Radical Review' of 1954 which reorientated the navy towards the waging of the Cold War. The 'Radical Reviews' carried out by the Conservative governments built on the logic of the 'Global Strategy' papers of 1950 and 1952, which had argued that in the atomic age there was little point in preparing for a long-drawn-out war and that British defence policy should therefore focus on three prioritised tasks: waging the Cold War; the maintenance of forces to deter war; and the maintenance of forces needed in a short 'Hot War'. The explosion of the American hydrogen bomb, reinforced by a realisation of the strain imposed on the British economy by the rearmament programme (in terms of cost, the balance of payments and the friction between civilian and military metal-using industries), forced the Churchill government to the conclusion that it should concentrate on waging the Cold War and maintaining the deterrent while making minimal preparations for 'Hot War'.[14]

This represented a threat to the very existence of the Royal Navy in its traditional role of protecting Britain's vulnerable sea communications, reflected in the curtailing of the frigate and minesweeper programmes. The Admiralty, however, was remarkably successful in maintaining its position by arguing that a carrier-based navy, with its combination of mobility, flexibility and striking power, was the ideal weapon for waging both the Cold War and limited wars, and that, fortuitously, such a navy could also be a

127

useful insurance in the event of *either* nuclear stalemate following the outbreak of conventional war *or* 'broken-backed warfare' continuing after the initial and devastating thermonuclear exchanges.[15] So successful was the navy in lobbying for the continuation of a carrier-based navy that even Duncan Sandys's 1957 White Paper acknowledged its utility in limited wars, police actions and the Cold War.[16] In effect the navy was now committed to the maintenance of an active fleet centred upon carrier groups, supported by guided missile escorts (both cruisers and destroyers), frigates and submarines. A paper of 1956 projected the fleet to 1966 and envisaged the construction of three guided weapon carriers, three guided weapon cruisers and sixteen guided weapon destroyers as well as miscellaneous fleet escorts at an annual new construction cost (excluding aircraft) of £41 million in 1959/60, rising to £45 million in 1964/5.[17]

The cost of these strategic re-adjustments was the almost total reduction of the ageing reserve fleet. From being a pool which the navy could mobilise in time of war, the reserve fleet was slimmed down through a process of sales and scrappings to the point where it functioned merely to provide cover for the refit and repair cycle of the active fleet in peacetime. Casualties of the 1950s included the surviving *King George V* battleships, the war-built armoured deck carriers and many of the unmodernised cruisers including the 5.25-inch anti-aircraft cruisers.[18]

It was not until the role of the navy was settled that the Admiralty could embark with any degree of confidence upon a construction programme that would support the active fleet. However, a glance at the type of vessels completed reveals that the brave hopes of the Admiralty for a balanced carrier-group based navy were to evaporate in the face of the harsh resource constraints imposed by the Conservative governments (see Figure 7.5).[19]

As the Admiralty themselves recognised, the most vulnerable elements of the Naval Estimates were Votes 8 and 9—the production estimates—and within this the most vulnerable element to any cost-cutting Chancellor was the New Construction Programme. The 'capital' ship replacement programme was to disappear as guided weapon carriers, guided weapon cruisers and ultimately aircraft-carriers themselves were axed on financial grounds.[20] Even the County class guided missile destroyer programme was halved to eight ships from the envisaged sixteen, and what was left was a reduced construction programme which focused on the provision of anti-submarine frigates (the Rothesay class, a repeat of the previous

Date

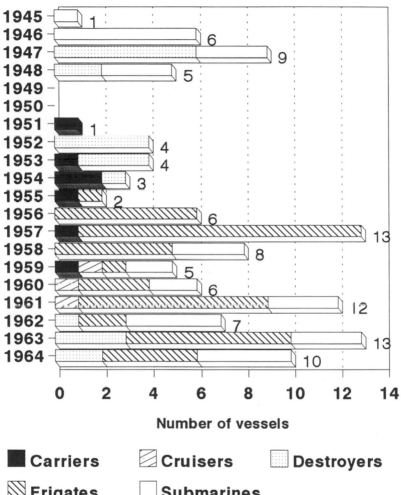

7.5 Warships by Completion, 1945–1964 (derived from Conways)

Whitby class) and the revival of the general purpose frigate—the Tribal and Leander classes—to prosecute the Cold War and limited wars.

For the shipbuilding industry of the late 1950s, which was beginning to be concerned about long-term prospects (as its share of the world market plummeted and its order books thinned), this was alarming. If the only major Admiralty programme was frigates— and then only an average of four per year, employing on Admiralty estimates 250 men for three years each—this was not going to mop up much in the way of surplus capacity, particularly as the modernisation, conversion and repair programme of war-built ships was coming to an end. What was needed was the construction of 'capital' ships, namely aircraft-carriers—and it was precisely these which were the casualties of the resource constraints of the postwar period.[21]

Although the bulk of the postwar carrier fleet—the 45,000-ton fleet carriers *Eagle, Ark Royal, Victorious,* and the 22,000-ton intermediate carriers *Albion, Bulwark, Centaur* and *Hermes*—was completed after the war and entered service in the period 1951–9, replacing the stopgap light fleet carriers, these new ships were essentially war-built. This posed a major problem: even with modernisations, costing an estimated £14.5 million for *Eagle* in 1958, they would need replacement. Two specific drawbacks with the carrier fleet can be identified. Firstly, the hulls were ageing with most running out in the late 1960s. Secondly, they were too small to operate a significant air group of the generation of aircraft beyond the *Sea Vixen* and *Buccaneer*. The cost in both money and manpower meant that the navy's ambitions to retain the class of ship that made it something more than a continental navy was ultimately doomed. Estimates for the provision of four replacement carriers and their air groups in 1964 reached £400 million. In the context of the financial and manpower implications, let alone the strategic and tactical arguments, it is little wonder that CVA-01 (the first postwar-designed carrier) was cancelled leaving an ever-diminishing carrier force in the late 1960s and early 1970s.[22]

In the constantly changing world between 1945 and 1964, it was therefore a difficult if not impossible task for the Admiralty to arrive at the settled construction programme that was the basis of any support for the shipbuilding industry. Long-running strategic questions continually shifted the priorities in terms of types of ships required, while continual resource constraints meant that the active fleet shrank ever smaller with the consequent reduction of the new construction programmes below the numbers required to provide support for the shipbuilding industry.

Naval shipbuilding had become an important element in the UK industry in the years before the First World War when the proportion of naval to merchant output reached 18 per cent, a record period for both numbers of ships and for the UK's share of total world merchant output.[23] During the First World War a large number of additional shipyards were drawn into naval production and the established warship firms reacted by increasing capacity, capitalisation and further measures of both horizontal and vertical integration. The end of the war, however, brought a spate of cancellations in its wake and the naval disarmament agreements of the interwar period, combined with severe financial stringency, effectively capped the Royal Navy's demands. In a much-depressed mercantile market the proportion of naval to merchant build fell to 9 per cent, half the pre-1913 figure. Naval specialisation was thus revealed as a double edged sword: Beardmore's—the most modern yard on the Clyde and specially laid and fitted out to build warships—closed, as did Palmers on the Tyne, and the giant Armstrong-Whitworth enterprise was forced into rationalisation with Vickers taking over the Elswick Yard. Essentially, the government was able to stave off a total collapse in some areas in the interwar period by providing naval orders; but given the scale of the depression in shipbuilding and the competing claims from yards and regions the impact was little more than marginal.[24]

Rearmament and the Second World War led to a substantial revival of fortunes in shipbuilding. The workforce recovered from an interwar low of 88,000 in 1932 to 247,000 by 1945, and the industry built over 6 million grt of merchant vessels between 1939 and 1945. As was noted in the introduction to this chapter, however, the two reports on the industry during the war—the Barlow and Bentham reports—both recommended large-scale modernisation in almost all aspects: layouts, prefabrication and welding, better fitting out berths, cranage, improved deployment of labour and more professional management structures.[25] Moreover, as early as 1942 and throughout 1944, talks were held between the Admiralty, the Ministry of War Transport and the shipbuilders where it was agreed that in the postwar period there should be some form of co-ordination between merchant and naval construction with naval orders being placed when merchant orders slackened off.[26] This would, according to A.V. Alexander, the First Lord of the

Admiralty, avoid the 'chaotic conditions' of the past. This decision was codified at Admiralty Board and Cabinet level in 1945.

Postwar, however, the shipbuilders were not much concerned with this in the short-term. Rather their main concern was clearing naval work from their slipways and berths in order to maximise their potential share in the postwar merchant building boom. The Admiralty tried, in 1946, to slow the launching and completion of the aircraft carriers *Eagle*, *Centaur* and *Bulwark*, leading Harland and Wolff to complain that:

> We could not under any circumstances agree that such valuable building berths with their cranes and other equipment should be tied up in this way. It would represent a very serious handicap in our efforts to secure contracts for new shipbuilding tonnage and would lead to serious dismissals of our workpeople, as well as a financial loss to ourselves which could not be disregarded.[27]

Swan Hunter expressed similar views with respect to the *Albion*.

Indeed, this attitude merely reflected government priorities, with it being estimated that it would take up to three years before the mercantile marine recovered its position and, as the Director of Dockyards noted in a 1946 report, not only was there likely to be hostility towards the Admiralty in terms of new construction occupying valuable slipways but even refitting was considered a distraction from the main objective of restoring the merchant marine.[28] In any case slowing completion was not to prove cost-effective. The provisional price for the light fleet carrier HMS *Albion* had been some £2.8 million on order in 1943, was estimated at £3.55 million in 1952, but totalled £7.6 million on completion in 1954.[29] This, however, was dwarfed by the cost of the larger fleet carrier HMS *Eagle*, which appeared in the 1952 Naval Estimates at a cost of £15.75 million. This drew from Emrys Hughes, MP for Ayr, a withering attack on the Admiralty. After dwelling at some length on the 'luxurious' fittings within the vessel he continued:

> I warn the First Lord not to bring that ship off the coast of Ayrshire. If the miners I represent, who live in far less salubrious dwellings than that, knew that the ship was anchored off the coast of Ayrshire, they would make a desperate attempt to capture it and use it for housing purposes.

On an altogether more serious note he continued:

This aircraft carrier was built in Harland and Wolff's yard in Belfast. No businessman would agree to give a contract in the way this ship has been built ... I would like to know the exact relationship between the Admiralty and Harland and Wolff Ltd. These are not contract prices. It appears that these prices alter from week to week and month to month and that at the end of ten years the Admiralty is presented with a huge bill of £15 million ... the result is that we have this enormous sum of money being spent and demanded from this house at a time when we are practically bankrupt.[30]

To be fair, this was not a situation which either the Admiralty or the Treasury was willing to tolerate indefinitely. The problem was, however, that the contractual conditions that obtained in the war—nominated firms building for the Admiralty with 'contracts' and prices only being fixed on delivery—had to continue through the 1950s boom as warship building competed for capacity with mercantile building. It was not until 1959, when the shipbuilding industry began to worry about falling orders and their declining world share of the shipbuilding market, that the Admiralty was able to return to the competitive tendering for warships (except for the captive market of submarines) that had prevailed in the interwar period.

Korean War rearmament led to an upturn in naval orders and a temporary plateau of merchant orders. Revealed inadequacies in the existing minesweeper fleet led to a substantial number of orders for new vessels. In the main these went to smaller shipyards, builders of yachts, coasters and fishing vessels, to sustain employment and create the requisite skills required to build these composite hulled vessels. Only Harland and Wolff, Thornycroft and White's from the major yards received any substantial share of this programme, but even here the employment factor played a part in the decision to build 15 in Belfast to offset potential job losses from the cancellation of an aircraft programme at Shorts.[31]

The Korean War led to the laying down of new frigates, most of which were launched between 1953 and 1955 (see Figure 7.7). Even here the Admiralty noted that 'progress on the frigates ... has been less rapid than was hoped, partly owing to production difficulties which are being overcome, and partly owing to problems inevitable with ships of new design'.[32] This programme though was to receive an early check as the head of the military branch noted in June 1954: 'it is clear that the Chancellor is going to press very hard

7.6 HMS *Lynx* under construction in 1954 in John Brown's Yard (courtesy of the Keeper of the Records of Scotland)

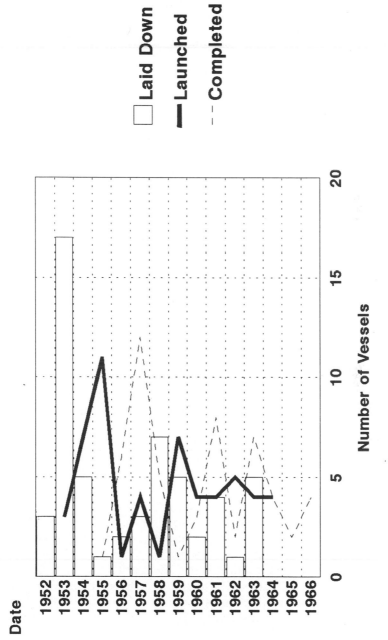

7.7 Frigate Programme Progress, 1952–1966 (derived from Conways)

indeed to get some decisions about methods of reducing defence expenditure before the end of the month'.[33] Indeed the pressure was for cuts of between £150 and £200 million in 1955–6. Whilst this financial pressure mounted the Navy Board was reporting shortfalls in expenditure on new construction. The production difficulties centred upon the vexed question of steel plate. This had been an issue since 1945, but the cost and shortage of plate was having an impact in the form of declining orders for merchant tonnage and increasing cancellations: indeed in 1954–5 some 99,000 grt had been cancelled, half by British owners. The government was sufficiently worried by the situation to begin a series of confidential enquiries into the industry.[34]

Far from being over-concerned with contra-cyclical building and sustaining the warship group, the Admiralty began to reveal a more hard-headed approach, noting that 'the Warship Group's collective representations appear always to be aimed at retarding the rational approach to future production'.[35] A paper on 'The present weakness of marine engineering industry and its consequences' identified only two 'progressive' firms in British shipbuilding, Yarrow and Cammell Laird, commenting on the rest of the industry that 'some undoubtedly recognise that change is required, but few have the vigorous management necessary to do anything about it'.[36] The paper also identified the Admiralty's postwar contractual practice and full-order books as being inimical to efficiency and forecast that the approaching end to the seller's market was the best force working for change. Despite the situation the seller's market had not as yet become a buyer's market. As an inter-departmental committee noted on the 1956–7 new construction programme, which spread six Type 12 A/S frigates between four yards, there was 'no alternative to the dispositions proposed. It was becoming increasingly difficult to place orders at all with shipbuilders for completion by planned dates.'[37]

This in turn led to a joint meeting between the Treasury and the Admiralty which pointed out the need for wholesale modernisation of yards in terms of layouts, plant and equipment, which it was felt had constrained pre-fabrication. It was also noted that British costs were comparatively high in international terms and that the return on capital employed and investment rates were poor. It noted restrictive practices but also observed that there was a lack of skilled labour in the industry, to the extent that an actual shortage of skilled labour was obvious. Moreover, this in turn was responsible for the British single-shift system, with consequently expensive overtime compared with the double-shift system which prevailed on the Continent and in Japan. Noting the problems, however, was one thing; doing anything about them was quite another.[38]

Against such a background, in autumn 1956, Lord Hailsham, the First Lord of the Admiralty, told Anthony Head, the Minister of Defence, that future cruisers would have to be sacrificed and that future aircraft-carriers were under threat as he gloomily forecast 'the end of our world-wide naval power'.[39] Meanwhile, the Admiralty continued to pursue the issues of prices and profits. While the Admiralty was trying to evolve a position where the upper profit limit was 10 per cent, profit rates for anti-submarine frigates were 12.5 per cent and those for anti-aircraft frigates were 15 per cent. At the same time the Admiralty recognised that it was 'nowadays a marginal customer of an industry in which the builders can obtain plenty of alternative commercial work of a more profitable nature. In these circumstances the Admiralty is not in a position to call the tune.'[40] No sooner was this observation made than the Admiralty was trying to devise productivity schemes for submarine construction—where 15 per cent for a good performance and 8 per cent for a substandard performance was considered—but here again 'there are orders in plenty for straightforward commercial vessels on which good profits can be comfortably earned. A shipbuilder can only be expected to give special attention to complicated submarine construction provided he is given adequate inducement to do so'.[41] In its turn, the discussion on profit rates resulted in a letter from the Shipbuilding Conference to the Admiralty warning that: 'while the warship building programme remains so emasculated and so frequently is only able to proceed on slow motion lines the Admiralty must not expect to get anything like the same low rates of profit terms as have applied when they were the predominant users of the shipbuilders facilities'.[42] This was ill-timed, however, as the seller's market was about to turn into a buyer's market and turn with a vengeance.

In 1958 the Cabinet and Admiralty's main concern was still bringing forward some measures to alleviate unemployment in the shipbuilding regions. Noting that there were 'few items which can be commenced now', the Admiralty suggested that the current building programme of one cruiser and eight frigates which had been slowed down that year because of budgetary constraints should be restored to the original completion dates. This would, the Admiralty stated, 'result in increased employment in the yards concerned ... [although] the amount of increased employment is difficult to determine without detailed investigation but the increase at peak would amount to about 1000 men'.[43] The difficulty, therefore, of using naval orders to increase employment were obvious with the employment gain of 1,000 men being distributed around seven shipyards.

Indeed, by 1959 the buyer's market had arrived and the Economic Policy Committee of the Cabinet noted that the position was 'disturbing': it was 'questionable whether we ... [could] retain even our current percentage of world shipbuilding ... [and that] the industry would begin to encounter acute difficulties in 1960'. It was suggested that the government should examine the possibility of phasing orders in a manner helpful to the industry but there was also a developing view that the industry had to 'contract and re-organise'.[44] With the buyer's market came the predictable appeals from the shipbuilding industry for the government to phase its orders: the Shipbuilding Policy Advisory Report of 1959 recommended that 'Government orders should be adjusted to compensate for fluctuations in the demand for merchant shipping'.[45] However, any help from the naval sector could only be minimal: as the Ministry of Transport noted, 'the pattern of employment on ships building on present plans for the Royal Navy will not change drastically during 1960–1961 and will not significantly alter the picture of the future based on merchant work only'.[46]

This was especially the case in that the Treasury continued to impose strict restraints, arguing in 1960/1 that the Admiralty did not seem to be giving due consideration as to whether 'a fleet of this size was required and could be afforded'. However, in an attempt to counter this the Admiralty took advantage of new market conditions and moved to competitive tendering. As W. Darracott noted to the Treasury, fixed prices were 'the spur to build with the greatest efficiency and economy',[47] while a thoroughly new approach to contra-cyclical building was also revealed:

> Some of the less efficient firms who have come to rely on Admiralty work to an important extent, can be expected to press for the placing of orders for Warships to continue on the old basis ... Among these are some old established firms with long records of building ships for the Admiralty. Resort to competitive tendering may therefore be criticised as inconsistent with the aim of tackling local pockets of unemployment: the invitation of tenders would not, however, bind the Admiralty to accept any particular offer, so that local unemployment

problems could still be taken into account in allocating orders. On the other hand it is no longer Government policy to retain a reserve potential for an emergency, and the number of warship building firms has in fact become an embarrassment, in as much as the naval programme these days is not large enough to make it possible to give all of them a continuity of orders.[48]

There could be no starker admission that, in the emergent market conditions of the 1960s, a contra-cyclical policy was useless. But just in case this fact was still not clear, the Treasury reinforced it by commenting that 'nearly all of the firms of a calibre capable of constructing a warship were in areas of high unemployment and that ... it would be immaterial where the contract went'.[49] Thus, the combination of a collapsing mercantile market—and consequently a buyer's market—and continuing budgetary stringency allowed the Admiralty to move towards competitive tendering, and at the same time admit that the prospect of any serious impact on employment in the shipbuilding sector being achieved by naval ordering was minimal. Indeed, with only 250 plus men being employed on the construction of a frigate over three years, the total man-year employment was only approximately 1,000.

The problem, however, was not simply mopping up unemployment, but was also reflected in the retention of skills. As a memo from K.T. Nash (at Military Branch 1 of the Admiralty) to Peck at the Treasury argued, the country had four submarine specialists: Vickers, Cammell Laird, Scott's and the Royal Dockyard at Chatham. In 1961 Vickers had two nuclear and two conventional submarines in hand; Cammell Laird, Scott's and Chatham all had two conventional submarines in progress. The Admiralty wished to order a further two conventional submarines—one from Scott's and one from Chatham—to keep the highly skilled workforces together. But Nash was quick to concede that, when a decision was made on the balance of nuclear and conventional submarines, there might not be a need for 'so many as four submarine building yards in the future'.[50] By May 1961 the decision had been made to 'go nuclear' and as Nash commented:

a building programme of one nuclear submarine a year will not call for keeping alive four building yards (or even perhaps three?); and if the writing is on the wall why order two conventional submarines this year to keep them all going a bit longer ? ... It is needless to say that the money would be very welcome for other purposes in 1962 and thereafter.[51]

In 1962 the dimensions of the collapse of the mercantile sector were becoming obvious and the Shipbuilding Conference was arguing that there was 'nothing ... to justify the maintenance of the present size of the shipbuilding industry'.[52] The Conference urged upon the government a revamped form of the National Shipbuilders Security Limited to reduce capacity by as much as 25 per cent. Whilst the government recognised that rationalisation was necessary, it baulked at the potential political ramifications of the industry's scheme, although the government itself could see no solution to the problem: the dilemma was one of being blamed for not getting involved or blamed for being involved. As to government ordering, it was conceded that 'any relief of this kind could not be expected to have more than a purely temporary effect', and that the First Lord of the Admiralty was to hold discussions with the Warship Building Group 'in which the subject of rationalisation within the Group would receive attention'.[53] Although having made this point it was also acknowledged that with the decline of 'commercial work Admiralty orders are becoming relatively more and more important ... [and] the industry are now inclined to look to the Admiralty as the only hope of averting something approaching a collapse'.[54]

Indeed, in 1962 the chairmen of the warship building firms had resorted to an old staple method of attempting to pressurise the government, a letter to *The Times*. The builders noted that the emerging crisis in merchant shipbuilding—surplus capacity, idle shipping, lack of demand for new tonnage, credit terms and foreign subsidies—was not the concern of the letter, but rather 'the pitifully small volume of naval work of every kind available to our shipyards'. They exhorted the government to take advantage of low ship prices and bring forward an 'imaginative and much needed naval shipbuilding programme' which would keep yards open and teams of highly skilled men together.[55] Essentially, though, the problem remained what it had been for many years: the lack of a policy decision on the navy's role resulted in an uncertain construction programme.[56]

Three issues in the early 1960s illustrate the complex relationship between the Admiralty and the shipbuilding industry: the nuclear submarine programme; the replacement aircraft-carrier programme; and the destroyer/frigate programme. Firstly, increasing stress was laid from the second half of the 1950s on nuclear-powered submarines capable of launching Intermediate Range Ballistic Missiles, which it was argued 'offered the Royal Navy the only means of making a significant contribution to the

Nuclear Deterrent which can be adequately supported by the country's economy'.[57] This was the genesis of *Dreadnought*, the first nuclear-powered submarine which was to be a trial for the eventual Polaris missile launching R class. The question as to whether the country could support this was moot as it was recognised that substantial US expertise in atomic powerplants would need to be purchased, given that Dounreay (the first British nuclear reactor) was not yet in commission. It was estimated that the total cost of the *Dreadnought* hull, the purchase of US equipment and continuing expenditure on Dounreay would reach £36 million by 1965, to which the Treasury saw 'no objection'.[58] Additionally, Vickers estimated that the total cost of altering their yard at Barrow for nuclear construction was some £1.1 million, and against this background the Admiralty began to warn of the prospect of 'nuclear blackmail by private firms'.[59] However, this was offset by the fact that the final bill for *Dreadnought* was just over £17.5 million, some £10 million of which was dollar expenditure to Westinghouse for the steam raising plant (reactor and propulsion machinery). Vickers' 9 per cent profit on the remaining items was considered something of a triumph for the Admiralty when set against profit rates ranging from 10 to 12.4 per cent for conventional submarines (which cost just under £2 million each). As the Admiralty stated, the settlement compared 'favourably ... with those on conventional submarines generally'.[60]

While money for prestige nuclear projects seemed easy to find, the opposite proved to be the case with the navy's other prestige project—the new generation of aircraft-carriers—typified by the struggle over CVA-01. This issue was complicated by the decision to retain two carriers East of Suez. The Cabinet had accepted that a new carrier was required but getting agreement to spend on research and development, design contracts and long-lead items was furiously contested. Set alongside the Polaris expenditure, and against developing balance of payments problems, the Treasury was 'strenuously looking for economies within the broad framework of present defence policy'.[61] The struggle over CVA-01 continued throughout 1963 and 1964 and the delay was such that the Admiralty conceded that there was no possibility of the vessel being ordered until 1966 at the earliest. By that stage, of course, the Conservatives had fallen and the new Labour government confronted a balance of payments crisis of major proportions which further pressurised the defence budget leading to the cancellation of CVA-01.

The third issue which was a cause of considerable concern was the detraction from the 'conventional navy' of destroyers and frigates posed by the *Dreadnought* and aircraft-carrier programmes. As the First Lord of the Admiralty, Earl Jellicoe, made clear in 1964 to the Minister of Defence, Peter Thorneycroft, 'at the moment I can point to no single conventional warship which we have authority to order': he therefore requested authority for the continuation of the Leander class frigate and the County class destroyer programmes.[62] At some £4 million each the Leanders were comparatively 'cheap', but ordering three per year spread around 13 private yards plus two dockyards could do little to alleviate any grave problem in employment in the shipbuilding industry. Perhaps the most telling comment on this issue is revealed by the tender for FSA31 (HMS *Juno*) from Thornycroft's in 1964. The Admiralty was staggered by a quoted price of £2.9 million and asked its principal accountant to investigate the tender. He reported that:

> On account of the present conditions in the yard, and having regard to the foreseeable future, the company may well be involved in a substantial under recovery of overheads on FSA31. It is noted that on the basis of the quotation the company is also prepared to forego any profit as an identifiable item.[63]

In other words there had been a return to the practises of the interwar period: shipbuilders were now building at a loss simply to remain open.

Laudable, therefore, as the contra-cyclical strategy may have been as an ideal, it could provide little defence against the vicissitudes of the market. The scale of naval shipbuilding was simply not large enough to impact seriously on the general market. Naval orders were 18 per cent of total orders in UK shipyards before the First World War, 9 per cent in the interwar period, and approximately 4 per cent in the post-Second World War era.[64]

A total of 121 warships (excluding minesweepers) over 19 years averaged just over six ships per year, distributed amongst 14 private shipyards and three dockyards (see Figure 7.8). The scope, therefore, for any contra-cyclical impact was minimal. Whilst recognising the importance of naval contracts, the Geddes Report of 1965–6 concluded that the spread of naval orders amongst 12 firms was assisting neither the yards nor the Admiralty, and it recommended not only the slimming down of the Warship Group but also a comprehensive rationalisation and what it termed the 'virtual segregation of sophisticated work in specialised yards

Yard

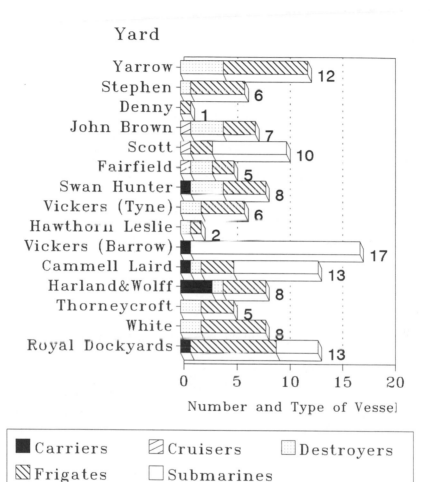

7.8 Construction by Yard and Type, 1945–1964 (derived from Conways)

concentrating on home and overseas naval orders'.[65] The Geddes Report was one of an increasing number of reports into the industry as its wholesale collapse began. Its recommendations would take some time to be realised.

NOTES

1. The focus of this chapter is on the *construction*, rather than the modernisation or conversion, for the Royal Navy of warships of the size of frigates and above including submarines, rather than auxiliaries however defined. In the main we will be dealing with vessels laid down and launched in the period from 1945 to 1964. However, we will also be including in our consideration some vessels which were laid down and launched in the war but were not completed until after the war, including various aircraft carriers, the Tiger class cruisers, the Weapon and Battle class destroyers and the A class submarines. We will not be discussing refit and repair work (the staple of the Royal Dockyards), except peripherally where it impacted upon new construction.

2. P. Kennedy, *The Rise and Fall of British Naval Mastery* (London, 1976); G.A.H. Gordon, *British Sea Power and Procurement Between the Wars* (London, 1988); E. Grove, *Vanguard to Trident: British Naval Policy since World War II* (Annapolis, 1987).

3. D.K. Brown, *A Century of Naval Construction* (London, 1983).

4. For a full discussion of the interwar period see Gordon, *British Sea Power.*

5. PRO, CAB 128/2 CM (45)56 minute 1, 27 November 1945. Unless otherwise stated, all archival references are to material held at the Public Record Office, Kew.

6. See L. Johnman, 'The Shipbuilding Industry', in H. Mercer, N. Rollings, and J. Tomlinson (eds), *Labour Governments and Private Industry: The Experience of 1945–1951* (Edinburgh, 1992), 188–9.

7. Johnman, 'Shipbuilding',187–8.

8. ADM 167/124, Director of Plans Future Building Committee: 1945 New Construction Programme, March 1945.

9. ADM 167/141 B.953, Naval Construction Programme 1952–1956, 4 January 1955.

10. See ADM 1/26067, A Review of Naval Policy 1955; and T 225/1159, Long-Term Defence Programme, 12 October 1955.

11. See Grove, *Vanguard*, 78–126.

12. See ADM 167/129 B520, *Naval Peace-Time Requirements*, 26 July 1947.

13. ADM 167/136 file.

14. See for example CAB 131/9 DO (50) 45, 7 June 1950; CAB 131/13 D(53)13th minute 4 discussing D(53)47; Grove, *Vanguard*, 78–126; and PREM 11/49 COS(52)362, 15 July 1952.

15. ADM 1/26068 memorandum, Where are we going, unsigned, 9 June 1955.
16. Defence Outline of Future Policy, Cmnd 124, April 1957; and Report on Defence. Britain's Contribution to Peace and Security, Cmnd 363, February 1958.
17. ADM 167/148, B1056, January 1956.
18. See DEFE 11/103 DP(54)12, 3 July 1954.
19. T 225/1159 Letter from the First Lord of the Admiralty, Lord Hailsham, to the Minister of Defence, Walter Monckton, 10 October 1956.
20. ADM 167/149, 5111, 11 April 1957.
21. Uncertainty over the future of the conventional gun-armed cruiser led to the suspension of the *Tiger* class at the end of the war. Replacements for the ageing *Colony* and *Town* class were the subject of controversy as the Admiralty struggled to evolve a design which embraced the new guided weapon technologies at an affordable price. This was a struggle which ultimately the Admiralty was to abandon in 1957 on grounds of their cost and manpower demands.
22. See discussions on the future of the carrier force 1961–3 in ADM 205/192. For papers on CVA-01 see ADM 1/28639 and ADM 1/29052. But as has been commented 'it was ... fortunate that CVA-01 was cancelled before her constraints of size, undue novelty and production problems had led to a costly and unsatisfactory ship'. Brown, *Century of Naval Construction*, 229.
23. Comparisons are rendered difficult by the measurements used for the two kinds of vessel. Mercantile construction is measured in gross tonnage, a measure of volume with 100 cubic feet being taken as 1 ton, whereas warship tonnage is expressed in displacement tons, i.e. the weight of water displaced by the vessel floating on it. Full load displacement tonnage for cargo vessels translates to approximately 2.25 gross tonnage and the conventional comparison is that one displacement ton has the same size implication as two gross tons.
24. D. Todd, 'Regional Variations in Naval Construction: The British Experience 1895-1966', *Regional Studies*, 15 (2), 126–33.
25. Johnman, 'Shipbuilding', 188–191.
26. National Maritime Museum, Shipbuilders and Repairers National Association papers, SRNA/SC/1/12, Note of a meeting with the Minister of Reconstruction, 10 February 1944; and Report of a meeting of the Executive Board of the Shipbuilding Conference, 23 February 1944.
27. ADM 205/64, letter from Harland and Wolff Ltd to the Secretary of the Admiralty, 4 June 1946.
28. ADM 205/64, Report by the Director of Dockyards, C.P. Talbot, 15 November 1946.
29. ADM 1/27644, HMS *Albion* Contract, 1952–6.
30. Hansard, Navy Estimates Debate, 6–7 March 1952, cols 845–8.

31. CAB 128/27 CC(54)73rd min 1, 5 November 1954.
32. ADM 1/25791, New Construction, undated but 1954.
33. ADM 1/25787, memo by Head of Military Branch, 17 June 1954.
34. See ADM 1/26455, Standing Committee on the Shipbuilding and Shiprepairing Industries, 1955, where the Shipbuilding Advisory Committee is described as being unable 'to produce any ideas of its own'. And ADM 205/106, Present Weakness of the Marine Engineering Industry and its Consequences 1955.
35. ADM 205/106, Machinery for the New Construction Programme, Memo from the Engineer in Chief of the Fleet to the Secretary to the First Sea Lord, 29 July 1955.
36. ADM 205/106, Present Weakness of the Marine Engineering Industry and Its Consequences,Report by Mr MacLean, 1955.
37. ADM 1/26455, Minutes of Inter-Departmental Working Party, 1956.
38. ADM 1/26455, Shipbuilding: Note of a Meeting Held at the Treasury, 25 April 1956.
39. T 225/1159, Letter from the First Lord of the Admiralty to the Minister of Defence, 10 November 1956.
40. ADM 1/26487, File Note to Meetings between Representatives of Frigate Builders and the Director of Navy Contracts and Colleagues, November 1956.
41. ADM1/26487, Profit Rate for Submarine Work, Memo by Bernard Pool, Director of Construction, 13 July 1956.
42. ADM 1/26487, Letter from A. Belch of the Shipbuilding Conference to the Secretary of the Admiralty, May 1956.
43. T 225/880 Admiralty: Short-term Reflationary Measures to Alleviate Unemployment, 13 November 1958.
44. BT 291/76, Cabinet: EPC meeting EA(59)14th, 8 July 1959.
45. BT 291/77, Brief Notes on Remedies for the Shipbuilding Industry, memo by A.B. Birnie, 16 February 1960.
46. BT 291/77, Immediate Prospects of Shipbuilding and Shiprepairing Industries, memo by the Ministry of Transport, 12 January 1960.
47. ADM 1/27498, Letters between A.W. Peck, Treasury, and W. Darracott, Admiralty, February 1960.
48. T 225/1281, W. Darracott to A.W. Peck, February 1960.
49. T 225/1281, Competitive Tendering for Warships, note by R.J. Allwood, 22 January 1960. See also T 234/632, Competitive Tendering for Warships, note by C.W. Fogarty, 22 February 1960.
50. ADM 1/27872, Frigates and Submarines, letter from K.T. Nash to A.W. Peck, 28 April 1961.
51. ADM 1/27842, Frigate and Submarine Building Programme, memo by K.T. Nash, 26 May 1961.
52. BT 291/1, Note of a Meeting with the Shipbuilding Conference, 31 July 1962.
53. BT 291/1, Economic Policy Committee EA62, 30 August 1962.
54. BT 291/138, Notes for EPC Meeting, 24 November 1962.

55. Letter to *The Times* reprinted in *Fairplay Shipping Journal*, 6 December 1962. See also Sir Eric Yarrow, 'Hard Times Ahead in the Shipyards', *Glasgow Herald Trade Review*, January 1963.

56. T 234/632, Competitive Tendering for Warships.

57. ADM 1/27479, The Role of the Submarine, Flag Officer Submarines to Secretary of the Admiralty, 20 December 1957.

58. T 225/1192, Purchase of US Nuclear Submarine Plant and Know-How, Memo by D.R. Serpell, 25 November 1958. See also ADM 167/149 5129 for an early recognition of the cost of a naval contribution to the nuclear deterrent.

59. T 225/1194, V-A Barrow Dreadnought—Plant extension. Letter from Forbes, Material Branch 1 to M.G.F. Hall, Treasury, 1 October 1959.

60. ADM 1/28410, Minute Sheet, January 1963.

61. ADM 1/29052, New Aircraft Carriers, J. Boyd-Carpenter, Chief Secretary to the Treasury, to the Prime Minister, 4 October 1963.

62. DEFE 24/1, DLG and Leander Orders, First Lord of the Admiralty to Minister of Defence, 11 March 1964.

63. ADM 1/29017, Leander Class Frigate FSA31 (Juno), Breakdown of Contract Price, 1964.

64. It is undoubtedly the case that naval shipbuilding had a higher value added content than merchant work. Realising accurate comparisons between value and profit rates on naval work and mercantile work is difficult given the very different natures of the products. What can be said is that profit rates tended to be higher and more stable for naval work than for mercantile work. Taking, for example, the P class submarine *Narwhal* and the cargo vessel *Memmon*, both completed by Vickers in 1959, a useful comparison can be drawn. The selling price of *Narwhal*'s hull was £992,000 as against £1,179,000 for *Memmon*. The final selling price for *Narwhal* was £1,450,000 as against £1,831,000 for *Memmon*. The final profit figures were £81,000 for *Narwhal* and £80,000 for *Memmon* with percentage profits being 5.6 per cent for *Narwhal* (8.2 per cent on the hull only) and 4.4 per cent for *Memmon* (6.8 per cent on the hull only). University of Cambridge, Vickers Papers, Vickers 1344, Chief Accountants Notes on Accounts for Half-Year ended June 1959.

65. Shipbuilding Enquiry Committee Report 1965–6, Cmnd 2937, 137. The difference between the figures of 14 private shipyards quoted in the text and the 12 quoted by Geddes is accounted for by the fact that Denny's on the Clyde and White's of Cowes had closed in 1962 and 1965 respectively.

CHAPTER 8

The Development of the British Distant-Water Trawling Industry, 1880–1939

Robb Robinson

Between 1840 and 1880 the British fish trade underwent a radical transformation. Output greatly increased as the marketing opportunities provided by the creation of a national railway network were exploited. Many of the old inland transportation constraints, which had previously restricted the conveyance of this perishable commodity, were removed and fresh fish finally became an article of cheap mass consumption in the burgeoning inland towns and cities. All sectors of the British fishing industry gained, but the trawling trade benefited more than most. Until 1840 most of the white fish landed in Britain had been taken by baited hook on hand and then long lines, but by 1860 the majority were caught in the trawl.[1] The beam trawl was not new, variations of the trawl net having existed since at least the fourteenth century. However, the technology proved particularly suitable for the marketing conditions created by the advent of the railways. The trawl net took large quantities of the cheaper varieties of fish—haddock, plaice and small cod, for example—which had previously been unable to bear the high cost of transportation but henceforward enjoyed a growing demand among the urban masses. Demand for such fish was to continue to expand through to the 1930s.[2]

The result was a rapid expansion in the numbers of trawlers and trawlermen and the opening up of new trawling grounds all round the English and Welsh coasts, most notably across the North Sea from the 'new' fishing ports of Hull and Grimsby as well as traditional centres such as Scarborough and Yarmouth. Much, though not all, of this expansion was fuelled by Devon fishermen who played a key role in the development of the activity at many ports.[3] Until the 1880s the trade relied principally on the sailing smack, the design of which was further refined and developed over these decades. Though they represented a considerable capital investment, many such vessels were owned by their skippers or small firms. Working fishermen found that by hard work and thrift they could purchase their own sailing smack.[4]

Trawling was a controversial activity and many traditional line fishermen, especially those working the inshore fishing grounds, tended to view the practice with resentment. They often complained that trawling was wasteful and destructive. Despite the great increase in the number of trawlers working from English ports, representatives of the trade asserted that the trawl could not harm fish stocks.[5] This belief was officially supported as early as 1866 when the Report of the Royal Commission on Sea Fisheries accepted the contemporary scientific belief that the sea was so large and the number of fish in it so great that the actions of man could have little effect on stocks. When the Commission reported, there was still a great deal of legislation on the statute book which sought to restrict or regulate the fisheries. In many instances such legislation was not enforced but its mere existence often ran counter to the prevailing free market philosophy. As a result of the Royal Commission's recommendations, the government passed the 1868 Sea Fisheries Act which swept away many of the regulations restricting fishing activities. This represented, in the words of R.H. Barback, 'the true and final apotheosis of classical laissez faire'.[6] Henceforward, the only constraints on fishing were to be those imposed by demand on the open market and the technology available to capture fish.

The Royal Commission also recommended a clearer definition of the high seas. Throughout the rest of the nineteenth century the British government was a prime mover in securing international recognition of a three-mile territorial and fishery limit. Restricting the limit of state control of the seas to three miles not only fitted in with Britian's traditional interpretation of international waters, it also sat well with a philosophy that sought to limit state intervention in economic activity.

The Emergence of the Steam Trawler

It was only in the last years of the 1870s that experiments with paddle tugs trawling from ports on the English north-east coast demonstrated that steam fishing could be a commercial proposition.[7] During the following decade the first successful purpose-built steam fishing vessels were constructed. The steam trawler, especially after the introduction of the triple expansion marine engine in the late

1880s, not only proved to be profitable, but it was also a far more efficient catcher of fish than the conventional sailing smack and potentially had a much greater range. Its emergence offered new opportunities to the British trawling trade in areas beyond the North Sea and British coastal waters, adding a highly significant distant-water dimension to the business.

The 1880s—when the purpose-built steam trawler was introduced—proved to be a time of crisis for the trawling industry. Indeed, the trade's expansive trend exhibited signs of faltering. The catching sector was still dominated by the sailing smack, the design of which offered little opportunity for further technological improvement. While it seems likely that when the trawlers first arrived at the east coast ports there had been considerable scope for increasing the exploitation of North Sea fish stocks, it is also evident that many of the grounds which had been opened up to trawling in earlier decades were now suffering from over-fishing,[8] and there were frequent reports of declining catches. A typical response of the trawling sector to falling landings was either to seek out new grounds or else fish more intensively.

Initially, this led to an intensification of the practice of fleeting across the North Sea in the late 1870s and early 1880s. Fleets of sailing trawlers worked on the fishing grounds for up to eight weeks at a time and were serviced by fast steam cutters which took their catches to port on a daily basis. The smacks could therefore maximise their fishing effort by reducing the number of individual voyages to and from port. At the same time, because fish was ferried to port so regularly, there was less need to spend money on ice to preserve the catch. However, fleeting merely provided an interim respite. By fishing more intensively larger landings were made in the short term; but this strategy merely aggravated the underlying problem of stock depletion across the North Sea, and in the medium term decline was resumed.

As catches declined in North Sea and other waters adjacent to the British Isles, smack profits fell. The trawling sector, hitherto strong opponents of state intervention, began to call for much wider regulation of the North Sea grounds. A series of national conferences was held during the late 1880s and early 1890s.[9] These meetings invariably called for regulation of the fishing effort.

When the Royal Commission on Trawling began collecting evidence in 1883 a number of the trade's representatives, who had previously denied that trawling could affect stocks, claimed that catches were now falling off on traditional grounds and that this was pushing trawlers ever further afield. Though this Royal Commission's report in 1885 did concede that trawling on narrow and inshore grounds might affect stocks, it stopped short of saying that man's activities could damage the resource base across the North Sea.[10] Moreover, many of these activities were carried out in international waters beyond the three-mile limit and therefore outside the orbit of government legislation.

Nevertheless, complaints about falling catches and profits from sailing smacks continued, with many owners still calling for regulation to ensure the conservation of stocks. This represented a considerable shift from the sector's previous position of supporting freedom of fishing across the seas. A group called the National Sea-Fisheries Protection Association had been formed in the early 1880s and the issue of stock depletion was always high on its agenda. Its 1888 conference urged the government to start negotiations with continental countries to secure international regulation of fishing grounds. The Association's later conferences tried to agree some form of self-regulation but this soon broke down. In 1891, at a hitherto unprecedented international conference attended by representatives from Belgium, France, Germany, Holland and Spain, the Association called for a convention on the international landing and sale of immature fish.[11] The State did work with other countries on a number of issues but many of these were related to maintaining good conduct and law and order, including a convention aimed at the suppression of the North Sea liquor traffic with trawlers. However, another initiative promoted by Sweden in 1899 encouraged greater international scientific discourse and led to the foundation in 1902 of the International Council for the Exploration of the Sea.

Even though an apparent interest in conservation had emerged, in actual practice trawling continued to be managed as an extractive activity and, despite the shortcomings of the fleeting system, the trade still attempted to maximise output by expanding the strength of the fleet and increasing catching efficiency. As noted above, the trawling smack was close to the limits of technological improvement and the search for unexploited grounds took these two-masted sailing vessels close to the maximum practical range from which they could return to port with catches of fresh fish. Small wonder that smackowners found conservation an attractive option for the first time.

However, the emergence of the purpose-built steam screw trawler altered the equation. At first, these vessels were largely confined to North Sea grounds, but even here they proved to be far more efficient than their sailing counterparts, being able to tow larger trawls and work in weather that the smacks could not endure. The commercial success of the otter trawl and its almost wholesale adoption by steam trawlers during the summer of 1895[12] widened their advantage over the smacks as this new gear, which was formidably more efficient than the old beam trawl, could only be used by steam trawlers.

The depletion of North Sea fish stocks encouraged some of the new steam trawlers to voyage further afield in search of new grounds. A number of Hull and Grimsby vessels worked off the west coast of Ireland in the early 1890s, whilst a Hull fleet tried fishing for hake in the Bay of Biscay in 1893 and ran catches into Plymouth.[13] But it was those trawlers which began exploring the potential of northerly grounds off the Faroes and Iceland that proved the most successful.

British fishermen had gone line fishing off Faroe and Iceland for centuries—the English interest in Iceland dates back to around 1400—and Grimsby had strengthened its interest in that direction in the 1880s, especially after the introduction of steam lining vessels. However, until the late 1880s, vessels had not been able to bring home what might be described as fresh fish from such grounds— except when wells had been used. A few English lining vessls may have experimented with trawling off Iceland during the summer of 1889 but a German vessel, *President Herwig*, can lay claim to being the first steam trawler there.[14] Unfortunately, its first voyage was curtailed when it trawled over a submarine lava field which tore its gear to pieces, necessitating a return to port without a catch. In 1891, however, the Grimsby Steam Trawling Company sent the steam trawler *Aquarius* to Iceland and, after working off Ingol's Hofde Huk, the vessel returned with a good catch of plaice and haddock.[15] In the summer of 1892 nine trawlers voyaged to the Icelandic grounds and made good catches each trip. These pioneering steamers were working at the very edge of their operational limit and when they sailed north from the Humber they not only carried coal in their bunkers and fish rooms but also in every possible spare space. Deterioration of the catch was reduced by mixing ice with the fish as it was stowed below deck.

In the early years these trawlers limited their activities to the seas off south-east Iceland, rarely venturing further afield than the Westmann Islands. Initially, only summer voyages were made and the craft concentrated on fishing off the Faroes during the winter.

Soon larger vessels were being built and the pressure was on to extend the Icelandic season. The marine insurance companies, which were initially dubious about the venture, gradually eased their restrictions on winter voyages and soon British trawlers were fishing right round Iceland.[16] By 1903, 80 Hull trawlers were working off Iceland along with nearly 70 from Grimsby.[17]

Off Iceland the trawlermen encountered a native fishing industry that was far less developed and capitalised. Though largely reliant on open boats and some decked sailing vessels, it was vital to the domestic economy.[18] Even before the trawlers arrived, the Icelanders had anticipated their impact, and in 1889 a law had been passed banning trawling in territorial waters. During the 1890s the threat posed by foreign trawlers caused considerable concern to Icelanders. They felt that many of the visiting trawlers appeared to pay little regard to the island's territorial limits and there were numerous complaints about trawlers sweeping away the lines of Icelandic fishermen. Iceland, like the Faroes, was then part of the Kingdom of Denmark and called upon the Danes to be more vigorous in their policing of the fisheries. One particular bone of contention was the fishery limit. The Icelanders regarded this as four miles while the Danish government had already joined with other European states to agree a three-mile limit for North Sea waters. Though the British trawling trade had recently seemed keen on encouraging state regulation in the North Sea, it began to take a different line as landings from the Icelandic grounds grew in importance. In the late 1890s there were calls in Iceland for the prohibition of trawl fishing on the rich grounds of the Bay of Faxa. The only concession some sections of the British trade were prepared to consider was a reciprocal agreement whereby they would stay out of the Bay of Faxa in return for permission to work within territorial limits on a different section of coast.[19] However, as the leading sector of the trawling trade specialised increasingly in taking fish on grounds close to the shores of far-off countries, most distant water trawler owners came to regard any suggestions of tampering with territorial waters and fishery limits as potentially damaging to their long-term interests.

The Icelandic legislation of 1889 proved to be largely ineffective and numerous complaints were made about foreign trawlers working well within exisiting limits. In 1894 Iceland passed a much stronger law which, in effect, sought to ban vessels with trawls from entering territorial waters or putting in at Icelandic ports except in emergencies. This Act was a significant step for

Iceland—and is indicative of the strength of native feeling on this issue—for it was the first time the Icelandic Althing had taken the lead in relations with a foreign country without first consulting Denmark.[20]

Danish naval vessels intensified their policing of Icelandic inshore waters and a string of foreign trawlers—many of them British—were arrested during the next few years. A number of skippers were fined and had their gear confiscated. British trawler owners complained bitterly to Parliament and the issue clouded relations between Britain and Denmark. Discussions eventually led to the Anglo-Danish Territorial Waters Treaty of 1901. This treaty in effect recognised three miles as the limit of territorial waters and fishery limits around Iceland, the Faroes and Greenland. Thereafter, relationships between the two countries improved again, though the Treaty became a focus for the resentment of those Icelanders who considered that the Danes had been prepared to sacrifice their fishing interests in order to facilitate easy access to the British market for Danish dairy products.[21] It was resentments such as these that fuelled later drives for independence. Indeed, seven years after becoming fully independent of Denmark in 1944, Iceland was to abrogate this Treaty. In the meantime, British and other foreign trawlers had unrestricted access to within three miles of the coast.

Demand and Distant-Water Trawling

Demand for fish in the United Kingdom grew throughout the Edwardian era and into the 1920s as the retail fish-frying sector continued to expand. The opening up of Icelandic grounds allowed British white fish landings to match increased demand even though catches of white fish from the North Sea at first stagnated and then declined. In 1905, for example, landings of such fish from the North Sea by British vessels at English ports amounted to 4,351,429 cwt. The comparative figure for 1913 was 3,385,459 cwt and by 1929 landings were down to 2,620,609 cwt. In contrast, British vessels landing at English ports had brought 1,661,190 cwt from Iceland in 1905. In 1929 they brought 2,720,750 cwt and were to surpass 3½ million cwt in 1937 (see Table 8.1).

During the Edwardian era new distant water grounds were also explored. The Barents Sea grounds were first visited in 1905 and before the First World War steam trawlers from Hull and Grimsby had voyaged to the Grand Banks, Newfoundland, as well as the Greenland coast. Working distant water grounds meant increasing the time taken steaming to and fro but once there the rewards were certainly great. It took, for example, five days to steam to the Barents Sea grounds but the catch taken more than compensated for the long journey. In 1906, the catch per day's absence from port on the Barent Sea grounds was 40.2 cwt while that from the North Sea was only 17.6 cwt.[22] True, the fish taken on the distant water grounds was much coarser and less valuable than that taken in the North Sea, but the Arctic cod proved particularly suitable for the increasingly popular fish-frying retail outlets. Such demand helped make the distant water trade so profitable.

Table 8.1: Demersal Fish Landings by British Vessels in England and Wales from Selected Grounds, 1909–1937 (annual average, cwt)

	1909–1912	1919–1923	1924–1928	1929–1933	1934–1937*
English Channel	190,000	224,000	191,000	155,000	127,000
North Sea	3,783,000	3,915,000	3,023,000	2,665,000	1,833,000
Faroe	615,000	366,000	763,000	804,000	820,000
Iceland	1,159,000	1,633,000	2,516,000	3,337,000	3,509,000
Barents Sea	273,000	131,000	277,000	568,000	1,331,000
Bear Island /Spitzbergen	-	-	-	758,000	1,627,000
Greenland	-	-	-	112,000	89,000
Norwegian Coast	-	-	-	44,000	355,000

Note: * Four-year period only.
Sources: Sea Fisheries Statistical Tables; R. Robinson, *Trawling: The Rise and Fall of British Trawl Fishery* (Exeter, 1996).

The development of middle and distant water grounds and the adoption of steam trawling technology in the late 1880s and 1890s had brought about a radical restucturing of the trade. Steam trawlers were expensive to construct and required a capital investment generally beyond the means of an individual fisherman or small owners. New joint stock limited liability steam trawling companies were formed and these mobilised capital and resources from outside of the trawling sector. Many of the smaller smackowners had gone to the wall or had become shareholders in the new companies as they sold off their old smacks. By the early twentieth century the ports of Hull and Grimsby had sold off all of their sailing smacks while the 'newer' trawling ports of North Shields and Aberdeen, which had grown to prominence in the 1880s, based their expansion almost completely on steam vessels.

Steam trawling required access to supplies of coal, marine engineering back-up, and modern harbour facilities. Larger crews were carried and there was also less demand for trades based on traditional maritime technology such as sail and blockmaking and subsequently a greater call for blacksmiths and engineers. Many of the older and smaller shipyards which had turned out wooden smacks lost out to newer and larger builders who constructed iron-hulled steam vessels. Ports such as Scarborough or Brixham which lacked lavish marine engineering facilities and possessed only modest harbour accommodation tended to stagnate and during the Edwardian era activity was increasingly concentrated on the larger centres. Within the steam trawling ports, however, a pattern began to emerge: Hull and, to a lesser extent Grimsby, developed the distant water grounds, whilst Aberdeen, Fleetwood and North Shields made much more of middle water grounds, especially off Faroe and the west coast of Scotland.

Table 8.2: British Landings of White Fish by Port, 1930

	Trawl	Great or Long Lines	Danish Seine	Total	
	(cwt)	(cwt)	(cwt)	(cwt)	(£)
Hull	4,077,465	31,128	-	4,108,593	2,688,564
Grimsby	3,354,878	229,790	121,479	3,709,981	4,038,384
Aberdeen	1,381,776	231,525	4,955	1,629,199	1,645,653
Fleetwood	1,127,702	2,073	-	1,121,407	1,623,778
Milford Haven	651,899	24,009	-	675,908	1,141,878
Granton	468,847	-	-	468,847	399,935
London (Billingsgate)	359,455	-	-	359,455	388,762
North Shields	277,796	35,378	102	313,672	371,715
Lowestoft	276,029	68	2,461	279,336	512,935
Swansea	183,418	-	-	183,418	263,327
Cardiff	145,176	-	-	145,266	187,250
Hartlepool	107,695	7,560	78	116,772	137,200
Other Ports	533,247	126,547	74,502	1,024,891	1,305,318
Total	12,945,383	688,078	203,577	14,146,745	14,704,699

Source: *Report of Committee of Fishing Industry* 1932, CMD 4012.

The First World War greatly disrupted operations with many vessels being called up for naval service as minesweepers and for a time there was very little fishing done by British vessels in distant waters.[23] After the Armistice, and the gradual demobilisation of the steam trawling vessels, all sections of the trade enjoyed a brief period of boom thanks to high prices and good catches being made on grounds which had seen little fishing for four years. Throughout the interwar period, however, British white fish landings from all sources tended to be increasingly concentrated in about a dozen ports. Indeed, by 1930 only about 7 per cent of landings were being made by British vessels at other ports. Out of a total white fish catch of nearly 14,150,000 cwt little more than 840,000 cwt were taken by British vessels using methods other than trawling (see Table 8.2).

About 18 months after the Armistice, the short postwar boom ended, catches began to fall in North Sea waters once more and prices soon entered a decline that was to last for most of the interwar period. The near water and middle distance fisheries were especially affected and for those ports which concentrated on these activities the interwar period was largely a time of at best stagnation and often decline. However, the distant water sector continued to expand and here activity tended to be concentrated on Hull.

Hull was able to improve its performance by specialising in supplying the thriving fish-frying trade. Though prices were low, catches were high and the port continued throughout the interwar period to invest in ever larger and more powerful steam trawlers. A series of technological developments cut costs allowing distant water trawling operations to cope with the downward trend in fish prices. Hull's fishing industry also maximised the return that could be made from the catch. It was the first port to introduce large-scale filleting straight after landing.[24] Previously, fish had usually been filleted on reaching an inland destination. Filleting at the port reduced transport costs as the fillet represented only 40 per cent of the weight of the fish, and it also meant that the large quantities of offal were produced as a by-product and by processing this in the fish meal and oil factory further income could be earned. By 1930 the Hull Fish Meal and Oil Company was processing 80,000 tons of offal per year.

Thanks largely to the success of Hull, English landings of demersal fish continued to expand throughout the interwar period (see Table 8.3). New grounds were opened up. The Icelandic grounds remained an important source and the Barents Sea grounds grew in significance. An amelioration of the Arctic climate led to a retreat of the ice in the late 1920s and trawlers took advantage and pushed further north, visiting Spitzbergen, Cape Kanin and Novaya Zemlya.[25] The prolific Bear Island grounds were trawled from 1929 and henceforward became an important supplier of fish landed on the Humber. The Lofoten Islands also became an important fishery from 1929. As noted earlier, Hull came to dominate the white fish sector in terms of landings, while Fleetwood, Aberdeen and Grimsby concentrated on middle water fisheries, and devoted only limited efforts to working distant waters. Hull became almost exclusively a distant water port and finally sold off most of its remaining North Sea trawlers in 1936. In 1913 Hull had accounted for only 12 per cent of English white fish landings but by 1938 the proportion had risen to 45 per cent.[26]

Table 8.3: Demersal Fish Landings in Britain by British Vessels, 1912–1938 (cwt)

Year	England and Wales	Scotland	Total
1912	8,749,591	2,862,586	11,612,177
1913	8,360,769	2,735,252	11,096,021
1921	7,867,037	2,639,642	10,506,679
1922	9,007,004	2,828,945	11,835,949
1923	8,121,970	2,069,160	10,191,130
1924	8,569,270	2,310,981	10,880,251
1925	9,287,404	2,468,208	11,755,612
1926	8,556,946	2,404,281	10,961,227
1927	9,307,968	2,619,319	11,927,287
1928	9,016,620	2,553,212	11,569,832
1929	9,732,270	2,591,612	12,323,882
1930	11,454,125	2,692,620	14,146,745
1931	11,109,473	2,778,759	13,888,232
1932	11,125,727	2,795,622	13,921,349
1933	10,941,278	2,680,849	13,622,127
1934	10,920,390	2,479,078	13,399,468
1935	11,396,644	2,395,683	13,792,327
1936	12,637,573	2,275,711	14,913,284
1937	13,333,342	2,481,731	15,815,073
1938*	12,644,000	2,976,000	15,620,000

Note: * rounded to nearest '000.
Source: Sea Fisheries Statistical Tables.

The continual development of the distant waters called not only for newer but also more sophisticated trawlers. Steam trawlers of up to 140 feet in length had been constructed during and immediately after the Great War and there was little real change until the early 1930s. However, as economic conditions worsened and profit

8.1 The *Bayflower*, built in 1933 by Cochranes of Selby for Yorkshire Steam Fishing Company (courtesy of Hull Maritime Museum, Cartlidge Collection)

margins were squeezed, the Hull owners began to order larger and faster vessels able to make the trip in practically all weathers. While a capacity of 2,000 kits of ten stone could be carried by vessels constructed in the 1920s, the new generation of vessels could carry double that cargo. The standard 140-foot vessels became obsolete and new 150-foot vessels were built. Another new development was the cruiser stern which had been pioneered with smaller vessels working from South Wales ports. The first Hull vessel with a cruiser stern, the *Beachflower*, was built in 1931. The cruiser stern gave a half knot advantage over other trawlers with the same engine power.[27] Various engine improvements were incorporated, including superheaters which made vessels more economical and faster. By 1936 the latest distant water trawlers had a one knot advantage on vessels built a decade earlier and were more economical.

While landings at Hull continued on an upward trend, those at the other trawling ports stagnated. It is not too clear why other ports failed to follow Hull's lead—indeed, it was not until the late 1930s that Grimsby began to modernise its fleet extensively. One factor may have been the type of firm to be found at Hull. Hull trawler firms were generally larger than those at other ports and had access to greater sources of capital. Moreover, firms in the Hull trawler industry were involved in a far greater level of mutual activity than was the case with other ports. Hull trawler owners, fish merchants, curers and wholesalers financed a whole range of jointly owned concerns, including ice factories, fish meal and manure plants, as well as a cod liver oil refinery and mutual insurance companies. The end result was that the profit margins maintained by Hull's steam trawlers were consistently better than those of vessels from other ports.[28]

Despite the growing importance of new distant water grounds, including Spitzbergen and Bear Island, Iceland remained the most important distant water fishery, ranking second only to the North Sea in terms of demersal fish landings. Britain was also the largest foreign catcher of fish off Iceland, taking 35 per cent of landings from those grounds during the years 1934–8 compared with 21 per cent by German vessels. Iceland caught only slightly more fish (35.1 per cent) than Britain during these years.[29] Throughout the interwar period British distant water fishing effort was clearly intensifying.

The sheer success of Hull's effort in distant waters caused problems for other sectors of the industry: 1930 was a record year for landings of demersal fish thanks in particular to the exploitation of the new Bear Island grounds; and it was also a year when all

8.2 St Andrew's Fish Dock, Hull, *c.* 1935: bobbers unloading trawler (courtesy of Hull Maritime Museum, Cartlidge Collection)

prices fell. While food prices continued to decline during 1931 and 1932 as the world economic depression tightened its grip, landings

Table 8.4: Earnings and Profits/Losses of Vessels Trawling in Near and Middle Waters, 1929–1934 (£, per vessel)

	Hull	Grimsby	Aberdeen	Fleetwood	Milford Haven
Gross Earnings					
1929	8,657	7,171	6,628	11,042	8,644
1930	7,690	6,147	5,876	9,445	8,254
1931	6,741	5,677	5,579	8,112	7,750
1932	6,115	5,565	5,360	7,901	6,876
1933	6,011	5,972	5,608	8,552	7,170
1934	6,342	5,911	5,932	8,398	8,510
Net Profits (+) or Losses (-)					
1929	+1,137	+344	+277	+1,284	+472
1930	+274	-279	-260	+164	-21
1931	+89	-333	-459	-335	-452
1932	+17	-170	-345	-39	-294
1933	+376	+81	-176	+233	-311
1934	+345	+9	+70	+71	+331

Source: Sea Fish Commission for UK, Second Report 'The White Fish Industry', 1938.

from the distant water sector remained high. Though fish consumption per head continued to increase over the interwar period it is clear that by the early 1930s landings were outrunning the capacity of the market. Only Hull, with its modern practices and highly efficient fleet, could make a profit during the worst years of the depression and over-production remained a problem until the outbreak of war. While Hull continued to prosper, many other ports remained in the doldrums until after the Second World War (see Tables 8.4 and 8.5). A government report in 1932 led to the Sea Fishing Industry Act of 1933 and the introduction of orders which sought to restrict distant water catches during the summer months and laid down restrictions on the catching and landing of immature fish, even those caught on the open seas. It also imposed quotas and restrictions on landings and imports of foreign caught fish. In essence, this was a partial reversal of the freedoms granted by the 1868 Sea Fisheries Act.[30] One other result was the creation of a Sea Fish Commission which was given the job of investigating all branches of the trade, including the herring fishery which was in an even more parlous condition. A further Sea Fisheries Act was passed as a result of its recommendations, leading, after the Second World War, to the creation of the White Fish Authority.

Table 8.5: Earnings and Profits/Losses of Vessels Trawling in Distant Waters, 1929–1934 (£, per vessel)

	Hull	Grimsby
Gross Earnings		
1929	15,569	13,132
1930	13,327	12,093
1931	11,894	10,547
1932	11,429	10,292
1933	12,081	10,962
1934	13,070	12,427
Net Profits (+) or Losses (-)		
1929	+2,601	+1,157
1930	+1,373	+396
1931	+957	-300
1932	+816	-434
1933	+1,202	+192
1934	+1,834	+744

Source: Sea Fish Commission for UK, Second Report 'The White Fish Industry', 1938.

The years 1901–39 might also be seen as the high-water mark of the three-mile limit which so favoured British distant water fishing. After the dispute with Iceland had been ended by treaty in 1901, Britain—and several other European countries—came to believe that their concept of fishery limits was enshrined in international law. However, international acceptance of the three-mile limit was general rather than universal. Portugal and Spain, for example, had always maintained a six-mile tradition, while Norway and Sweden claimed four miles. Nevertheless, all Icelandic attempts to secure a reconsideration of its limits came to naught in the interwar period. After the Second World War support for the three-mile limit was to be undermined by a number of factors. It was becoming obvious, for example, that the seas and the seabed contained valuable and potentially exploitable resources other than fish and this added a new dimension to arguments over access and ownership. The strategic importance of access to oil supplies had been highlighted by the war and the United States had become particularly concerned about securing rights to the exploitation of a range of economic resources in and below the seas adjacent to its coasts. In 1946 the United States government issued two declarations which became known as the Truman Proclamations.[31] These claimed jurisdiction over continental shelf resources and asserted rights to establish fishery conservation zones in open seas. In 1951 the International Court of Justice in the Hague upheld Norway's claim, contested by Britain, to a four-mile limit. This brought into question the existing definition of territorial waters and fishery limits which many European states thought were long settled. Henceforward, a number of states pushed to extend the area of their exclusive economic interest adjacent to their coasts.[32] During the 1950s, 1960s and 1970s fishery limits—or rather what became known as Exclusive Economic Zones—were gradually but relentlessly extended to 200 miles and this led to the exclusion of distant water fleets from the grounds they had once dominated. After 1945 Britain's distant water sector was able to regain and then maintain its interwar position until the mid-1950s but there was no further marked expansion. Thereafter, it entered into a gradual decline which turned into a wholesale collapse after the last Cod Wars with Iceland in the early and mid-1970s.

Conclusion

The period 1890–1939 saw the establishment of a method of distant water fishing that allowed Britain to increase greatly her supplies of fish and keep pace with demand. This encouraged the concentration of activity in a limited number of ports which had access to the requisite combination of capital, labour, marine engineering, management and marketing resources. Ultimately, this caused the trade to focus increasingly on the Humber ports and Hull in particular. Its strategy, however, was still based largely on matching—and thus often maximising—the extraction and exploitation of commercially valuable species to market demand rather than the conservation and management of the fish stocks in line with existing resources. The vitality of the British trawling industry was therefore crucially dependent on the high seas being recognised as international waters—global commons—open to all.

NOTES

1.	R. Robinson, 'The Rise of Trawling on the Dogger Bank Grounds', *Mariner's Mirror*, 75 (1989), 79–80.
2.	J.K. Walton, *Fish and Chips and the British Working Class 1870–1940* (Leicester, 1991), 35–43.
3.	D.H. Cushing, *The Arctic Cod: A Study of Research into the British Trawl Fisheries* (Oxford, 1966), 4–9.
4.	Royal Commission (R.C.) Sea Fisheries, 1866 XVII–XVIII, Minutes of Evidence, qq. 7484, 7789, 7792.
5.	R.C. Sea Fisheries, 1866 XVII–XVIII, Report, ciii.
6.	R.H. Barback, *The Political Economy of the Fisheries* (Hull, 1966), 18–19.
7.	R. Robinson, 'The Development of the British North Sea Steam Trawling Fleet 1877–1900', in J. Edwards, H. Nordvik, S. Palmer, and D. Williams, (eds.), *The North Sea: Resources and Seaways*, (Aberdeen, 1997).
8.	W. Garstang, 'The Impoverishment of the Sea', *Journal of the Marine Biological Association*, 6 (1900), 1–3. Also R. Robinson, 'The English Fishing Industry 1790–1914: A Case Study of the Yorkshire Coast', (Hull Univ. Ph.D. 1985), 275–98.
9.	Robinson, thesis, 294–5.
10.	R.C. on Trawling, 1885 XVI, Report, xliii.
11.	J.T. Jenkins, *The Sea Fisheries* (London, 1920), 151–5.
12.	North Eastern District Sea Fisheries Committee, *Minutes*, July 1896.
13.	Annual Report of the Inspector of Fisheries, 1893, 3–5.
14.	J. Th. Thor, 'The Beginnings of British Steam-Trawling in Icelandic Waters', *Mariner's Mirror*, 74 (1989), 268–9.
15.	E.W.L. Holt, 'On the Icelandic Trawl Fishery', *Journal of the Marine Biological Association*, 3 (1893), 129–32.
16.	Humber Steam Trawlers Mutual Insurance and Protecting Company, *Minutes*, 12 December 1900 and 31 October 1901.
17.	Report on English and Welsh Sea Fisheries for 1903, 5.
18.	J.Th. Thor, *British Trawlers and Iceland 1919-1976* (Esbjerg, 1995), 46–7.
19.	*The Times*, 13 April 1897.
20.	Thor, *British Trawlers*, 46.
21.	H. Jonsson, *Friends in Conflict: The Anglo-Icelandic Cod Wars and the Law of the Sea* (London, 1982), 38.
22.	Robinson, 'The Development', 377.
23.	Report on the Sea Fisheries, England and Wales, 1915–18, 1–4.
24.	Report of the Imperial Committee on the Marketing and Preparation of Food, *Fifth Report*, 1927, 39.
25.	Cushing, *Arctic Cod*, 22–3; and J. Nicholson, *Food From The Sea* (London, 1979), 86–7.
26.	R. Robinson, *Trawling: the Rise and Fall of the British Trawl Fishery* (Exeter, 1996), 151.

27. A. Addy, 'Fifty Years of Progress in the Fishing Industry at Hull', *Hull Association of Engineers Journal*, 17 (1949), 5.
28. Sea Fish Commission for the United Kingdom, *Second Report, The White Fish Industry 1936*, 55–9. See also Tables 8.4 and 8.5.
29. Thor, *British Trawlers*, 71–81.
30. E. Ford, *Nation's Sea Fish Supply* (London, 1937), 11–12.
31. Jonsson, *Friends*, 40–41.
32. F.T. Christy and A. Scott, *The Commonwealth of Ocean Fisheries* (Baltimore, 1965), 156–60. See also Robinson, *Trawling*.

CHAPTER 9

Yachting in Britain, 1890–1960

Janet Cusack

'Yachting' may be defined as the use for pleasure of privately owned vessels, propelled by sail, or powered by steam, diesel or petrol engines. This maritime recreational activity, which comprised two principal modes, racing and cruising, developed significantly between 1890 and 1960. Not only was there a huge increase in the number of vessels deployed as yachts, but the size and cost of the average craft diminished. There were technical changes in yacht design, in the materials and methods used in yacht building, in the development of power units, and in the instrumentation available to yachtsmen. Changes also took place in the modes of yacht use and in the institutions and organisation of the sport, although the pace of social change was limited by some conservatism in the traditional yachting establishment. This chapter examines and attempts to explain the development of yachting in Britain between 1890 and 1960, focusing on the extent and character of the activity, and the economic, technical and social factors which conditioned the pace and pattern of its growth.

The Extent and Character of Yachting, 1890–1960

While a precise calculation of the total number of yachts active in Britain between 1890 and 1960 is not attainable due to the inadequacy of primary source materials, sufficient data exist to provide an indication of the size and composition of the British yachting 'fleet'. Lloyd's Register of Yachts, for instance, offers a wealth of information on pleasure boats of 1 ton or more, although not all yachts were listed. As Table 9.1 shows, the number of yachts entered in the register rose from 3,087 to 3,889 between 1890 and 1914, an increase of some 26 per cent. This expansion was due entirely to the

167

growth of steam yachting, which experienced an increase from 735 to 1,584 vessels between 1890 and 1914, though in 1914 some 1,240 of

Table 9.1: The number, Construction and Tonnage of Yachts Owned in the United Kingdom, 1890–1914

	1890	1895	1900	1905	1910	1914
Steam yachts						
Iron, steel or composite (no.)	287	361	389	394	376	344
Average tonnage	194	208	200	228	255	268
Wood (no.)	448	515	491	527	841	1,240
Average tonnage	40	36	37	32	20	19
Total	735	876	880	921	1,217	1,584
Sailing yachts						
Iron, steel or composite (no.)	85	113	28	112	80	52
Average tonnage	65	67	76	77	91	140
Wood (no.)	2,267	2,752	2,935	2,865	2,643	2,253
Average tonnage	24	19	17	17	15	13
Total (no.)	2,352	2,865	3,063	2,977	2,723	2,305
Grand total (no.)	3,087	3,741	3,943	3,898	3,940	3,889

Source: *Lloyd's Registers of Yachts*, 1890–1914.

these vessels, or 78 per cent, were wooden-hulled, while their average size was just 19 tons. In contrast, the population of sailing yachts increased during the 1890s before contracting from 3,063 to 2,305 vessels between 1900 and 1914, the vast majority being wooden-hulled. The average size of wooden sailing yachts also diminished from 40 tons in 1890 to 13 tons in 1914. Yachting continued to expand in the interwar years. By 1930, as Table 9.2 shows, nearly 7,000 yachts were listed in *Lloyd's Register of Yachts*, the figure rising to 8,062 in 1939, of which 65 per cent were under 15 tons, and 47 per cent under 10 tons. The Second World War interrupted this upward trend, with the yacht fleet declining to 7,501 vessels in 1950, when expansion commenced once again. With nearly 9,000 vessels detailed in *Lloyd's Register*, yachting activity reached an unprecedented level in 1960, though over 66 per cent of these craft were of 14 tons or less. At the other end of the spectrum, there was a fall in the number of yachts of 200 tons and above, from 349, or 5 per cent, in 1930, to just 97, 1 per cent of the total in 1960.

Such statistics neglect a major component of British yachting, the sailing and racing of small open day boats and centre-board dinghies. Data on these vessels, again, is incomplete. Some racing dinghies were listed in the often inaccessible records of clubs, class associations, or individual boatyards and traders, while many owners of small yachts and dinghies neither belonged to a club, nor entered their craft on a register. However, there is clear evidence that this facet of the yachting world expanded between 1890 and 1914. For instance, in 1885 *Hunt's Universal Yacht List* listed 58 major yacht clubs and 24 clubs formed to race small boats. In 1913 *Lloyd's Register of Yachts* recorded 53 major yacht clubs and 90 small yacht and sailing clubs. Some geographical areas set up specialist organisations to co-ordinate small boat racing, an example being the West of England Conference, established in 1890 with a membership of eight sailing clubs, which had expanded to a membership of 20 clubs by 1899.[1]

Table 9.2: The Size of Yachts Entered in *Lloyd's Registers of Yachts*, 1930–1960

Tonnage	1930	1935	1939	1947	1950	1955	1960
400+	188	198	158	88	52	36	36
200–399	161	168	128	85	64	64	61
100–199	206	223	223	233	239	264	216
50–99	396	457	353	495	456	431	401
30–49	502	522	621	593	565	632	655
20–29	527	511	660	692	588	735	771
15–19	520	540	643	625	598	1,100	884
10–14	1,127	1,230	1,489	1,472	1,416	1,867	2,069
0–9	3,303	3,138	3,782	3,536	3,523	3,592	3,810
Totals	6,930	6,987	8,057	7,819	7,501	8,721	8,903

Source: *Lloyd's Registers of Yachts*, 1930–1960.

Before 1914 the Royal Yachting Association, the co-ordinating body of British yacht racing, showed little interest in dinghy sailing. However, between the wars it not only accepted, but positively encouraged the activity. The Association promoted the establishment of some national one-design classes, and sponsored high-profile events such as the race for the Prince of Wales Cup, held for the National 12' class in 1927. No reliable estimate of dinghy numbers can be made for the years between 1919 and 1939. In contrast, there is strong evidence that the number of boat owners and sailing clubs increased between 1945 and 1960. Membership of the Royal Yachting Association rose from 250 recognised clubs in 1945 to 715 in 1955, 831 in 1958, and 978 in 1960, while the number of individual members increased from 235 in 1945 to 5,212 in 1958, and 9,703 in 1960. However, the Association estimated in 1958 that '220,000 people mess about in boats in Britain', so that its membership only included 2.5 per cent of the total of amateur sailors.[2] Some confirmation of these trends can be found in *Lloyd's Register of Yachts*. For example, as Table 9.3 shows, the number of sailing dinghies registered for racing in selected national and international classes increased greatly between 1950 and 1960. While the 'Firefly' and 'Merlin Rocket' classes virtually doubled in number in each five-year period, the most impressive growth was that of the 'Enterprise', which was only launched in 1955 but by 1960 extended to 3,325 registered vessels.

Table 9.3: The Number of Sailing Dinghies in Some National and International Racing Classes, 1950–60

	1950	1955	1960
National Firefly	698	1,398	2,441
National 18'	100	183	229
Merlin Rocket	-	577	1,017
National 12'	809	1,277	1,780
International 14'	570	653	715
Enterprise	-	-	3,325

Source: *Lloyd's Registers of Yachts*, 1950, 1955, 1960.

In terms of its composition, Britain's yacht population can be divided into racing and cruising vessels. While these principal modes of yachting became more clearly differentiated during the 1890–1960 era, both developed along similar lines. In each mode, for instance, there was a decline in the relative significance of the larger, more expensive vessel, as the number of yachts and owners increased through the period. Before the First World War, large racing vessels were prominent in the yacht fleet: fine examples of such vessels were the *Britannia* (221 tons), owned by the Prince of Wales, from 1893; the *Thistle*, later the *Meteor* (170 tons), built in 1887 and owned first by James Bell, and later by the German Emperor; a second *Meteor* (236 tons), built in 1895 for the Emperor; Lord Dunraven's *Valkyrie I, II*, and *III* (94, 220 and 263 tons), built between

1893 and 1895; and the 130-ton *Shamrocks* built by Sir Thomas Lipton in 1899, 1901 and 1903. Some very large yachts, including the America's Cup challengers *Shamrock IV* and *V*, built in 1920 and 1930, the 143-ton *Endeavour I* and the 163-ton *Endeavour II*, built in 1934 and 1937, were still produced between the two wars. In contrast, the major racing yachts of the post-1945 era were fewer in number, and much less lavish than their predecessors. For example, the *Endeavour II*, which challenged for the America's Cup in 1937, had a length overall of 136 feet, was 163 tons, and had a sail area of 7,543 square feet. In contrast, the 1958 challenger, the *Sceptre*, was only 30 tons, 69 feet overall, and had a sail area of 1,832 square feet.

However, although the average size of major racing craft decreased, a territorial change took place after 1945 in their racing. Most pre-1939 large class racing, including that for the America's Cup, was essentially day-sailing, where races started and finished on the same day, usually in sheltered waters. Much postwar racing used offshore courses and races often lasted for a week or more. Ocean racing was not, of course, new in 1945. For instance, a transatlantic race took place as early as 1866, the Fastnet Race was started in 1925, and the Little Ship Club organised North Sea races for both sail and motor yachts in the 1930s. However, offshore and ocean racing increased after 1945. The Fastnet Race continued, the Transatlantic Race was added in 1958, and much yacht racing has since become fully international, and under the control of the International Yacht Racing Union.[3]

British yachtsmen, under sail and steam, cruised world-wide throughout the period 1890–1960. Between 1890 and 1914, numerous large steam yachts were active, some recording notable cruising feats. For instance, between 1891 and 1905 the steam yacht *Santa Maria* (340 tons), owned by Lord Llangatock, cruised a total of 40,544 miles, to destinations which varied from Sevastopol to the North Cape. This was bettered by Mrs Watney, whose steam yacht *Palatine* (350 tons) visited Denmark, Norway, St Petersburg, the Scilly Islands and Constantinople, in the course of completing some 49,153 miles between 1889 and 1902. Mrs Watney noted with satisfaction in her journal in 1905 that she had cruised 'a mileage [that] is about <u>twice</u> round the world'. These yachts were manned by large paid crews, with Lord Llangatock engaging a crew of 16, while Mrs Watney employed 24 men.[4] Substantial cruising yachts were, like large racing yachts, still a noted part of the yacht fleet before 1939. For instance, the Duke of Westminster built a four-masted 1,195-ton schooner, the *Flying Cloud,* in 1923 for cruising, and in the interwar

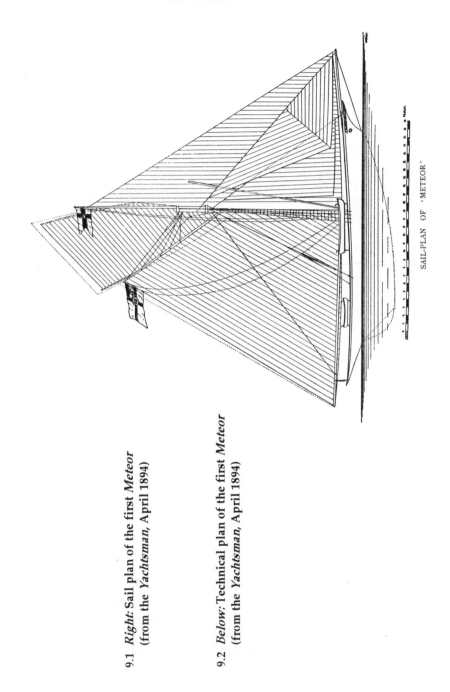

SAIL-PLAN OF 'METEOR'

9.1 *Right:* Sail plan of the first *Meteor* (from the *Yachtsman*, April 1894)

9.2 *Below:* Technical plan of the first *Meteor* (from the *Yachtsman*, April 1894)

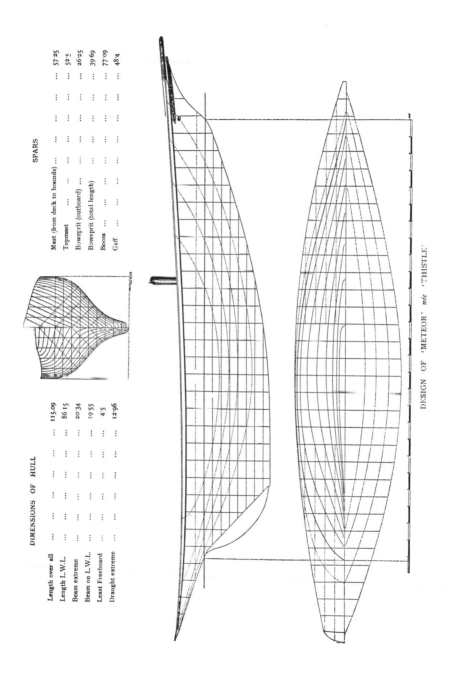

DIMENSIONS OF HULL

Length over all	115·09
Length L.W.L.	86·15
Beam extreme	20·34
Beam on L.W.L.	19·55
Least Freeboard	4·5
Draught extreme	12·96

SPARS

Mast (from deck to hounds)	57·25
Topmast	52·5
Bowsprit (outboard)	26·25
Bowsprit (total length)	39·69
Boom	77·09
Gaff	48·4

DESIGN OF 'METEOR' *née* 'THISTLE'

173

years some large steam yachts such as the *Xarifa II* (731 tons), built by J.S. White of Cowes for R.M. Singer, and the *Nahlin*, later used by King Edward VIII and Mrs Simpson for Mediterranean cruising, were still constructed. But they were increasingly being supplanted by motor cruisers, while internal combustion engines were also installed as auxiliaries in sailing cruisers, some of which were large, as in the case of the 611-ton barque *Belem*.[5]

However, as the evidence presented in Tables 9.1, 9.2 and 9.3 indicates, the principal growth points in British yachting during the 1890–1960 period were located in the smaller classes of vessel. This trend was forecast as early as 1892 when Lord Dunraven suggested that 'racing in the large classes is dead', and that that the future would see a move to small racing vessels, linked to a preference for steam cruising. He considered that if a yacht was wanted solely for racing, small classes were attractive since: 'The cost is infinitely less and the proportion of prize money to expenses far greater. The sport to be gained in proportion to expenses and trouble is much greater also.' Regatta programmes continued to offer some races for yachts of 15, 20, 40 tons or larger in the years between 1890 and 1960, but an increasing number of races were for smaller craft, and amateur crews.[6]

An important aspect of this expansion of small classes was the introduction in the 1890s of one-design class racing. This involved competition between fleets of identical yachts built on strictly regulated lines, a system adopted to prevent the domination of small boat racing by those whose depth of purse enabled them to build new yachts at frequent intervals with radical changes of design. One-design classes, usually designed to suit specific conditions, were sponsored and adopted by yacht or sailing clubs, so that a wide variety of local racing classes developed in British waters by 1914, examples being the 'Solent One-Design' class, which had 20 members by 1899, the 'Yorkshire One-Design' (1897) and the 'Broads One-Design' (1900). Between the wars a number of national classes were introduced, an example being the 'National 12'. In the post-1945 era, small boat racing was further stimulated by the availability of one-design dinghies sold in kit form for home assembly. As Table 9.4 indicates, these vessels varied in size and price from the 10-foot 'Cadet', where a £30 kit could build a hull normally costing £85, to craft such as the 16-foot 'Hornet', where home construction saved £116. The quality of boats built from these kits depended, of course, on the skills of the builder, but the construction was sufficiently simple for an amateur with limited practical skill to produce a reasonable hull.[7] While some kit boats raced with considerable success, many, particularly in the 'Heron' and 'G.P.14' classes, became family cruisers.

Table 9.4: Dinghies Sponsored by the *Yachting World* between 1945 and 1954

	Length (feet)	Sail area (sq. feet)	Boat	Price (£) Kit of parts	Sails
Cadet	10½	55	85	30	28
Heron	11	70	75	30	20
G.P.14	14	102	120	60	37
Hornet	16	121	176	60	37

Source: *Yachting World*, 106 (1954), 215.

Comparatively modest cruising vessels, which varied greatly in size, design and origin, also became an increasingly important facet of the yacht fleet as the twentieth century progressed. Some cruisers were converted from other marine functions, or were second-hand pleasure boats. Amongst the used vessels advertised for sale in 1926, for instance, were an 80-foot ex-Admiralty motor launch, and, for inshore cruising, a 26-foot, two-berth 'smart cabin motor boat'. Fifty Brixham sailing trawlers were sold as yachts between 1911 and 1938, while in 1919 Maurice Griffiths bought the 2-ton sloop *Dabchick*, 'a converted ship's boat of uncertain age, 17 feet long'. Many amateur sailors used 'pocket cruisers', designed for inshore or Channel sailing, crewed by family or friends. British examples here were the range of small sailing, auxiliary and motor cruisers, ranging from 2 to 30 tons, advertised by David Hillyard of Littlehampton in 1929, while some small cruisers were imported, notably from Sweden and Finland.[8]

The equipment in some 'pocket cruisers' was very limited, as demonstrated by a 1938 inventory published by Francis Cooke, who wrote extensively on small boat cruising in the 1930s. No electrical instruments were listed, except a torch worked by dry batteries, and there were no signal lamps, flags, or even emergency rockets. Navigation was by compass, with a gimballed candlestick for night use, and there was a lead and line, but no trailing log. It is interesting that Cooke's recommended equipment in 1938 was apparently more sparse than that listed in 1895 by the *Yachtsman's Handy Book*. This described the use of compass, patent log, lead and line, and artificial horizon, and gave instruction in the use of rockets, flag signals, Morse and semaphore. Cooke suggested, however, that the yachtsman should carry binoculars and, if there was sufficient room, a wireless receiver to obtain weather forecasts, and enable 'one to keep in touch with the news of the day, to say nothing of its entertainment value'. Paid crew for small cruisers were deemed unnecessary by Cooke. 'A paid hand is an expensive luxury ... [at] £3 per week, and often expects the owner to find him in food as well.' He did suggest, however, that owners should employ a boat husband, to care for the boat at moorings, for about 3 shillings per week.[9]

Other yachtsmen preferred to recruit crew, though it became common for owners to enlist amateur crew who might be willing to contribute to the expenses of a voyage. Thus, in 1939, the owner of the *Seaplane*, a converted Brixham ketch, advertised that he was planning a three-year cruise to make 35 mm films and thereby 'get away from Nazis, newspapers, neon lights, neighbours and other nuisances'; to assist in this scheme he required a 'tough guy not more than 28 years of age and able to contribute £3 a week to the common store'. The Little Ship Club provided a service for yachtsmen in that it put potential amateur crews in touch with those planning yachting trips, though some owners and crews chose to advertise. In 1927, for instance, one hopeful traveller described himself as

> an Englishman, Public School, aged 36, good sailor, wishes passage, cruising yacht, any destination, Feb. to June 1927, in exchange for free services as navigator and general help. Thorough knowledge of pilotage, signalling, usual social accomplishments.[10]

After the Second World War the size of the average cruiser tended to contract still further, while very few yachtsmen now employed paid crew. There were, however, signs of the design and technical improvements that had taken place since the days of Francis Cooke. Most cruisers were still built of wood, but this was now often ply, and many were powered by two-stroke outboard engines rather than inboard units. A 1963 guide-book for small boat owners discussed the merits of moulded and hard-chine plywood boats, self-draining cockpits, bilge keels, and small cruising catamarans. Instructions were given on the use of rockets, and on road trailing, while inboard or outboard auxiliary engines were taken for granted, and the recommended equipment included personal life-lines, fire extinguishers and life jackets, but still, at this date, no ship-to-shore radio.[11]

Possibly the most interesting development in postwar cruising was that, just as racing moved offshore, there was considerable expansion of long-distance cruising undertaken single-handed or by family teams in small boats. This was not, of course, completely new. For instance, Frank Knight with a small crew took the *Falcon* to the River Plate in 1880 and Slocum went round the world in 1895–8. After 1950, however, long-distance voyages increased in number, examples being those of Bill Tillman in 1955, and the Smeeton family in the *Hang*, who were wrecked off South America in 1957. Tom and Anne Worth in the early 1950s took their 43-foot yacht the *Beyond* via Panama to New Zealand, in 1952 the Hiscocks made a three-year circumnavigation in the *Wanderer III*, and Anne Davidson crossed the Atlantic in the 23-foot sloop *Felicity Ann* in the same year.[12]

If the 1890–1960 period witnessed changes in the extent of yachting activity and developments in the design, power units, construction and equipment of yachts, the social milieu in which much yachting was conducted altered only slightly, the long-established 'Royal' clubs continuing to dominate the sport. This reflected and, in turn, sustained the social and gender exclusivity which marked yachting before 1960. In the late nineteenth century yachting and membership of the major yacht clubs was essentially the province of the rich, well-to-do and socially well connected. These clubs were influential male organisations comprising yacht owners and their social peers, elected by ballot. For example, in 1900 the list of the Royal Western Yacht Club of England, at Plymouth, the senior and most socially distinguished yacht club in South Devon, comprised 388 members, of whom 56 owned yachts. Among those listed were two earls; three lords; one viscount; six baronets; two knights; seven honourables; 82 army officers, including 14 generals and 18 colonels; 46 Royal Navy officers, including 12 admirals; seven doctors; six clergy; five barristers, including two judges; two MPs; three engineers; and a master of foxhounds. The membership of established and influential clubs tended to be stable and conservative, not only in social and economic patterns of recruitment, but in long individual memberships. For instance, the 1928 list of the Royal Western Yacht Club, Plymouth, included the Senior Member, elected in 1864, and 57 others elected before 1900, while the Royal Southwestern Yacht Club in 1937 still had one foundation member from 1890, and 22 elected before 1914.[13]

Wealthy businessmen and manufacturers also resorted to yachting, as demonstrated by the membership lists of the three major South Devon Royal Yacht Clubs, at Plymouth, Dartmouth and Torquay, between 1890 and 1914. These included William Garfit MP, director of the Capital and Counties Bank; Edward Baring, later Lord Revelstoke, also a banker; Sir Donald Currie, the head of the Castle Shipping Line, and Sir William Pearce, the Clyde shipbuilder. Manufacturing money was represented by the sons of Isaac Merill Singer, inventor of the Singer sewing machine, who settled at Paignton and took out British nationality in 1901; commerce by Frank C. Capel of J. Capel and Co. of London; and building by Sir Thomas Freake, whose father had built Grosvenor Square and much of South Kensington. South Devon yachting was, in fact, typical of the national yachting establishment in that industrial and business fortunes were not only socially acceptable, but played a vital role, as it was increasingly only commercial and manufacturing fortunes that were capable of financing major projects such as challenges for the America's Cup. For instance, James Bell, who challenged with the *Thistle* in 1887, was a Glasgow merchant at the head of a syndicate. From 1899 to 1930 five challenges were mounted by the grocer, Sir Thomas Lipton, and the 1934 and 1937 challenges were mounted by T.O.M. Sopwith, whose fortune was based on aviation.[14]

The increase in the numbers of smaller and cheaper yachts did not significantly change the social composition of the major clubs between 1890 and 1914. At the same time, new yacht and sailing clubs formed to cater specifically for small boat racing often had a similarly restricted social spectrum and ethos among their members like the traditional clubs. For example, Salcombe Yacht Club, founded in 1894 as a small boat club, had the aim of 'not only fostering sailing in the vicinity of Salcombe ... but creating in Salcombe something which the town lacked, a social meeting place for gentlemen'. Moreover, some yachtsmen were members of both types of club. Accordingly, in the 1890s the Torbay Sailing Club was largely composed of members of private means, and the committee in 1894 consisted of one general, two lieutenant-colonels, and three civilians, and included the honorary secretary and two committee members of the Royal Dart Yacht Club. However, there was a slight expansion of the social spectrum of members, as some boat-builders and a few wealthy local tradesmen joined. The Teign Corinthian Sailing Club had a rather wider membership, and in 1897 the club list included doctors, brewers, solicitors, military officers, an auctioneer, a sanitary inspector, an architect, and the local income tax collector.[15] Working-class participation in yachting was rare, and in fact many club rules specifically excluded manual workers. In 1894 the Royal Yachting Association adopted a policy of 'recognition' of yacht and sailing clubs, 'organised by yacht owners for the promotion of properly conducted yacht matches, and which do not enrol mechanics and labourers as members'. Similarly, the 1899 rules of the Royal Plymouth Corinthian Yacht Club excluded 'any artisan, handicraftsman, or other similar person in the habit of working for wages'.[16]

The British yacht club system changed little between the two wars. It is true that some simpler clubs were started. For example, at Salcombe, the Salcombe Yacht Club survived as a 'gentlemen's club', but a second group, the Salcombe Sailing Club, was formed in 1922 to race small boats, and catered for 'a younger element, male and female, and the local boat-builders, who wanted a club of their own formed simply to provide facilities and organisation for racing'.[17] However, most established yacht clubs maintained their customs, traditions and rituals, and had no wish or appetite for social change. This is demonstrated by the reluctant reaction of many traditional and some new yacht clubs to female aspirants to membership. Women, of course, had sailed as passengers and on family yachts from the very early days of yachting. Some became yacht owners, one example being Mrs Yorke, who cruised her steamers *Garland II* and *Garland III* from the Mediterranean to the Norwegian fiords in the early twentieth century. In the 1880s and 1890s some ladies wished to take out the club memberships which would provide the cruising privileges and access to racing programmes enjoyed by male club members. A few of these women were allowed to race, although many clubs restricted them to 'Ladies Races', organised as social events for the relatives of members, and separate from the normal racing programme. A very few women, examples in Devon being Miss Tew of the Dart Boat Sailing Club, and Miss Carus Wilson, later Mrs Morgan Giles, became well-known dinghy sailors, competing on equal terms with men, well before 1914. Progress towards full club membership was slow both before and after the two wars. Some clubs admitted women members, though often at first on restricted terms without voting rights, and grudging access only to limited areas of the club house. For instance, the Salcombe Yacht Club, which in the 1890s refused to allow women (or dogs) into the clubhouse, admitted the female companions of members and visiting yachtsmen to a lounge in the entrance hall in 1939, and gave full membership to women in 1947.

Women were declared ineligible for the General Committee in 1948, but a woman became Hon. Sailing Secretary between 1952 and 1964. The Royal Yacht Squadron opened changing rooms for ladies only in 1964, and a Lady Associate membership was introduced in 1969. Although some women raced with considerable success, national and local prejudice often refused official recognition of their skill. Thus Helen Pritchard, one of the first three ladies accepted by the Royal Dart Yacht Club to full membership in 1936, established herself as a skilled helm in the 1930s. Her obituary in the Royal Dart Yacht Club Newsheet noted that when in 1948 she reached the final selection trials in the Dragon class for the Olympic Games, 'Women's Lib had not penetrated the world of sailing and, as a lady, it was not the done thing to compete, and she was allowed to go no further'. By 1955, however, Helen Pritchard was allowed to enter, and had outstanding success in the National Firefly Championships.[18]

The Development of Yachting: Causal Factors

Various factors interacted to condition the pace and pattern of change in British yachting. Perhaps the most influential of these forces was economic. At the macro level, yachting, as a facet of the leisure market, was generally stimulated by improvements in the standard of living of the British population during the 1890–1960 period. With rising real earnings, and a growth in the number of white-collar workers from 18.7 per cent of the total occupied population in 1911 to 35.8 per cent in 1961,[19] people had more money to spend on recreational activities such as yachting as the twentieth century progressed. While this broad influence underpinned the growth in demand for yachts and yachting, micro-economic factors improved the supply side of the market. Before the First World War, both racing and cruising were largely the preserve of the wealthy. For instance, in 1894 Sir Edward Sullivan analysed the crew costs of 'a modern racing yacht' of about 150–170 tons, with a crew of 50 men. He considered that a successful racing yacht would 'easily knock a hole in £1,000 for racing wages alone, to say nothing of the cost of spars and sails and gear etc.'. Sir Edward did add: 'Of course, in comparison with keeping a pack of hounds, or a deer forest, or a good grouse moor, or to pheasant preserving on a very large scale, the expense of yacht racing even at its worst is modest'. Racing at the highest national and international level, of course, continued to be expensive in the twentieth century. It has been noted above that many large racing yachts were supported between 1890 and 1939 by wealthy businessmen and manufacturers, but after 1945 syndicates funded much large class racing. Thus the *Sceptre*, which challenged for the America's Cup in 1958, was owned by Hugh Goodson and a syndicate, and in 1955 the Royal Thames Yacht Club formed a syndicate of 234 members to build the 6-metre yacht, the *Royal Thames*, 'to carry the British flag in international events'. Sponsorship, the modern method of dealing with high racing costs, did not take place in public before 1960, but started in the 1960s in events such as single-handed transatlantic races, which were outside the jurisdiction of the International Yacht Racing Union, which forbade the painting of logos on yachts before 1964.[20]

At a more modest level, it was suggested in 1894 that a beginner in Solent racing should start with 'a second-hand 1-rater, costing from £50–80, such a boat being new would cost £100–£150'. The novice was advised to hire a 16-year-old boy as crew and boat husband, at a weekly wage of 16–20 shillings, supplemented by 'racing money' of 5s. for a first and 2s. 6d. for a second prize. The boy should also be provided with a suit of clothes, the property of the yacht. Slightly larger yachts were estimated to be more expensive, so that a new 2½-rater would cost £300, and need two paid hands, while a 5-rater could be purchased new for £500, complete with sails, and could be maintained for 20 weeks of the 1894 racing season for £100–£150, 'from which may be deducted the value of the prizes won, less entrance fees and racing money'. One-design racing craft were modestly priced throughout the period. Thus, in 1898, the Seabird, a 20-foot gunter-rigged ballasted centre-board sloop, cost £35, and in 1902 the 22-foot Belfast Fairies were built for £50. In 1936 the cost of the RYA-sponsored clinker-built National 12 dinghy was £45 complete, but that of the National 14 was £150, so that the latter became known as the 'rich man's' dinghy'.[21]

Like racing, cruising in the late nineteenth century could be expensive. Large steam yachts, in particular, gave their owners great opportunities for a display of personal wealth. Clyde-built steamers such as Mr Vanderbilt's *Valiant* (2,184 tons) were reported to cost 'considerably over £100,000', while the *Valhalla* (1,490 tons), barque-rigged, was estimated to have cost between £55,000 and £70,000. Yachts in this range were built at about £40 per ton. Steam yachts were always larger and more expensive than sailing vessels which offered equivalent accommodation for owner and guests, since space had to be found in the hull for engines, boilers, and fuel, and a crew which included engineers and stokers. The yacht designer

HILLYARD 2½ TON SAILING SLOOP, ACCOMMODATION AND SAIL PLAN

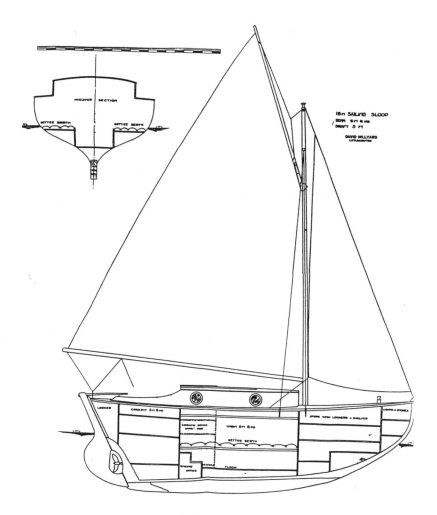

9.3 Sail plan and accommodation of a Hillyard sailing sloop (from Francis Cooke, *Weekend Yachting*, London, 1933)

Dixon Kemp estimated in 1890 that a sailing yacht of 200 tons would provide equivalent accommodation to a steam yacht of 300 tons. The 200-ton sailing yacht could be purchased for £7,000 and operated at an annual coast of £861, assuming a 16-week sailing season, while the steam yacht would cost £12,500, with an operating cost of £1,170. These figures include wages for seamen and engine room staff, but not for domestics.[22] In the interwar years many cruising yachts were less expensive. For example, second-hand steam yachts advertised in 1926 included a 450-ton vessel, with triple expansion engines, four large saloons and six staterooms at £4,000. For £450, however, a purchaser was offered a 37-ton steam yacht, having a large saloon with a piano, two exceptional staterooms, seven bedrooms, electric light, a 'nearly new boiler', and the yacht was claimed to be 'cheaper than a motor to run'. In fact, in the 1920s and 1930s steam engines for cruising lost popularity and the use of internal combustion engines increased. Second-hand motor yachts advertised in 1926 covered a wide price range, from a 102-ton twin-screw yacht, described as 'built for royalty, very little used', at £8,000, to small cabin cruisers and yachts fitted with outboard engines. Cruising yachtsmen in 1927 had a wide variety of outboard engines available for small yachts or tenders. Among others on the market were a range offered by Evinrude, including a ⅔ hp Utility engine at £34, a 2½ hp Sportwin (44 lb) at £36, a 4 hp Fastwin (49 lb) at 35 guineas., and an 8 hp Speeditwin (70 lb) at 45 guineas. The small 'pocket cruisers' described earlier were inexpensive. Francis Cooke listed the prices of some new 'pocket cruisers' in 1938. Among these was a Blackwater sloop, (2½ tons), at £155, a Hillyard yacht (2½ tons) at £125, and a 'Z' cruiser (4 tons), which cost £339 complete, including a 6½ hp engine. Cooke estimated that in 1935 a second-hand small cruiser could be purchased for about £70, that a mooring could cost as much as £5 a year, but was an unavoidable expense, and that yearly maintenance should not exceed £52 for a boat used all the year, and this could be reduced for an owner sailing only April to September.[23]

The growing use of smaller and cheaper yachts was facilitated by parallel developments in the availability, power, and expense of motor vehicles. Initially cars competed with yachting for the attention of the wealthy. In 1902, for example, King Edward VII remarked that he was 'afraid that all this motor car business is going to have a bad effect on yachting. Everyone is going mad on motoring, and apparently they enjoy it more than cruising in their yachts.' Four years later the report of the Torquay Regatta also considered that the poor attendance of large yachts was probably attributable to the great interest in, and expenditure on, motor cars as a form of recreation for the wealthy. The report concluded, however: 'Automobilism should not prove a lasting hobby'. Nevertheless, even though motor vehicles were rare, luxury articles in 1913, over 2,000,000 were privately owned in 1939, the figure rising to 2,258,000 in 1950, 3,526,000 in 1955 and 5,526,000 in 1960.[24] As cars became more popular, the increase in personal mobility they brought, together with the fact that postwar small family cars had sufficient power to tow a small boat, encouraged the use of small, light, de-mountable dinghies, which could be trailed or put on roof racks. The yachting journals responded to the fashion by providing instruction on trailers and towing techniques, For instance, in 1950 the *Yachtsman* suggested fuel economy measures, such as the carriage of two Fireflies on one trailer, and described how the 12-metre *Chuckles* had been towed from Itchen to the east coast, crossing central London, towed by two family cars linked by a steel bar. Trailers were available from several firms by 1950. By 1959 it was assumed that family cars could tow larger boats, and the 'Atalanta' cruiser was advertised as a dual-purpose investment. The 'Atalanta' had accommodation for four adults and two children, and drew only 18 inches with keels retracted, so could 'explore remote creeks and rivers'. It was also suggested that the yacht could be used on a trailer as a caravan. Cars and trailers were used by members of clubs and class associations to transport racing dinghies between regattas. It should be noted, however, that they also enabled much pleasure sailing to take place outside a club framework. Percy Blandford commented in 1963:

> One of the greatest changes in the boating world during the last ten years has been the emergence of the boat and trailer outfit which the motorist keeps at home and takes to the waterway of his choice ... a great many people now enjoy the sport and recreation without having a fixed base.[25]

The absence of a fixed base meant that, for many, yachting was a private family pursuit rather than a social activity.

Technological developments served to stimulate yachting activity throughout the 1890–1960 period. This was partly due to their role in increasing efficiency and cutting costs, but also because technical improvements, particularly in the field of communications, instrumentation, and weather protection, enhanced safety standards. While innovations in yacht construction were evident before the Second World War, such as the introduction of steel hulls during the 1880s, aluminium and other alloys in the 1890s, and the use of duralumin for masts in the 1930s,[26] the pace of development accelerated between 1945 and 1960. The majority of pre-1939 yachts of all sizes were built as individual items by craftsmen. However, the construction of the 'Redwing' in 1938 gave the builder Charles Nicholson of Gosport an opportunity to experiment with the assembly line production of 16 vessels. Many of the postwar developments in dinghy construction were made possible by advances in the use of waterproof glues and plywoods in aircraft production during the war, combined with the adoption of mass production. An early postwar innovation in boat-building was the use of plywood, both in sheet form for hard chine boats, and in moulded form. The *Yachting World* presented the concept of moulded ply yacht construction as a revolutionary American invention in 1945: '[This will] present yachtsmen with craft, from dinghies upward, which will prove to be a tremendous jump ahead of those planked on timbers ... boats will be developed of hitherto undreamed of performance'. Possibly the best known moulded ply dinghy was the Firefly, originally designed for the 1948 Olympic Games, and priced in 1946 at £65 plus purchase tax.[27]

By the late 1950s some synthetic boats were available, a foretaste of the innovation that was to transform yachting after 1960. For example, in 1957 a reinforced plastics cabin cruiser, 22 feet long, with an inboard engine, accommodation for four people, and a two-wheel trailer suitable for towing by a private car, was advertised for £1,350. Sails were improved in efficiency, and their care simplified, by the use of synthetic materials. In 1954 the *Yachtsman* printed an article by an employee of ICI on 'sailcloth made from terylene polyester fibre'. Readers were told that terylene sailcloth would be in very limited supply in 1954, more would be available in 1955, and it should be easily obtainable in 1956. Yachtsmen were quick to appreciate the potential of terylene sails, so that by 1955 it was reported that, 'any modern yacht race includes several competitors with terylene sails', and by 1960, according to the *Yachting World*, 'cotton is a thing of the past'. For yachtsmen's greater comfort, synthetic waterproofs were available in the 1950s, with yachtsmen's smocks and trousers advertised in 1955 as being flexible vinyl sheeting, resistant to wear, tension and tearing, transparent, but not flammable. In 1959 pvc dinghy suits were advertised, in yellow, white or red, at £4 19s. 6d. per suit.[28]

The introduction of electrical power was a further significant technical development, contributing to both comfort and safety.

Before 1914 some of the larger yachts were fitted with electrical equipment: accordingly, the the 83-foot steam yacht *Seagull*, built by Simpson, Strickland and Co. of Dartmouth in 1907, was equipped with an electrical system provided by engine and dynamo, and a battery of accumulators so that the boat could be lighted throughout by electric power, with a 5,000 candle-power searchlight on the bridge and electric heaters in the cabins.[29] Even so, electrical equipment was not widely deployed before 1939, although, as noted earlier, some yachtsmen carried a radio receiver. As with the development of yacht building materials, electrical equipment developed for wartime service use was gradually adapted and made available for yachtsmen. Thus in 1945 the *Yachting World* discussed Decca navigation, and possible future applications of Decca systems to yachts, and in 1946 reported that Marconi had published a booklet on 'wireless aids for navigation' which described equipment available from the company, including echo sounders and radar units. In 1952 Pye advertised the Dolphin Radio Telephone: 'To connect you to home and office, or any number on the G.P.O. system'. However, little equipment was on the market until the late 1950s, when electronic instruments became more common on yachts, although still expensive. A battery-operated echo-sounder was advertised in 1956, which was claimed to work between three feet and 45 fathoms, and cost £75. Moreover, an advertisement in 1957 offered radio navigation for small ships, using a Heron direction-finding aerial. The receiver used with the Heron was remarkable technically in that it was 'the first communication receiver in England to use transistors in place of valves—transistors are believed to be everlasting'. It is interesting to note that a *Yachtsman* article in 1959 on helicopter rescue assumed that yachtsmen in distress would radio for help, although transmitters were rarely included in contemporary equipment lists for small cruisers.[30]

While economic and technical factors underpinned the growth of yachting between the late nineteenth century and the 1960s, countervailing factors were also at work. The two wars may have accelerated the technical changes which impacted upon yachting, but they also had short-term negative effects. In both conflicts, yachting was stopped, at least in the Channel, and many of the larger steam yachts were given or requisitioned for military service. Some 37 yachts from the Royal Yacht Squadron alone served between 1914 and 1918, of which seven were lost, while in the Second World War 58 served with nine losses. Some yachts were relocated by war, bombed, or rotted while unused. According to Peter Heaton, 'half of all the racing yachts existing in British waters were acquired during the First World War by owners in Scandinavia, many more were immobilised, and many just derelict'. On the other hand, after 1945 a number of yachts came to British waters as war prizes, and some of these 'Windfall Yachts' were distributed to the Services yacht clubs by the Admiralty.[31]

Recovery after 1918 was fairly quick, although Maurice Griffiths, in 1919, claimed that the war had raised cruiser prices to unreasonable heights so that 'anything that had a cabin of sorts and could float of its own free will was a yacht and fetched a high price'. The occasion of this bitter complaint was the £36 required for the purchase of a second-hand 2-ton sloop, a sentiment echoed by Francis Cooke, who considered that 'in the good old days before the Great War everything was much cheaper than it is now'.[32] Yachting was much more seriously affected by the Second World War. Prices for yachts of any kind rocketed compared with those before 1939, and in early 1945 the *Yachting World* commented that, although the war was still being fought, the second-hand yacht market was very active:

> While I know that the demand is due to many yachtsmen not wanting to be without a boat when war ends, I wonder how much of this is due to speculative buying. I heard recently of a yacht which has changed hands three times during the last six months, more than doubling her original price in the process.[33]

Some yachtsmen resented these price rises bitterly, one complaining in 1945 that it would take £3,000 to replace his 36-foot motor cruiser, built for £1,000 in 1937. The cruiser had been a Dunkirk casualty, for which he had received only £900 in compensation. Racing revived in 1945 but builders were restricted in the size and number of vessels they could produce by shortages of building materials, and government restrictions which prevented the use of these scarce resources for pleasure craft construction. Owners who were able to obtain new racing boats had to be content with smaller vessels than before 1939. For example, in 1946, W.L. Stephenson, purchaser of the *Valsheda* (204 tons) from Camper and Nicholson in 1933, was fortunate to get a 7-ton Dragon class yacht. In the same year, the *Yachting World* claimed that building costs were 75 per cent higher than prewar, largely on account of the high wages being paid in the boatyards, the chief cause of high prices, while an imposition of 33⅓ per cent purchase tax on boats raised prices further. This burden was relaxed in mid-summer 1946, but in November it was announced that no more licences for the building of pleasure craft would be granted. After vociferous trade protests, there was some relaxation of these restrictions, in that permits were granted for the building of pleasure craft for export, while a supply of timber would be authorised if it appeared that a firm would be put out of business without it. Even so, the shortage of new boats drove second-hand yacht prices to a very high level. In addition to high purchase prices the operating costs of yachts increased after 1945. Maurice Griffiths reviewed typical annual running costs in 1946 and 1947, suggesting that a 7-ton yawl, fitted with an 8 hp engine, where the owner did his own work, should cost £90, including moorings and insurance, while £230 was needed for a 20-ton sloop with a similar engine, boatyard-maintained, and £120 for a 30-foot motor cruiser with a 12–24 hp engine, maintained by the owner.[34]

Cruising also started slowly after 1945. Yachtsmen faced such factors as government restrictions on yacht movements, residual minefields, fuel shortages, and, above all, the same building restrictions that constrained racing. Cruising was not simple in the immediate postwar years, even for those who could obtain an operational vessel. Cruising range was limited by fuel shortages. A petrol ration was introduced in 1945, ranging from 1.5 gallons per month for a 1–3 bhp engine to seven gallons per month for an engine over 17 bhp. Like the small petrol ration for private cars, this was withdrawn in 1947, so that it was difficult for owners both to reach yachting centres, and to leave harbour. Further, in 1947, foreign travel was banned. Limited foreign currency was available in 1950, and the *Yachting World* described the attractions of Holland as a cruising destination, in spite of the fact that yachtsmen were limited to £50 per person, plus £25 for the boat.[35]

The impact of the war and its aftermath was summed up by the *Yachtsman* in 1951:

> The shattering effect of [the war] was not at first appreciated, because many yachtsmen still had money made before the war, and hoped to begin again where they left off; others accumulated money during the war and had it to spend; no one realised that maintenance and building costs would increase as they have; most people hoped for a reduction in taxation ... [however] rearmament, overlong delayed [caused] us once more to tighten our belts. The large motor yacht has all but vanished; no more have been built; the big racing classes have also gone by the board

... The tendency generally has been increasingly towards smaller yachts.[36]

However, 1950 probably marked the end of the period of maximum difficulty, and, as shown in Table 9.2, the new expansion of yachting began. In 1951, according to a report on Cowes week: 'This year the Royal Yacht Squadron was almost up to its prewar splendour, and the starting guns were responded to by classes of yachts which, if smaller than in the prewar days, were nevertheless bigger than in any year since the war'.[37]

Conclusion

In the years between 1890 and 1960 yachting was revolutionised. The construction, materials, size, design and power units of yachts changed, as did the navigational and personal equipment available to yachtsmen. The numbers of yachts increased, as did the number and types of yacht club. Both racing and cruising developed, and dinghy sailing, from a minority element of the sport in 1890, predominated in the 1950s. Paid crews virtually vanished, and women gained some, often begrudged, status in yacht clubs. However, yachting, particularly in the well-established clubs, retained a strong continuity of tradition and social practice, and despite the growth in yachting in the midst of the massive economic, social and technological changes of the era, British club yachting still retained many essentially Edwardian trappings and attitudes through the 1890–1960 period. The end of this era, in which wood construction had predominated, saw the start of the present-day era of the mass-produced synthetic hull. It is interesting that the yachting journals in 1960 apparently did not anticipate the massive expansion in yacht numbers which would arise from the use of synthetics, the strain which this growth would put upon the provision of yacht moorings, and the consequent need to devise alternative systems. An editorial in the *Yachtsman* in 1960 commented upon a proposal to establish a marina at Cowes, on the lines of the costly establishment at Bahia, Florida. The journal denied the suitability of marinas for England, 'with our tides and rather variable climate, the provision of suitable facilities would be even more expensive', and considered that English marinas should never be established, as the berthing cost to yachtsmen would be prohibitive.[38]

NOTES

1. *Hunt's Universal Yacht List,* 1885; *Lloyd's Register of Yachts,* 1913; Gordon Davis, *Dartmouth Royal Regatta: From 1834 to the Present* (Dartmouth, 1987), 74–5; H.C. Folkard, *The Sailing Boat* (5th Edn, London, 1901) 247–52.

2. Gordon Fairley, *Minute By Minute: The Story of the Royal Yachting Association, 1875–1982* (Shaftesbury, 1983) 64–9, 81–2, 121–31.

3. Ian Dear, *The America's Cup* (London, 1980), 178–82; Robin Knox-Johnston, *History of Yachting* (Oxford, 1990), 108–92; D. Rayner and Alan Wykes, *The Great Yacht Race* (London, 1966); J.J. Quill, 'North Sea Cruiser Race', *Journal of the Little Ship Club,* 13 (1938–9), 29–30.

4. Gwent Record Office, Cwmbran, Rolls Collection, F648, exercise book containing the mileage record of the Steam Yacht *Santa Maria,* 1891–1905; F62.2, Seaman's wages account; Devon Record Office, Exeter, 2065 Madd/F309, Log of steam yacht *Palatine.* This is not the official ship's log, but a journal kept for the owner, Mrs Watney, by her secretary, Edgar Bailsa, and annotated by Mrs Watney.

5. Ian Dear, *The Royal Yacht Squadron, 1815–1985* (London, 1985) 115–61; David Couling, *Steam Yachts* (London, 1980) 110–13.

6. Royal Yacht Squadron Library, Cowes, Lord Dunraven, 'The Changed Character of Yacht Racing', *North American Review,* cited by *Hants Advertiser,* 14 December 1892, in Castle Yacht Club Scrap Book, 75; see, for example, *Torquay Directory,* 17 August. 1887, programme of Royal Torbay Yacht Club Regatta; 27 August 1890, report of Torbay Royal Regatta; Davis, *Dartmouth Royal Regatta,* Figures 10–12, being analyses of yacht entries in Dartmouth Royal Regatta, 1860–1986.

7. Jack Coote, *Classic One-designs* (Shrewsbury, 1994), 7–8, 16, 23; Comments on kits from author's personal experience.

8. *Yacht Sales and Charters,* 2 (1926–7), 25; 1 (1925–6) 126, 80; Adrian Small, Brixham, Register of Brixham Fishing Smacks, unpublished; Maurice Griffiths, *Magic of the Swatchways* (London, 1932), 14; David Hillyard, Yacht, Launch and Boat builder, Littlehampton, *Catalogue for Shipping Exhibition, Olympia, 1929; Journal of the Little Ship Club,* 13 (1938–9) 39, 67, 12, 165.

9. Francis B. Cooke, *Pocket Cruisers* (London, 1938), 404; and *Cruising Hints* (London, 1935), 404, 24; W.H. Rosser, *The Yachtsman's Handy Book for Sea Use* (London 1895).

10. *Journal of the Little Ship Club,* 13 (1938–9), 96; *Yacht Sails and Charters,* 2 (1926–7), 97.

11. D. Sleightholme, *Pocket Cruisers: A New Approach* (London, 1963).

12. Johnson, *Encyclopaedia,* 31, 41, 36; Eric Hiscock, *Cruising under Sail* (London, 1981), 200–05; Anne Davidson, *My Ship is so Small* (London, 1957).

13. Royal Western Yacht Club of England, Plymouth, membership lists, 1900, 1928; Royal South Western Yacht Club, membership list, 1937; *Hunt's Universal Yacht Lists*, 1890–1914.

14. Compiled by *The Yachtsman, British Yachts and Yachtsmen* (1907), 430; Ivor Smart, *Dartmouth Industry and Banking: The Story from 1795 to 1925* (London, 1995), 28; *Yacht Racing Calendar and Review*, 18 December 1888; Percy Russell, *Dartmouth: A History of the Port and Town* (Dartmouth, 1982), 159; *Brixham Guardian*, 31 July 1902; Ray Freeman, *The Story of Warfleet* (Dartmouth, 1993), 51; Dear, *America's Cup*, 178–80.

15. Sonia F.G. Parkinson, *Salcombe Yacht Club: The First Hundred Years* (Salcombe, 1995), 5; Torbay Sailing Club, membership list, 1894; Teign Corinthian Yacht Club, subscription list, 1897.

16. Dixon Kemp, 1894, cited by Roger Ryan, *A History of the West Lancashire Yacht Club: 1894–1990* (Preston, 1993), 3; Royal Plymouth Corinthian Yacht Club, Minute Book, Annual General Meeting, 10 March 1899.

17. Parkinson, *Salcombe Yacht Club*, 15.

18. Marquess of Ailsa, 'Some Prominent Yachtsmen' in *The Sportsman: British Sports and Sportsmen* (London, 1916), 187–336; see, for example, Royal Plymouth Corinthian Yacht Club, Minute Books, arrangements for Ladies Races, 1890–1905, newspaper reports of yacht racing in South Devon, 1891–1911; Parkinson, *Salcombe Yacht Club*, 26–7; Dear, *Royal Yacht Squadron*, 100; Obituary of Miss Helen Pritchard, Royal Dart Yacht Club newsletter, September 1995, 2.

19. Chris Cook and John Stevenson, *The Longman Handbook of Modern British History* (London, 1988), 155.

20. Sir Edward Sullivan, 'Introduction', in Duke of Beaufort and Alfred E.T. Watson (eds.), *Yachting* (London, 1894), 1–17; Dear, *America's Cup*, 182; Douglas Phillips-Burt, *The Cumberland Fleet: Two Hundred Years of Yachting, 1775–1975* (London, 1978), 134–5; Knox-Johnston, *History of Yachting*, 129.

21. 'Thalassa', 'Small Yacht Racing on the Solent', in Beaufort and Watson, (eds.), *Yachting*, 222–85, 278, 285; J.H. Coote, 'One-design Dinghy Racing', in BBC, *Under Sail* (London, 1986), 102–28; Fairley, *Minute by Minute*, 87.

22. *Torquay Times*, 3 June 1898; John Leather, (ed.), *Dixon Kemp's Manual of Yacht and Boat Sailing* (Southampton, 1988), 459.

23. *Yacht Sales and Charters*, 2 (1926–7), 25; 3 (1927–8), 561; Cooke, *Cruising Hints*, 23–4, 42; Cooke, *Pocket Cruisers*, 23, 100–1.

24. J.B. Atkins, *Further Memorials of the Royal Yacht Squadron* (London, 1939), 27; *Torquay Times*, 31 August 1906; Francois Bederida, *A Social History of England, 1851–1875* (London, 1979), 180; Cook and Stevenson, *Longman Handbook*, 22.

25. *Yachtsman*, 104 (1950), 67–76, 210–12; 113 (1959), 67–76; Percy Blandford, *Tackle Trailer Boating This Way* (London, 1963), note on dust jacket.

26. Leather (ed.), *Dixon Kemp's Manual*, 487; *Marine Engineer*, 1 May 1888; Dear, *America's Cup*, 102.

27. Fairley, *Minute by Minute*, 94, 99; *Yachting World*, 97 (1945), 200–1.

28. *Yachtsman*, 111 (1957), 51; 113 (1959), 51, 113; 108 (1954), 83–7; 109 (1955), 69–75; *Yachting World Annual* (1960), 7.

29. Steam Boat Association, *Catalogue of Simpson, Strickland and Co., Dartmouth*, 1907; Brixham Museum, A/SS 2427, Specification of the *Seagull*, built for H. Loeffler, 1907.

30. *Yachting World*, 97 (1945); 98 (1946), 255; *Yachting World Annual*, (1951–2), 64; *Yachtsman*, 110 (1956), 105; 111 (1957), 64; 113 (1959), 64–6.

31. Dear, *Royal Yacht Squadron*, 159–87; Peter Heaton, *Yachting: A History* (London, 1955), 204, 234.

32. Griffiths, *Swatchways*, 14; Cooke, *Cruising Hints*, 23.

33. *Yachting World*, 97 (1945), 92.

34. *Yachting World*, 97 (1945), 62; 98 (1946), 402; William Collier, University of Liverpool, Camper and Nicholson Yard List; Letters from Charles Nicholson to Redwing Association, March 1946; *Yachtsman*, 105 (1950); Eric C. Hiscock, (ed.), *The Yachting Year* II (London, 1947–8), 129; Maurice Griffiths, *Post-War Yachting* (London, 1948).

35. *Yachting World*, 97 (1945), 240; 99 (1947), 351, 421; 102 (1950), 244–5.

36. *Yachtsman*, 105 (1951), 1.

37. *Yachtsman*, 105 (1951), 121.

38. *Yachtsman*, 114 (1960), 11.

CHAPTER 10

Welsh Seaside Resort Regeneration Strategies: Changing Times, Changing Needs at the End of the Twentieth Century[1]

Nigel J. Morgan

As the structure of their economies change, particularly through the decline of many traditional activities including agriculture, fishing, shipbuilding and defence, many of the UK's coastal communities are facing extremely difficult times. In this context, tourism and leisure have long been recognised by central, regional and local government as having a vital regenerative role as long-term growth sectors with a low threshold of entry. However, many seaside resorts, arguably now also part of a traditional industry in the UK, are similarly in need of renewal and revitalisation.

Seaside resorts have been the dominant facet of the British holiday product throughout the twentieth century and, despite their recent relative decline, are still a vital component of the tourism industry. Currently they account for about one-quarter of all tourism trips and a third of domestic spending, a dominance which is even more pronounced in Wales.[2] Domestic tourism in the UK, and particularly in Wales, is for many people a seaside experience, and its dominance has only been threatened in recent decades by wider changes in tourism behaviour and tourism provision. In view of the importance of the seaside, this chapter reviews a number of key issues which have implications for the future prosperity of the Welsh seaside resort. Firstly, it discusses the market context of Welsh resorts and highlights that unlike their English counterparts, resorts in Wales have retained their share of the tourism market in recent decades. This suggests that it is misleading for commentators to talk of a British resort experience in these decades, since resort experiences have been so diverse. Secondly, the chapter reviews the resort regeneration policies of the Wales Tourist Board (WTB), the key strategic player in the tourism industry in Wales, and of the resort local authorities, the main implementation agents. Between 1988 and 2001 the WTB, in partnership with local authorities, will have assisted a large number of resorts, some of which are geographically isolated and seem to have little future. Although politically very difficult, it may have been in the long-term interests of Welsh tourism to have adopted a more selective, targeted approach. Moreover, an examination of recent resort strategies reveals that many are very similar, and if implemented, may undermine the individual character of the resorts, creating an undifferentiated product in an era when tourism consumers seem to be demanding destinations able to project a distinctive image and product.

Wales as a Tourism Destination

Wales has a population of 2.87 million and occupies an area of 20,768 square kilometres. Together with England, Scotland and Northern Ireland, it forms the United Kingdom and has a degree of administrative autonomy centred on the Secretary of State for Wales. At the local level, Wales is governed by 22 unitary authorities which are responsible for the delivery of all services, including tourism and economic development.[3] The WTB, established by the Development of Tourism Act in 1969, is the country's statutory body for tourism and receives the bulk of its resources from central government, via the Welsh Office.

Table 10.1: All Tourism Trips in the UK(millions)

	UK	England	N. Ireland	Scotland	Wales
1990	95.3	77.7	1.6	7.7	8.3
1991	94.4	76.0	1.4	8.2	8.7
1992	95.6	77.2	1.1	8.9	8.3
1993	90.9	73.0	1.3	9.0	7.7
1994	109.8	90.2	1.2	8.5	9.8

Source: English, Scottish, Wales and Northern Ireland Tourist Boards, *United Kingdom Tourism Survey*, 1990–94.

During the last two decades the Welsh economy, in common with that of the rest of the UK, has experienced major structural change, with the traditional heavy industries of coal, iron and steel being replaced by a more diversified pattern of manufacturing and service-based industries. This shift has reinforced the role of tourism as a key source of income and employment for communities in Wales. Although small in comparison with England, Wales's tourism industry is a major force in the country's economy (see Table 10.1). Tourism now generates over £1.5 billion annually in Wales and receipts from staying visitors make up almost 5 per cent of the Welsh gross domestic product, compared to about 3.5 per cent in England. It is also responsible for sustaining 95,000 jobs, 9 per cent of the total Welsh workforce.[4]

Wales as a destination has an impressive range of tourism products as well as a rich and varied natural environment. It has three national parks, each with its own character, one of which is Britain's only coastal park. Approximately 25 per cent of the land area and 70 per cent of the coastline carry some form of official designation to protect and manage the landscape. It is also readily accessible to its traditional domestic markets in England. Particular core image strengths include its beautiful unspoilt scenery; peace and quiet; a variety of holiday products; accessibility; and its varied coastline and seaside.

As a distinctive country with its own cultural and linguistic identity, Wales also offers a potentially unique destination for both the UK domestic holiday market and the overseas market. Wales is a country of two languages—English is spoken universally, while over a fifth of the population speak Welsh. In many rural areas more than two in three are able to speak Welsh.[5] This is reinforced by Wales's built heritage which stretches back into prehistory. Of particular importance are its castles, and Celtic and Roman remains, all of which are strong selling points for Wales overseas.[6]

The Place of the Seaside

Seaside resorts have dominated the Welsh, like the British, holiday industry for decades, although much less has been written on them.[7] The pattern of resort development in Wales also mirrors that in England. Their small-scale early development accelerated considerably in the second half of the nineteenth century with the expansion of the rail network, and in the twentieth century the overall shape of the industry has changed little, with road improvements merely confirming the traditional links. Thus, the catchment areas have remained constant during the postwar decades and today most of Wales's visitors come from north-west England, the West Midlands and South Wales, much the same as in the 1950s, 1960s and 1970s

There is also a pattern of resort specialisation similar to that of England and many of the Welsh resorts which emerged to serve specific markets have successfully maintained their original purpose. Resorts such as Rhyl and Prestatyn, Pwllheli and Barry Island continue to cater for visitors requiring fun, excitement and a wide range of entertainments at a reasonable cost. At the opposite end of the spectrum are resorts typified by the genteel Victorian-style resort of Llandudno in the north, known as 'The Queen of Welsh Resorts'. Others, including Tenby and a series of smaller resorts in the north-west and south-west, provide traditional family seaside holidays with safe sandy beaches and a wide range of supporting attractions and facilities.

Just as in the rest of the UK, there are a large number of resorts in Wales. At the end of the 1970s there were around 70 recognised seaside resorts in England and Wales, although most were small and only about 40 are estimated to have had over 1,000 letting bedrooms. By the end of the 1980s there were no more than 15–20 nationally known resorts which were capable of sustaining 500,000 or more staying visitors per annum and only a dozen resorts which formed the core of the seaside industry.[8] In Wales in 1992 27 resorts were identified by the WTB (see Map 10.1).[9] However, many of these were very small and today only three can be legitimately described as of national importance: Rhyl, Llandudno and Tenby, whilst Porthcawl and Barry Island are also significant day-trip destinations.

These resorts all have widely different products and markets. Llandudno has a high-quality environment and promenade, a range of good-quality hotels, extensive entertainments and retailing and cultural facilities, with the added dimension of mountain tours in nearby Snowdonia. These attributes have made it Wales's most important resort and conference centre and the most popular coaching destination in the UK, benefiting recently from road improvements to north-west England. Llandudno alone accounts for about 15 per cent of Wales's total serviced accommodation stock, the next most significant accommodation stock being found in the family resort of Tenby, which has 5 per cent.[10] Barry Island and Porthcawl, both on Wales's south coast and both with fun-fairs, continue to attract day visitors, mainly, but not solely, from South Wales. It is probably only the north coast resort of Rhyl which can truly be placed in the category of a national holiday and day-trip destination alongside resorts such as Blackpool, Great Yarmouth or

10.1 Tenby: South-West Wales beaches (courtesy of the Wales Tourist Board)

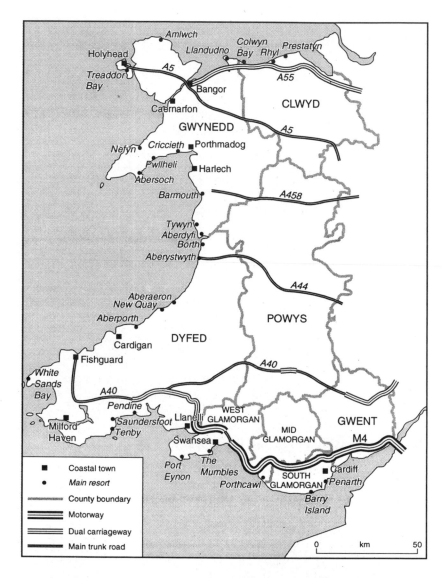

10.1 **Principal Communication Links and Location of Main Resorts and Coastal Towns (from PA Cambridge Economic Consultants, *Prospects for Coastal Resorts*, Cardiff, 1992)**

Brighton and it is the only Welsh resort attracting substantial investment from the main leisure companies.

The modern heyday of most UK resorts was in the 1950s, when, freed from the deprivations of war and rationing, British holidaymakers flocked to the seaside. Yet the virtually continuous expansion of the 1950s, 1960s and 1970s was to prove illusory and whilst on the surface, the seaside resorts were thriving up to the end of the 1970s, deeper analysis reveals that their deep-seated problems began in the mid-1960s. Indeed, many resorts experienced an almost continuous year on year decline in domestic holiday nights throughout the mid and late 1970s. The main reasons for this change are well documented elsewhere; for example, in its 1991 report on the problems of the smaller seaside resorts, the English Tourist Board (ETB) talked about the serious 'legacy of neglect' caused by 25 years of market decline.

The continuous loss of visitors over that time led to the widespread closure of hotels and made redundant many traditional attractions and entertainment facilities. In turn low levels of confidence and investment accelerated the rate of physical decay and obsolescence, and threatened the resorts' appeal.[11] At the same time, the trends towards low cost packages to the Mediterranean, which offered more modern accommodation, guaranteed sunshine, value for money and the glamour of foreign travel, further undermined the UK resorts. This overseas competition was also assisted by a shift towards second and short breaks which favoured city and inland locations, and by a notable lack of quality in the domestic seaside resorts.[12]

The Welsh Seaside Product in the 1980s and 1990s

While such a 'bleak and pessimistic assessment is perhaps justified in respect of several English resorts which are continuing to be hit hard by the recession', the most comprehensive recent report on the role and status of the Welsh seaside resorts argues that 'it should not be taken as indicative of the state of resort tourism in Wales'.[13] In fact, the seaside in Wales has retained its position as the leading tourism product, and Wales, with 24 per cent of total seaside visitor nights, is now only second in its volume of visitors to the West Country, which has 40 per cent.[14]

During the period 1978–88 seaside holidays in Britain were reduced by 39 million visitor nights, a fall of 27 per cent; yet Wales fared better than average, declining by only 13 per cent and retaining market share. More recent surveys suggest that the seaside in Wales continues to be by far the most significant holiday product, although its overall share is declining. This situation is very different from that experienced by England and Scotland, although Northern Ireland exhibits a similar dependence on the seaside with much smaller base numbers of tourists (see Table 10.2).

Table 10.2: Trips to the Seaside as a Percentage of all Domestic Trips Taken in the UK

	UK	England	N. Ireland	Scotland	Wales
1991	29	27	49	23	53
1992	28	27	42	22	48
1993	27	26	36	22	42
1994	27	25	46	21	45

Source: English, Scottish, Wales and Northern Ireland Tourist Boards, *United Kingdom Tourism Survey*, 1990–94.

There are a number of reasons why the Welsh resorts fared better than their English counterparts. Firstly, three-quarters of Welsh seaside bedspaces are in the low cost self-catering sector, a sector less severely hit in the recession of the early 1990s. During this period this sector recorded relatively high and consistent levels of occupancy, benefiting from the tendencies of tourists to 'trade down'. Secondly, in contrast to England, many Welsh resorts are marketed jointly with their hinterlands. This means that the potential tourist is offered a more diverse tourism product, often including the scenic beauty of national parks, or the appeal of heritage attractions and theme parks. Finally, and most importantly, grant aid for both public and private sector schemes has been more available in Wales because of the remits of 'quangos' like the WTB, the Welsh Development Agency, and the Development Board for Rural Wales. In particular, the opportunity to award grant aid under Section 4 of the Development of Tourism Act (1969), lost to the English and Scottish Tourist Boards, still remains available to the WTB.

However, despite this overall tendency for the Welsh resorts to retain market share, the effects of decline have still been evident at the Welsh seaside since the late 1970s. Resorts saw a decay in their physical fabric as the contraction of demand meant that many hotels, guest houses, shops, cafes and places of entertainment became redundant. Some found satisfactory alternative uses, but many did not. Hotels and guest houses, particularly in resorts such as Llandudno and Rhyl, were converted into nursing homes or low-cost housing provision for the unemployed, a development which has served to undermine both the infrastructure of tourism and the 'social tone' of the resorts. All too often, the owners of these properties in multiple occupation did not invest in maintenance and many took on a run-down appearance, becoming a blight on the townscapes and contributing to the poor-quality environments. Alternative uses were more often found for some of the redundant piers, arcades, concert halls and cinemas in Wales's resorts. In many, however, the new uses were typified by what has elsewhere been referred to as the 'drift down-market' with low quality retailers, fast-food outlets and slot machine amusements.[15]

The seaside clearly has an enduring appeal and is the long-standing mainstay of the tourism industry in Wales. Yet its decaying infrastructure and the impact of foreign competition has severely affected its fortunes. This situation is further complicated by the link between the tourism fortunes of large and small seaside resorts. Surrounding the larger resorts are many smaller resorts whose tourism fortunes are linked to the performance of the larger resorts. If the larger resorts decline any further in the 1990s the effect on the feeder resorts would be significant. This 'ripple' effect makes the traditional seaside resorts rather more important to domestic tourism than a superficial view of their market volume and share suggests. It also means that hundreds of visitor attractions around the resorts relying on resort visitors for a significant proportion of their annual revenue will prosper or decline with their larger neighbours.[16] Of equal concern, it has been suggested that the prospects for growth in seaside resorts is severely limited with growth opportunities restricted to perhaps a dozen resort areas in England and Wales. In the many smaller resorts around the coasts the investment prospects are certainly very limited. Many of them no longer rank as significant holiday centres and it seems certain that their remaining markets will decline further in the future.[17]

The situation is further exacerbated by the fact that seaside resorts in the UK are not modern self-contained tourism resorts, like a Center Parc or a Disneyland, which are entities organised around customers' needs. This, of course, is in complete contrast to the fragmented nature of traditional seaside resorts, which are also urban centres dominated by competing residents' interests, often with significant numbers of retired residents, and sometimes with light industrial development. The main concern of seaside resorts in Wales, as throughout the UK, has to be the quality of visitor experience, especially in their frequently visited core areas, including promenades, piers, arcades, gardens and pleasure grounds. Provided largely by the public sector, often originally laid out in the Victorian and Edwardian eras, these facilities have long been in need of reinvestment. In addition, many resorts have dealt inadequately with the basic visitor-related problems of litter, petty vandalism and street and beach hygiene which often create a sense of dilapidation in public spaces.

The visitor experience reflects the perceived attraction and quality of the built environment within which visitors spend most of their time and money. Yet in the postwar decades, especially since the 1960s, resorts throughout the UK have witnessed a massive erosion of the quality of their core visitor areas. This has resulted from several factors, identified by a number of commentators. In particular, Victor Middleton has argued that English resorts have failed to manage the intrusion and the increasing demands of motor vehicles and failed to maintain the original harmony of their architectural style and quality. He also points to the influx of retirees opposed to change and development and to the gradual 'slide down-market' as lower incomes and narrower profit margins led to inadequate reinvestment in improved tourism facilities.[18] This decline in the quality of the resorts' physical environment has also been reinforced by increasing visitor awareness of the polluted state of UK beaches.[19] Together, these circumstances have combined to create a vicious spiral from which it is impossible for resorts to recover except through co-ordinated public and private sector partnerships.

Strategies for Welsh Resort Regeneration

In contrast to Middleton's perspective, however, there is no doubt that the seaside has an enduring appeal as a holiday destination, and indeed the history of mass holidaymaking in the UK has its roots planted firmly in this tradition.[20] In spite of the fact that the physical character of many has become degraded, much of the original infrastructure and many of the key attractions remain in place. Moreover, the seaside resort also has a tradition of convenience, friendliness and good value-for-money accommodation, entertainment and other facilities.

In view of the existing accommodation base, infrastructure and tradition of tourism at the resorts, it seems sensible for tourism policy-makers to continue to encourage development in these areas. This argument is supported by economic and social considerations, since many of these towns are heavily dependent on the tourism industry and their decline as resorts has had severe implications for the future of those communities. Thus, although the agencies responsible for tourism in Wales recognise the need to regenerate these seaside towns for tourism-related reasons, there are also overarching political considerations. This latter point has important implications since decisions may not necessarily be taken purely to promote successful tourism development but also to attempt to ensure the survival of such communities. This in turn has implications for the successful development and future of the tourism industry in Wales as a whole.

Since tourism is such an important sector in the economy, its survival and success is critical, and while there are some grounds for optimism in Welsh coastal tourism, there clearly are a number of issues which need addressing if resorts are to fulfil their potential, or in some cases continue in existence. The role of the public sector has always been vital in sustaining the pace of product development and maintaining the appeal of resorts.[21] Certainly in Wales, the ability of the WTB to offer financial assistance via Section 4 of the Development of Tourism Act (1969) has been a vital tool in influencing tourism development in the Welsh resorts.

There have been several programmes aimed at resort regeneration in the UK in the last two decades. Individual local authorities have worked in partnership with a range of organisations and agencies, including the statutory tourist boards, voluntary organisations and a number of government bodies, to revitalise resorts. At a national level, the most well known schemes have been the ETB's tourism development action plans, its 1985 Resorts 2000 competition (won by Bridlington and Torbay) and its recent Seaside Campaign which was largely a marketing campaign. In Wales the most well known scheme was the WTB's 1988 competitive Local Enterprise and Development Initiative (LEAD) programme, which was intended more to improve the seaside product via grant aid. Under this scheme three resorts—Barry Island, Rhyl and Tenby—received assistance.

The Wales Tourist Board LEAD Initiative

The LEAD initiative emanated from the WTB's 1988–93 strategy document, *Developing the Potential*.[22] Designed to 'stimulate the public and private sectors to jointly plan and implement co-ordinated development programmes', the initiative had a number of key objectives.[23] These included: creating new jobs; improving the accommodation base; improving the local environment, especially by utilising derelict land or buildings and easing traffic congestion; and 'pump priming' private sector investment in tourism projects. The LEAD projects formed 'part of a long term improvement of tourism infrastructure in Wales focused, in some instances, on areas that have long been in decline'.[24]

The major problem with the implementation of this scheme stemmed from a poor response from the private sector to the LEAD programme and to the projects outlined in the resorts' bids for LEAD grant aid. This, it has been argued, resulted mainly from the poor economic climate, but there were also other problems.[25] For instance, the WTB's evaluation of priorities for tourism development in Wales has always had major implications for the industry and its relationship with the Board. Some of its decisions have often created both puzzlement and resentment and this was also the case with LEAD. Firstly, the Board has been perceived as favouring large, 'high-profile' projects (often operated by organisations outside Wales) over smaller developments proposed by indigenous firms. Secondly, it has also been perceived to favour some towns and regions over areas which seem to be more in need of special assistance.[26]

However, despite these difficulties, the LEAD scheme did provide excellent value for money and a cost-effective mechanism for tourism development. An independent evaluation of the scheme argued that some 3,500 full-time equivalent jobs were created or safeguarded as a result of the grant aid, at a cost of between £4,100 and £7,200 per job. Moreover, the report concluded that a third of the tourism projects which were grant aided would not have proceeded without the intervention of LEAD.[27]

The success of LEAD lay in its role as a catalyst, often galvanising hitherto inactive local authorities and providing a framework for action. It created an atmosphere of positive public sector co-operation and an integrated approach to common problems. In fact, the public sector often delivered successful, exciting projects, but private sector schemes were not forthcoming, despite the availability of LEAD grants to reduce their risks. In this respect, of all the resorts which benefited from the LEAD initiative, perhaps Barry Island in South Wales best illustrates the problems encountered by the scheme.

A Case Study: Barry Island

Barry, approximately 15 miles south-west of Cardiff, is Wales's fifth largest urban centre, with a population of 46,000. It is the administrative and service centre of the Vale of Glamorgan, a major port on the Bristol Channel, and a centre of an expanding chemical industry. It also has major economic and social problems and is characterised by a high level of unemployment, which at 12 per cent is above the UK national average.[28]

Barry is also an established holiday destination as the town's resort area of Barry Island is one of the most popular of the coastal resorts in South Wales. The resort was very successful historically when thousands of day-trippers used to travel down from the South Wales valleys to enjoy its fairground, the sandy expanse of Whitmore Bay beach and the seaside fun of donkey rides and amusements. In the decades following the Second World War there seemed no reason to change that successful product, so Barry Island, like many British seaside resorts, remained unchanged. However, this lack of investment in its fabric, infrastructure and attractions, together with the competition of the package holiday boom, brought decline in the 1970s and 1980s.

The resort suffered particularly from the withdrawal of Butlins from the Island in the mid-1980s and from a reduction in its day-visitor market as a result of its poor image and dilapidated environment Of further damage to its image was its acquisition of a reputation for violence and drunkenness in the early 1980s. By the late 1980s Barry Island had become extremely run-down, 'a typical example of a once flourishing seaside resort which not only failed to move with the times but failed to realise that the times had changed'.[29]

The Vale of Glamorgan Borough Council, then the responsible local authority, recognised in the mid-1980s that unless Barry Island received major capital investment, its very future as a tourist resort was in doubt. This was confirmed in 1987 by an independent study which emphasised the need to promote tourism though proactive development and marketing. As a result, the authority appointed a tourism officer who successfully put together a bid for funding from the WTB under the LEAD initiative. In 1989 Barry Island was designated a Tourism Action Programme area by the Board and awarded £500,000. This money was the catalyst for the Borough Council to secure further grant aid for improvements. The Welsh Development Agency provided £1.6 million, the Welsh Office Urban Programme £100,000 and the European Regional Development

10.2 Barry Island Tourist Information Centre: visible evidence of resort regeneration strategies (courtesy of Nigel Morgan)

Fund £500,000. Over a five-year period the Barry Island Resort Action Programme (BIRAP) invested £2.5 million into a programme of environmental improvements to revitalise the sea front at Barry Island. This upgrading of the built environment was intended both 'to create a more positive image' and to provide 'a higher quality product ... to meet modern visitors' expectations'.[30] The schemes included enhanced car parking, lighting, paving and street furniture, and a new tourist information centre.[31]

Although BIRAP occurred at a time of flux and structural change in the tourism industry all the agencies involved claimed some successes from the initiative. The local council gained an improved environment at the resort and the WTB, a key facilitator of the revival via LEAD, although less enthusiastic because of the lack of private sector involvement, was also satisfied with the development.[32] The impact of the programme was assessed in 1993 when, as part of a larger economic regeneration initiative for Barry, a partnership of local authorities and public agencies undertook a tourism study to reappraise BIRAP and to identify opportunities for future development.[33] The study concluded that 'Barry Island's core market is primarily semi-skilled or unskilled manual workers with children, living in South Wales and visiting for the day, several times a year'. Recognising that this was probably to continue to be the major market, the study asked that 'expectations for the Island's future must be realistic: the Island is unlikely to be successfully repositioned as an upmarket resort. It must continue to do what it does best as a family fun resort.'[34] Despite this rather cautious comment, the report also revealed that Barry enjoyed a strong position within its traditional market.

As part of the study, market research was conducted with existing and potential visitors and in the resorts of Porthcawl and Weston-Super-Mare, Barry's main rivals.[35] This research produced some very encouraging findings. Barry Island's major strength was its high level of awareness amongst its visitors, with 75 per cent having visited the resort five or more times before. These findings clearly demonstrate the appeal and the consistent pulling power of the resort. However, the research also revealed the need to create a positive image amongst those who were not visitors to the Island and amongst potential private sector investors. The study concluded: 'Barry Island's ability to attract major investment projects is limited by ... the perception of Barry Island as a low quality and declining resort'.[36] This is a crucial point and is related to the primary failure of the LEAD scheme overall and the BIRAP scheme in particular—an inability to attract private sector investment in the seaside resort infrastructure.

Despite the undoubted success of some elements of the Barry Island scheme, particularly in improving the physical environment, it did fail to deliver its key objectives, principally because of this poor private sector response. This raises questions about the ability of public sector investment to do little more than marginally influence private sector business decisions. The evaluation of the BIRAP scheme revealed some key findings with which, for political reasons, both the WTB and the Vale of Glamorgan Borough Council were rather uncomfortable. In essence, despite considerable public sector funding, Barry has failed to attract significant new investment from the private sector, and while popular with its core market, still retains a negative image with non-visitors, a problem which improved marketing must overcome.

Thus, with the end of the LEAD initiative in 1993 the decision facing the WTB was whether to continue to support resorts like Barry and Rhyl which had already benefited from LEAD during 1988–93 or to focus on a further set of resorts. In the event, the Board selected six resorts which are evenly spread across Wales: two in the south (Mumbles and the Gower, and Porthcawl), two in mid Wales (Aberystwyth and Barmouth) and two in north Wales (Pwllhelli and the Llyn resorts, and Llandudno). Selected on the basis of the strength of the partnerships between their local authorities, communities, and local business organisations, each resort will receive grants not exceeding £1 million in a regeneration scheme to run from 1996 to 2001.

The Tourism 2000 Coastal Resorts Regeneration Programme

At this early stage it is not possible to provide an assessment of the impact of the new resort regeneration scheme. It is, however, useful to discuss the strategies on which the bids were based since they reveal not only the directions in which the resorts themselves wish to move, but also the priorities of the WTB. In December 1994 the WTB invited local authorities to bid for the resort funding and the Board received ten applications, each of which was based on a resort strategy. The resort areas which submitted applications were: Aberystwyth; Barmouth; Mumbles and the Gower; Barry Island; Tenby and Sandersfoot; Pwllhelli; the Llyn Resorts; Porthmadog; Penarth; Rhyl and Prestatyn.

Of these ten resort areas, the Board selected four to benefit from the resort regeneration scheme, announcing the winners on 5

10.3 Aberystwyth seafront by night (courtesy of the Wales Tourist Board)

May 1995. Unless there were excellent reasons to support the bid, those resorts which had benefited from the 1989–94 LEAD scheme would not be favoured under the new initiative. For this reason both Barry Island and Rhyl were excluded, although the latter's submission was in any case extremely weak. Those selected were: Mumbles and the Gower; Aberystwyth; Pwllheli and the Llyn resorts; and Barmouth. These four resorts would be targeted for regeneration by the WTB, together with Llandudno and Porthcawl, already previously selected. What is extremely interesting is that, although varying in quality, the strategies share a number of core objectives (see Table 10.3).

Table 10.3: Core Resort Strategy Objectives of the Tourism 2000 Resorts Regeneration Applications

Identified as a key objective	Percentage of strategies in which identified
extend the tourist season/short breaks	90
environmental improvements	90
develop/improve attractions	90
improve marketing	80
improve beach/water quality	70
upgrade accommodation	70
increase visitor spend	70
develop festivals, events	70
develop heritage/historical themes	40
encourage sustainable tourism	30
develop business/conference market	30
improve resort management	30
forge private/public partnerships	30
establish/reposition image	20
create/protect jobs	20
improve visitor services	10

Source: Ten Resort Strategies, Wales Tourist Board Resort Regeneration Programme files, 1994–95.

Clearly, although the resorts themselves are very individual in character, many of them are seeking to implement very similar regeneration strategies. This is, in part, a response to the common difficulties facing not only these resorts, but most resorts around the British coast. However, it is also due to a number of other reasons. Firstly, the similar strategies are a response to the stated objectives of the programme as formulated by the WTB. Secondly, their common core features are also a result of a similar process of strategy writing. For instance, some received input from staff in the WTB, whilst others were developed on the basis of consultants' reports and there are only about a half dozen consultancies which specialise in this kind of project. Together, these factors combine to produce very similar documents with very similar objectives.

Conclusions

There are clearly a number of generic problems facing Welsh seaside resorts, as there are facing UK resorts. They are all striving to offer a quality experience; to improve standards of beach hygiene, traffic and visitor management; and to market effectively the coastal product. Yet the experience of Wales also differs from that of England. The seaside remains a pre-eminent part of the Welsh tourism product and while there has been some diversification, particularly into countryside and activity-orientated holidays, the vast majority of tourism trips are still taken on the coast. Thus, the need to produce the right seaside resort product is, it could be argued, critical not only to the survival of a successful Welsh seaside industry, but also to the tourism industry of the country as a whole. The WTB, the agency charged with developing and promoting the tourism industry in Wales, is well aware of this need to upgrade and energise the seaside resorts of Wales. As this chapter has outlined, a number of schemes have been implemented which have provided practical programmes designed to achieve this regeneration, including the LEAD programme and the Tourism 2000 resorts regeneration scheme.

The success of such programmes can be analysed on a local, national and strategic level. At each level areas of significant success can be identified along with areas which may suggest fundamental weaknesses, some of which can be addressed by the WTB but others which are beyond its control. At a local level individual resorts can assess the specific impact of the grant aid, whereas at a national level the overall success of the schemes as employment generators and development catalysts can be established. Although it is too early to comment on the Tourism 2000 regeneration programme, it can be argued that it is perhaps at these levels where the LEAD scheme was most successful. It created approximately 3,500 jobs in the Welsh tourism industry, at considerably less expense than employment creation schemes in other industries. Furthermore, it also contributed to the regeneration of much of the infrastructure and environment of resorts in Wales, as the Barry Island case study illustrates.

Where LEAD did fail, however, was in generating investment from the private sector. Investment from this quarter is essential if the industry is to capitalise fully on the infrastructural and environmental improvements created by the public sector schemes supported by LEAD. Yet there is a reluctance to invest in the seaside in Wales, perhaps due to a lack of an entrepreneurial base in the resorts, certainly due to a failure by many businesses to reinvest profits in improving their product. Whatever the reason, potential outside investors are favouring resorts elsewhere which have already achieved the critical mass of tourist attractions and are capable of attracting further investment. In Wales only Rhyl on the northern coast has reached this level of activity.

This failure of the private sector to initiate complementary schemes must raise some worrying questions over the ability of the industry to meet the challenges of the next century. Moreover, at a strategic level, the success of these regeneration programmes, assessed in terms of their long-term impacts on the continued health and development of the tourism industry in Wales, may have to be tempered by a consideration of the overall imperatives governing the WTB.

Clearly, it must be recognised that there are overriding political imperatives which frame the public sector support of tourism. The development of tourism by the public sector, with its competing funding priorities, increasingly has to be justified as an economic development tool and there are major political considerations surrounding the allocation of regeneration funding. The WTB cannot make decisions purely on tourism development grounds. It seems to be striving to achieve an even geographical distribution of the funding around resorts in Wales, funding two each from the north, mid and south in 1995, possibly placing such considerations above the resorts' long-term ability to survive and prosper. Yet failure to support some of the struggling resorts would probably accelerate their demise, often in areas where there is no alternative to tourism employment. However, to satisfy these wider social and political considerations, the Board is taking funding away from the potential winners in the Welsh resort industry and therefore possibly undermining the long-term competitiveness of the tourism industry in Wales.

While understandable on a political level, the Board's decision not to continue in 1995 with those resorts which had already received aid under LEAD, some of which include Wales's most viable resorts, could be criticised. It does mean that without the continued stimulus of grant money in these resorts there is a danger that previously successful partnerships may be dissolved and efforts dissipated.[37] It must be questionable whether this approach of awarding funding to an entirely new tranche of resorts is creating a sustainable seaside industry in Wales. Firstly, by excluding the first tranche from further funding, the WTB is excluding some of the potential winners for Welsh tourism. Barry Island may not have been a complete success story, but other LEAD resorts, notably Rhyl and Tenby, are some of the mainstays of the Welsh seaside industry, and may have been more successful because of the grant aid.

Secondly, by attempting to distribute funds evenly on a geographical basis, the WTB is assisting resorts which, in direct competition, cannot both succeed. Thus in the first tranche the WTB supported Barry Island, whilst in the second tranche it is supporting Porthcawl, only 20 miles down the coast and a very similar family-orientated resort, struggling to maintain its market position. It would be an extremely difficult decision to decline to support such resorts, since although both are declining, their economies are very tourism-dependent. For example, each year there are almost a million tourism visits to Barry Island, creating an estimated total visitor spend of £9.6 million and sustaining 257 full-time and 1,200 part-time jobs.[38] Yet, despite the local importance of tourism in Barry Island, as in other similar resorts around Wales, the tourism policy-makers must be allowed to take a more strategic view in the interests of the long-term viability of tourism throughout Wales.

Finally, not only are these regeneration strategies in danger of propping up ailing resorts instead of supporting the more dynamic ones, they are also in danger of creating an undifferentiated seaside product. The similarity of the strategies submitted in 1994–95 is significant as 70 per cent were based around the same eight key objectives. At a more detailed level, two resorts within 20 miles of each other, Porthcawl and Barry Island, were basing their revival around plans to build a large-scale water-based attraction, proposals which, because of their geographical proximity, would not seem to be viable. Similarly, both Barry Island in the south and Porthmadog in the north suggest in their strategies that they could become a Welsh national centre for railway heritage. The sense of two or more resorts chasing similar schemes is highly questionable. Clearly, their similar strategies do reflect common solutions to common problems. Yet, there is also the suggestion of an 'off the shelf' solution as many of these resort strategies were produced by the same process of the WTB supervising a small number of consultants. Over recent decades, it is arguable that the strategies of the WTB, constrained by social and economic considerations and complicated by the influence of regional politics, have had the effect of sustaining a large number of mediocre resorts. The regeneration schemes have raised several resorts to a lowest common denominator, when perhaps a more targeted, selective approach could have created a smaller number of higher quality resorts capable of competing for the more discriminating visitors of the twenty-first century.

NOTES

1.   The author is grateful to Nigel Adams and Tim Beddoe of the Development Section in the Wales Tourist Board for access to Wales Tourist Board files, and to Annette Pritchard of the School of Leisure and Tourism at University of Wales Institute, Cardiff, for her valuable comments on this paper.
2.   V. Middleton, 'English Seaside Resorts', *Insights* (1989), B5–13.
3.   A. Pritchard and N.J. Morgan, 'Evaluating Vacation Destination Brochure Images: The Case of Local Authorities in Wales', *Journal of Vacation Marketing*, 2:1 (1995), 23–38.
4.   Wales Tourist Board, *Record of Achievement* (Cardiff, 1994).
5.   R.E. Owen, 'Towards Sustainable Tourism—The Experience of Wales', paper presented at 'Building a Sustainable World Through Tourism', IIPT Second Global Conference, Montreal, 12–16 September 1994.
6.   A. Pritchard and N.J. Morgan, 'Selling the Celtic Arc to the USA: A Comparative Analysis of the Destination Brochure Images used in the Marketing of Ireland, Scotland and Wales', *Journal of Vacation Marketing*, 2:4 (1996), 346–65.
7.   See P.A. Cambridge Economic Consultants, *Prospects for Coastal Resorts: A Paper for Consultation* (Cardiff , 1992); and N.J. Morgan and A. Pritchard, 'Welsh Seaside Resort Strategies: Creating a Viable Industry for the Next Century', paper presented at the Third International Urban History Conference, Budapest, August 1996.
8.   Middleton, 'English Seaside Resorts', B5–8.
9.   *Prospects for Coastal Resorts.*
10. Wales Tourist Board, *Tourism 2000: A Strategy for Wales* (Cardiff, 1994).
11. Building Design Partnership, Victor Middleton and Tony Wright, *The Future for England's Smaller Seaside Resorts* (English Tourist Board, 1991).
12. Middleton, 'English Seaside Resorts'.
13. *Prospects for Coastal Resorts*, 13.

14. English, Scottish, Wales and Northern Ireland Tourist Boards, *United Kingdom Tourism Survey* (London, 1990).
15. *Prospects for Coastal Resorts*, 13.
16. Middleton, 'English Seaside Resorts', B5–9.
17. Middleton, 'English Seaside Resorts', B5–1.
18. Middleton, 'English Seaside Resorts', B13.
19. See for instance J. Channon, 'Pollution and Resort Development: Teignmouth in the Twentieth Century, and Especially in Recent Years', in S. Fisher (ed.), *Man and the Maritime Environment* (Exeter, 1994), 180–98.
20. J.K. Walton, *The English Seaside Resort. A Social History 1750–1914* (Leicester, 1983).
21. N.J. Morgan, 'Perceptions, Patterns and Policies of Tourism: The Development of the Seaside Resorts of Devon 1900–1990, with Particular Reference to Torquay and Ilfracombe' (unpublished PhD thesis, University of Exeter, 1991).
22. Wales Tourist Board, *Developing the Potential* (Cardiff, 1988).
23. A. Pritchard, 'Marketing the Welsh Seaside', paper presented at the Tourism Society's 'Heritage and Culture at the Seaside' Conference, Scarborough, 1994.
24. Segal Quince Wicksteed Ltd, *Evaluation of Section 4 Assistance: A Report to the Wales Tourist Board* (Cardiff, 1992), 27.
25. *Evaluation of Section 4 Assistance*, 22
26. *Evaluation of Section 4 Assistance*, 27.
27. 'Section 4—An Independent Evaluation', *Tourism Wales* (1993), 18.
28. Coopers & Lybrand Consultants Ltd, *Barry Joint Venture Tourism Topic Report* (February 1994), 1.
29. 'Barry is Back! How a LEAD Programme Sparked a Resort's Revival', *Tourism Wales*, (Autumn 1993), 8–9.
30. Vale of Glamorgan Borough Council, *Barry Island Resort Action Programme—Opportunities for Investment* (Barry, 1994), 2.
31. For details of the initial success of BIRAP see contributions from N.J. Morgan, in *Leisure Management* (October 1992) and the *British Resorts Association Newsletter*, 47 (May 1993).
32. 'Barry is Back!', 9.
33. The Vale of Glamorgan Borough Council, the Welsh Development Agency and South Glamorgan County Council launched a regeneration initiative called the Barry Joint Venture in 1993. A key element in the regeneration was the planned redevelopment of number one dock, a derelict area of waterfront in the heart of the town. In 1994 the Venture was relaunched with the same partners as the Barry Action Venture Partnership.
34. *Barry Joint Venture Tourism Topic Report*, 15–16, 30.
35. For details of these surveys see M. Selby and N.J. Morgan, 'Reconstruing Place Image: a Case Study of its Role in Destination Market Research', *Tourism Management*, 17:4 (1996), 287–94.

36. *Barry Joint Venture Tourism Topic Report*, 15, 19.
37. *Evaluation of Section 4 Assistance*, 29.
38. *Barry Joint Venture Tourism Topic Report*, 15–16, 30.

Index